NAKED IN NEPAL

A YOUNG WOMAN'S JOURNEY

NAKED IN NEPAL

A YOUNG WOMAN'S JOURNEY

ROANNE LEGG

LAUGHING RAIN

Published by Laughing Rain Inc.

Naked in Nepal: A Young Woman's Journey / Roanne Legg

1.Non-fiction. 2. Legg, Roanne I. Title.

ISBN-13: 978-1-935070-28-3

ISBN-10: 1-935070-28-2

Front and back cover photos credit: Olav Myrholt. Used by permission.

A portion of the profits from the sale of this book will be donated to non-profits which benefit the Nepali people.

This is a window into my life that happened a long time ago, much of which has been drawn from my personal journals. I have done my best to put it in order from my memory, however, timelines may not be exact, dialogue has been re-created, names have been changed (except for mine) to protect the privacy of certain individuals, and locations have been recalled as well as I could. In order to make it more readable, a number of people were combined, creating composite characters who are genuine to the personalities involved. In all of this, I have remained true to the essence of the story. I apologize for any errors, omissions, or anything that is historically inaccurate.

RoanneLegg.com

For Brandt and Teakki Rain

"Mountains are not Stadiums where I
satisfy my ambitions to achieve, they are
the cathedrals where I practice my religion."
– Anatoli Boukreev

Modi Khola gorge on the way to Machapuchare base camp. Photo credit Olav Myrholt

"The rivers, the mountains, aren't hiding anything, that's their
secret." — Marty Rubin

PREFACE

I stared out into the wild blue sky, struggling to decipher the images and unanswered questions filling my heart and mind. Then, finally, my eyes softened to the plane's interior. Low chatter and creaks swallowed the dissonance. Nepal, my obsession, grew closer. A deeply accentuated experience waited, one I hoped would guide me to my true path.

Suddenly, turbulence shook the craft, igniting a line of fasten seat belt lights. I gripped the armrests. We disappeared into a cavernous wave of clouds. Once more a jostle, gasps from passengers, nothing but white, and then, mountain tops. The jagged, frosty tips of the Himalayas poked through, anchored in an endless realm of bitter wind. My heart tightened in excitement. I swallowed, tears wet and internal as I pressed my face to the window and saw my Shangri-La.

Before stepping on that plane and embarking on that monumental, life-changing journey, I had escaped the last two years of a conventional education to live on my own in Mendocino, California during high school, while my parents stayed in Wyoming. Then my mother had discovered a wonderfully alternative college, one I thought could lead me to my dream. Even though I appeared independent and strong, I really didn't know who I was or what I wanted—but I did know I needed to get out of this country, out of my home, out of this life. I don't remember how the idea of Nepal first lodged itself in my mind, but knew it was somewhere I belonged.

I've always had an unquenchable thirst to find out who I am and why I'm here, yet the steps to figuring that out created overwhelming anxiety. Maybe the cracks had begun early in my life, at age six, when my parents divorced.

The split left my two older sisters living with Dad while I went with Mom and her new guy as they gypsied their way across the country, making a living selling their art. The crumbling of my family left me in a guilty isolation. Perched in the back of our funky 1966 VW van, torn open and raw from the greatest loss I would experience in my life, the country passed by as we moved from the Green Mountains of Vermont to the Rocky Mountains of Wyoming.

Nine years after that cross-country odyssey, I left home again, this time on my own, to experience something different. America was too familiar and didn't fill the depth of worldliness I craved. An easy life seemed less authentic, so I was drawn to the hardships of poverty as an opportunity to feel the truth of existence and rawness of life, as well to mirror my own personal tragedy. A land of enchantment, Himalayas, abode of the gods, with an exotic language on the edge of the world roused my attention and beckoned a visit to experience its beauty and rustic culture. Nepal, with its attention to spirituality, monks, meditation, and Asian mystique, would start my adventure in the fall of 1987.

I couldn't wait to get into the snowy portals and icy crags of that foreign land, whose beautiful people carried huge loads on their backs and walked barefoot. Hopefully Nepal would tear me open so a mature, confident woman could emerge, even though, passing the hours before departure, I still felt like a child.

1

WHILE CLEARING SECURITY AT SAN FRANCISCO INTERNATIONAL Airport, eager to begin my journey, a burly airport guard abruptly jerked me out of my euphorically abstracted visions of the Himalayas, waving a six-inch dagger in front of me he'd pulled out of a bag I was carrying through.

I panicked and looked around wildly. "It isn't mine. I've never seen it before."

The agent waved the weapon, sheathed in an ornate leather casing, in front of me. "Whose is it?" they asked as another agent joined him.

I stuttered Carl's name. It was his knife, another ragamuffin-child and student like myself. I had naïvely agreed to carry his bag through security, having no idea what was inside. We were good friends, had baked bread together, walked in the hills above our college, and felt the same about many things.

"Where is he?"

I searched frantically. They eventually found him and took him away.

The next time I saw him was on the plane, when he sat down next to me. He'd always had a peculiar smell to him, something old, like newspaper that had been hanging around in a damp house too long.

"Sorry," Carl began, "I don't know what I was thinking. They kept it."

"Are you okay? Why did you have that knife?"

"I bring it everywhere."

Strange guy, I thought. *Maybe I don't know him that well.*

But I did. He was one of my best friends in college. His naïve sense was similar to mine, and like children, we resonated in a playful way—not a sexual way, though I think he wanted it to.

WORLD COLLEGE WEST, a visionary four-year institution in the rolling hills of northern California, offered a study-abroad program for second-year students. Total immersion in a language and culture helped prepare a student for life—at least that's what their brochure said—and that's what I wanted. The choices were China, Mexico, or Nepal. There was no doubt in my mind when I picked Nepal. China was too big, the language too difficult. Mexico, too close, too easy. Nepal, the name itself was mystical, the Himalayas—magnificent. And it was in Asia! That's where one went to find oneself, where transformation happened, and people got skinny without trying.

Nepali was a beautiful language to learn. Our teacher in the States devoted her life to it. She loved Nepali, and cooed over well-done homework of its letters and phrases practiced into sentences. It uses Devanagari Script, curly characters written below the line. I'd spent the previous summer riding my bicycle fifteen miles to and from work, repeating phrases, numbers, and songs until the lyrical language took root.

For the long flight, Carl sat on one side of me, Dave, our leader, on the other. Dave's clean-cut, wiry beard framed a rugged, yet delicately bony face. He had warm eyes, with a not-too-hidden hint of frivolity and carelessness. I felt protected with him, going to a place seven thousand miles away. Being a Canadian citizen with a green card, I was a foreigner growing up in the United States. It added to my oddness, and I liked that. It set me apart—although the financial aid audits, border checks, and immigration were always a hassle. So, other than a spontaneous ten days in Baja, Mexico, I had never left the United States. Nepal would also be my longest time away from home.

We fidgeted in the confined airline seats, reading and eating, talking and dozing. An intimacy of hopeful camaraderie surfaced unlike the kind we had already mastered in our freshmen year together.

As we traveled timelessly over seams of different zones, a whole day would pass in the air. The small window reflected in my eyes a dark moodiness, the radical and conventional sides of me as far-off lights and clouds dispersed above masses of land and water. College was normal and accepted as opposed to rough and dreamy Nepal— dangerously different, far away from everything and everyone familiar. I smiled at my reflection. College was usually the first place kids got to be adults, free from watchful parental eyes, but I had already lived that way. High school was driven by self-motivation, living on my own in a different state, working before and after classes, paying rent, preparing meals, and then receiving a diploma and two scholarships. Regardless, naïveté ran deep in my veins, pervasive, like a tincture or a dye. I wasn't shy or uneducated without manners, just a country girl wanting a new experience. I trusted the world, and yet, at the same time, didn't feel safe, even as I stepped recklessly into it.

San Francisco to Kathmandu. The first layover was in Hong Kong, not long enough to venture beyond the high-ceiling airport whose large, foggy windows was a barrier to a huge, grey, dank city. Its obtuse angles, strange, intangible culture, and deeply-etched urbane attitude hung like a haunt. I thought if I were to venture into its disenchanted, uncouth streets, I would not return—at least not as the same person, but rather in a colorless and alien aura. It was too foreign.

In the air again for another leg of our journey. The next landing, delirious, exhilarated, and starving, we were hustled onto a bus for an eighteen-kilometer ride to a hotel in Singapore. The steering wheel on the right side fascinated any first-timer, and I'd been waiting to see it for a long time. The city looked clean and modern. We checked into our rooms before meeting in the lobby to set out on foot into the strangely stark streets where cracked, intricate tile art nestled in folds of walls and Victorian buildings were overcome by high-rise modernity. A late dinner found us all packed around a narrow rectangular table eating rice so spicy I couldn't taste it or anything afterward, not even water. Our leader, Dave, toasted our adventure with red cheeks and an awkward smile.

The next day we explored the city in small groups, had the best fried tofu and noodles at the hawker stations, and checked out the youth hostel. I bought tiger balm, a medicinal herbal ointment, at Haw Par Villa Gardens, a theme park filled with statues of Chinese mythology. I did that only because it was one of the expected things to do, but it felt cheap and touristy.

Early the next morning we left that sophisticated and other-worldly slice of Singapore to catch a three-and-a-half-hour flight to Nepal, with a stopover in Dhaka, Bangladesh.

2

THE PLANE SLOWLY CAME TO A STOP AND IMMEDIATELY DHAKA closed in—sad and depressed. Large droplets of silvery rain stuck like greasy flies to the windows. Tightly muscled soldiers with steely slit eyes and weathered fatigues, gripping automatic guns, boarded and stood at either end of the aisles, feet apart, ready to shoot. Their brazen answer to commands and determined glares warned of a seriousness well beyond my comprehension, unsure as to why we had to remain in the plane, but knowing something much larger was at work. The cool, clammy interior held vacuum to an oppressive quiet as everyone eyed each other with questioning hushed voices. Only our leader, Dave, reading National Geographic, seemed unperturbed. Outside the small, humid windows, green fields stretched lonely and wet where thin, bent-over bodies worked under a bleak sky.

I felt somber staring out the window, having no idea of the actuality of war—brutality, inequality, death—until that moment in a torn country with its beautifully green and flooded fields. The injustice of the human heart didn't make sense. Hours later, a commotion and heated words brought me back. The plane's doors closed and we were in the air once again, leaving Bangladesh behind. My transformation had begun during those brief hours in that hollow land, thrust into a reality I had only read or heard about on the news.

After we departed, Dave quietly explained about the political unrest which had put Bangladesh into a state of emergency following opposition demonstrations and strikes. Tension and rumors of revolution were in the air. Muslims were consolidating their power in a move to make Islam the state religion. I felt troubled and sorry for the Bangladesh people. Not long after, floods devoured the area, causing tens of millions of people to become homeless, further devastating that fragile land.

Flying out of the Bangladesh hostility had been a relief, although I would have liked to help in some way. One couldn't ignore the depravity, frustration, and anger, but most of all, the absolute helplessness of the plight of those people trapped in a country in turmoil. Alone, in that small window seat, high above the world, my thoughts and feelings mirrored that stricken land.

Questions bubbled up: what percentage of children lived daily with the threat of war, the fear of abandonment, and only the education of artillery? Experiencing the media's coverage is not the same as witnessing a horrific hardness in a soldier's eyes whose emotional life had been stolen by circumstance. What does one feel in readiness to kill? How much of the world lives in some form of hostility or abuse? Does a child, a country, a population, ever recover from such trauma? Why is there such hatred and injustice? Where does ignorance, greed, and lack of common sense stem from?

Nearing Nepal, the country I had fantasized about for so long, delivered more questions about Third World politics, poverty, sickness, deprivation, and religious intensity. But stepping onto that sacred soil, twenty flight-hours from home, would be an awakening. I really had no idea what lay ahead and wished I'd had the guts to have gone alone. Hopefully Nepal would get me out of my good girl syndrome and shed an over-protected veneer so I could become the uninhibited adventurer I longed to be. But admitting the need for a group to allow me the space to experience this land without worrying about safe lodging and visas was deemed sensible. Letting the college handle the logistical aspect of foreign travel allowed me to absorb the art, language, and customs of the country. If I had taken on those necessary responsibilities, I might have easily messed up something really important.

3

FINALLY, WE WERE ON NEPALI SOIL. THE WIDE, LOW-LIT HALLS IN the Kathmandu airport were busy with women in wrinkled cotton saris hurrying about with kids. Entranced at nineteen, living my dream, I smiled at the sound of Nepali, spoken fast like a mystical orchestra.

The bathroom initiated Third World primitive lifestyle: two tiles on either side of a hole, squat, do your business, clean up with water from a bottle using your left hand (instead of toilet paper)—but not yet because I had a tissue. We nervously laughed, exchanged looks, and then raced back to our luggage, friends, and leader. He knew what to do, and we clung to him like chicks barely out of the nest.

Dollars were traded for rupees before gathering luggage, and we were out into the bright sun. People scurried, taxis pulled in and out, and buses loaded with all types of people in a scene of no skyscrapers, no manicured lawns, no smell of plastic or fast food. A swirl of dust, warm and sunlit, a proximity of scale that instantly made me feel big.

My eyes hungrily gazed on Kathmandu, a huge, sprawling, active city. It appeared small in stature. Its buildings didn't vie for attention. The people seemed accustomed to white skin, at least in that area. If staring was rude in our culture, Asian etiquette went beyond unspoken mores and unabashedly checked everything out. It was refreshing. I wanted to blend in, be local, and be brown. A bus pulled up, and we loaded our baggage and said namaste to the driver, who whisked us off to the Manaslu Hotel.

At the well-kept and traditionally built hotel, the teachers of the program handed out small Nepali coin purses and folders containing class schedules. They placed tika—red dye and rice made sticky with yoghurt—on our forehead between the eyebrows where the third eye was said to be. It is traditionally considered the center of awareness, and marking it portended its opening to help attain higher consciousness. The teachers were sweet and jubilant while placing the tika, which dripped and partly fell off as their fingers deftly pushed it on. Their smiles and modest words made us feel at ease.

Kathmandu, from the Sanskrit words "Kaasth" meaning wood and "Mandap" meaning beautiful shade, had a stimulating energy which left me feeling unusually calm and relaxed, yet excited, bringing me a sense of home, as though I'd been there before, immersed into the great Nepal civilization, yet buffered by stone walls and unkempt gardens. Melodic and clipped, the Nepali language tumbled from the hallways, spilled into the courtyard and joined the throb of a city crammed into tight spaces filled with things to sell and barter. Shops, more like stalls, were thick with scarves of every shade, undulating levels of handmade purses, bangles, and beads, watched over by friendly and smooth traders with coy smiles and slick phrases.

At the Manaslu Hotel, in a simple, comfortable room, my few possessions were strewn on a single bed: a journal, pens, passport, money, blank aerogrammes, and an address book which marked the beginning of my simplified life. I left what I had known behind and already loved being in a wild, somewhat undiscovered piece of the world. In 1987, Nepal remained largely trackless, undeveloped, and utterly different.

Having grown up in the mountains of western Wyoming, these lofty peaks made me feel safe and courageous. Unfortunately, I trusted easily, and was often confused or hurt by simple encounters. I had to learn that life was rough, to see the reality of it. It was not easy for a painfully sensitive and naïve child raised by two successful artists.

Nepal seemed an appropriate transition from my sheltered upbringing into a world that was big and beautiful, ugly and brutal, a world to make what I wanted it to be. I was ready to take it on, but scared lest anyone see me make a mistake.

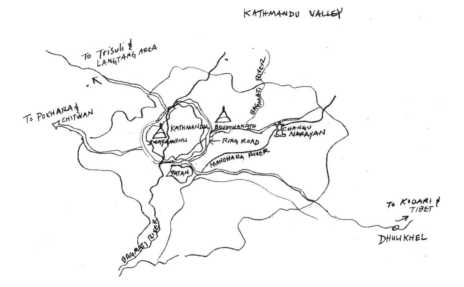

Hotel Manaslu, also known as the "Mountain of the Spirit," named after the eighth highest peak in the world, showed off quaint balconies with views of the Himalayas. On several evenings a few of the hotel workers found me riveted to the raspberry tinges of alpenglow after the sun set as they conversed in a little English, and I in a little Nepali.

"You like mountains?" a young boy dressed in neat, white hotel clothes asked in Nepali.

"I do love mountains, and these mountains are costo ramro (better than good). Have you been in them?" I asked in extremely limited Nepali.

"My village is in them. My father works for a company who takes people into them." He was proud but shy.

"Do you want to do that, too?" I asked him.

"Ho Didi (yes sister), I think, bye now."

JUST BEYOND THE doors of the Manaslu, in the area of Lazimpat, which bordered a touristy section of Kathmandu, was Thamel—a vibrant, funky, and popular hub. The shops were full of trekking supplies, pashminas (wool and cotton shawls), jewelry, music, handicrafts, as well as hip cafés offering good, cheap food—and yet the area possessed an undertone of darkness. Although considered a main tourist spot and hippie stomping ground, an eerie, slum-like reality subsisted in its crowded precinct. Getting lost in its jam-packed oddities, or people-watching from a café chair, would become some of my best times in Kathmandu. A dusty breeze through a taxi window carried my curiosity to noisy streets, where Carl and I made our way to Indra Chowk and Raki Bazaar, an area of glass beads.

Narrow, twisted alleyways were embedded in color from thick, swirled strands of hanging motii or potii (beads), with girls sewing and beading little purses, men sitting intently stringing and wrapping malas (necklaces), women discussing design. The commotion and dialogue absorbed inhibition and we stumbled through basic Nepali for the meaning of the Potey (or pote) malas—traditional necklaces worn by women of Nepal as a sacred symbol of marriage.

"You like?" a bespectacled man wearing a Dhaka topi (hat) asked through a thick beard.

"Ho," said Carl. "Kati parcha?" ("How much is it?")

The man answered quickly.

"Bistaari bhannus," ("Please speak slowly,") asked Carl. The man called out loudly to the next stall. A young guy came over and translated in English and slowed down Nepali.

"My grandfather did it, my father did it, I'm doing it, so is my son." The old man smiled while pointing back and forth from the young man to us. "Caste does not matter anymore." He tipped his head and held up the necklace.

We thanked them and said we'd come back.

"Didi," a young woman called to me while waving her hand at the beautiful pote malas in her stall. She seemed to think I needed to be wearing one. We laughed, exchanged simple words, and moved on.

"She thinks we're married," Carl said, winking at me. "At least that's what it appears."

He walked over to a stall where a man sat wrapping a bundle of stringed beads.

"Kasto ramro," Carl said pointing to the man's fingers. The man motioned to us to sit down. He showed how he wrapped delicate golden thread at the end of the necklace, binding it into a looped clasp, all while making it look effortless.

Carl and I shared the same thought over a cup of tea—Nepal was a paradox of wisdom and innocence, lost horizons, and wildness.

4

Atop Swayambu in Kathmandu, with a Rhesus monkey

WE SPENT A WEEK IN THE MANASLU HOTEL AS OUR NEPALI teachers helped us get accustomed to the new country before moving in with Nepali families for the first few months of our stay.

One of our outings was a visit to Swayambhunath, also known as the Monkey Temple, an important Buddhist and Hindu shrine in Kathmandu. As we entered through the well-trodden East entrance, three hundred and sixty-five worn, rocky steps rose ahead in a diminishing perspective. Sunlight hit their ancient chiseled surfaces, beckoning a pilgrimage one could not turn down.

We began the climb through a mystical forest where Rhesus monkeys appeared in great numbers, hanging from branches, flying from the railings, suggesting their right of territory as they sat on the steps, nibbling crumbs, curiously watching the hundreds of seekers ascending the ancient sanctuary.

Just below the conical cap of shiny copper were the famous Buddha eyes—all-seeing, wise, saintly, lazy and penetrating— painted on four sides, as big as a billboard. The curved line between, like a nose, represented the Nepali number one, meaning unity. Its presence descended on me like a concert—musical, visual, dynamic color in slow moving procession. I walked around the majestic dome touching the prayer wheels, their smooth ridges in etched copper carved with Tibetan letters. They were heavier than expected, and each spin counted as an uttered prayer. Touched by millions of different castes, traditions, races, and religions, they spun around and around, rolled written words packed inside. Below the prayer wheels were numerous small brass cups, each filled with melted liquid (ghee) in which a single flame arose from a floating wick. Light one, make a prayer, and let it go.

Many shrines stood around the stupa (literally "heap"), a dome-like structure that symbolized the Buddha sitting in meditation. They are based on ancient burial mounds, shaped as a free-stand-ing, dome building with a cone or spire rising from the top. They supposedly contained remains of the Buddha, sacred relics, Buddhist texts, and served as important places of puja (worship). Each structure had its own meaning, and was strewn with flower petals, colored powder, rice, and holy water, making the area appear chaotic, yet in ritualistic order. Crowds awaited tika from the priest. Gaunt dogs and a cacophony of pigeons vied for the rice and other food offerings.

I sat on top of the wall that surrounded the area and stared out at the magnificent view of Kathmandu below, pondering the centuries of culture that whirled around the mantra "Om-Mani-Padme-Hum," a message or prayer of love, compassion, forgiveness, tolerance, and self-discipline. It is the Buddhist's motto of transformation to infinite altruism and wisdom, as well as purification of one's body, mind, and speech, which is the basis of suffering from impure thought and emotion. The stupa was alive with rangi and changi cheez biz (colorful things), prayer flags flapping in the breeze in shredded pieces.

Prayer flags were made in five different colors: yellow, green, red, white, and blue. In that order, they represent the elements—earth, water, fire, air, and space. Buddhists believe spiritual vibrations are released like silent prayers when the flags are blown by the wind. They were hung everywhere, from river valleys, mountain passes, temples, anywhere people wanted protection or blessings, offering good luck, happiness, long life, and prosperity. They fluttered like butterflies, eliciting numerous openings into other realms and creating movement in an alluring manner. I wondered how often they needed to be changed.

Small, grubby hands from humble, brown-eyed children begged for rupees. I watched puja (worship) take place in the drone of chanting monks, clanging bells, and high-pitched ringing of Tibetan tingshas (small cymbals used in ritual and prayer). The constant rhythm of the drums from the monks kept my path in line around the famous Swayambhunath. Its piercing yet gentle eyes penetrated the human soul, bequeathing an odd sense of the world: of oneness, of peace, of change, of impermanence . . .

A Caucasian man walked up to me, commented on the view, then reached his hand out to shake mine. He was one of many, a Christian missionary maneuvering amongst the statues and people, preaching the language of their beliefs that Jesus is God.

"Nepali religion has been around a lot longer than Christianity," I openly, yet cordially said.

His hard, grey eyes narrowed slightly, then softened. "The Nepalese have been very open to adding a plaque of Jesus to their deities in their homes. We teach them to set aside all their gods because Jesus is truly all that is needed."

He was very pleased with himself. I looked at him, wondering where he found the nerve to convince these people of anything, especially concerning religion.

"Where are you from?" I asked.

"Salt Lake City." His pasty white face dimpled in a pudgy nod.

"Do you realize what you're doing? Do Nepali people come to *your* home and ask you to pray to *their* gods?"

"Of course not," he said with a shrewd smile, and then, knowing he was wasting his time, bid me good day. Those young missionaries were my age, on their two-year assignment to convert the Nepali people.

Monkeys, attracted to the flowing garb of those placid, white-cheeked proselytizers, grabbed at them, taunting. The missionaries were afraid of the little beasts, so human-like, with a mystique and power unpredictable and wild. The man of god walked away quickly, pulling at his frock. The monkeys looked upon the land and people through small beady eyes, keenly observing in a relaxed, superhuman way. They seemed to enjoy the monks practicing higher consciousness at the temple, watching their deliberate movements, the slowly rotating beads between fingers, the spinning prayer wheels, the chanting. It was a ritual the monkeys (and the monks) had always known: the incense, monotony of tasks, in forever order no matter what color of skin, taking off shoes, peering in, hushed whispers. The monkeys saw and heard everything— Nepal in essential form and syncopated time, pure and authentic, beneath the penetrating, lazy Buddha's eyes that adorned every stupa in the country.

5

I SAT IN MY ROOM, ABSORBING THIS NEW CULTURE. AS THE impact from the stares, smiles, humble gazes, and pushy nature of Kathmandu faded, I journaled, wanting to savor every detail of the day's experience.

JOURNAL ENTRY: September 1987, Kathmandu, Nepal.

An odd vernacular of the United States, and of Nepal impressed, malleable, and though I don't like to judge, I cannot help but feel what I feel. Comparing how I live in the States and living here in Nepal, only the physical aspect of place has changed. I am the same. I take in and accept things easily. Sitting in this comfortable room, in my own space and time.

Unlike previous brief encounters in Singapore and Dhaka, the Nepali people have a humble, soft quality. Of course, it's brutal and unfair to judge, but, none-theless, the instant feel of the place hits me first. Kathmandu impresses an ageless wonderment, one that crosses over easily, like music, or an interesting smell that piques all senses. It's not about what I did or chose to do in life, but because I did it.

Let the wise old Swayambhunath eyes witness this growth. Let them beguile me with what is ahead, and give me hints along the way. I desperately need to

know who I am. I have come here to be saturated in the brine of spiritual recon-
naissance. To recognize my path and know where I am going. If I could get out
of myself long enough to peek into life, perhaps I will see what I am here to do.
Now, a luscious descent of fatigue, and the joy of being able to rest, but first, I'll
draw a little. La.

"La"—a beautiful euphemism used in Nepal that stood for some-
thing like: *Well, since life was decreed, let's just smile, let everything go, and*
move on to whatever is next. It was usually accompanied with a tip of
the head to one side, a tired smile, and a quiet sense of the struggles
ahead; a playfully sweet ending to a Nepali conversation in its lyrical
quality with the determined energy to accept the impermanence of
life. I took "La" seriously to end my questions, comments, or private
conversations in my head.

In the week spent at the Manaslu Hotel, we attended classes as
relaxed outings held on rooftop balconies, dining areas, courtyards,
temples, restaurants, and even in the streets. In these classes our
teachers got to know us, and had given each of us a Nepali name. I
liked mine, *Sobha* (pronounced soe-bah), which meant *gentleness*. It
sounded soft as it easily rolled off the tongue. We were immersed
into the Nepali culture and enjoyed our time as we stayed up late
sharing this new experience of learning the Asian language and way
of life. But the culture was palpable beyond the crumbling walls,
and I wanted to get out there. It was easy to be adventurous while
under the influence of a curriculum.

We had four Nepali teachers. Two were women, one slightly
plump, possibly pregnant as her sad eyes reflected the tug between
mother and teacher, but she was sweet and patient with us, and I
could only imagine the huge burden of adding another child to her
family. The other, waif-like, simply elegant, with a regal air about
her, had no children. They both were quaint, refined, and earthy, as

well as strong adherents of punctual behavior and altruistic candor. Our other two Nepali teachers were men. One was thin, gentle, and soft-spoken. The other was hefty, not completely trustworthy, yet somewhat fatherly and protective. And then there was Shankar, who found host families for us and served as the go-between for everything. His cunning, smart, and kind personality didn't hide a hard-working man in his early thirties. They all offered guidance, helping us to assimilate and feel comfortable in the Nepali life.

A few days into my stay, Shankar had taken me on the back of his motorbike to meet one of two Nepali families he had chosen. It was a beginning of an orientation, to see if I could become part of their household and be considered their brother or sister, son or daughter. We were given code words to express our feelings: "taco" (yes, I want to stay), or "burrito" (no). At the first family I wanted to say no, something was not right, but a pressure to concede, not be difficult, made me agree as I uttered, "Taco."

The other family had two sisters, which instantly reminded me of *my* sisters, and I turned it down even before going there. I longed to have been able to have chosen that one, but the ripped emotions of my past prevented any clear understanding of the closed door I had slammed on that part of my life. I remembered my sisters well—so many good things. I idolized them. But thinking things through and settling too easily were hard patterns for me to break.

When that silent voice questioned, I wished I'd stop and listened —*damn it!*—but I was so impatient with myself and often didn't trust my feelings. This bad habit of making quick decisions, relying on a heightened sense of things, imposing a false time pressure, or worrying too much about the opinions of others debilitated any sense of reason. It could all be traced back to that life-changing decision when my sisters had left me to stay with our father after our parents' divorce, which had disfigured me emotionally.

Imagining Shankar might be tired of setting up those family interviews and taking us around on the back of his bike, I acquiesced to stay with the first family.

6

AT AGE FOUR, IN A STORYBOOK HOUSE IN THE HILLS OF STOWE, Vermont, I was the youngest of three girls when the lull of my idyllic childhood exploded. Our parents began regularly yelling uncontrollably, slamming doors, and filling our lives with tension. They divorced two years later. Unable to discuss the matter civilly, our parents left the cruel choice to my sisters, who were age nine and twelve, supposedly old enough to decide, who they wanted to live with. They chose Dad. I wanted to be with Mom *and* my sisters. Impossible. I was six. Too young. Mom made the decision for me— to go with her. I locked myself into the downstairs bathroom and cried for hours, sitting on the closed toilet seat as my gut wrenched with pain, slashed open and exposed. That ragged wound was too much to bear, never to bridge the gap. That bond, our love, was forever gone.

Before I left, my sisters and I would visit our father on weekends at the mountain cabin he bought near our new house in Vermont, which was called the Tinker House, named after the prior owners. I felt unattached and separated from my body. It didn't seem right being with either my mother or father, and as children often do, I blamed myself for their breakup. With all my might, I resisted the feelings that surrounded me—discord, betrayal, grief, silence, anger. "Unfair!" I screamed silently at everything that had gone wrong. My wounded parents' inability to communicate compounded the tragic ripping apart of my family and the loss of my sisters. Mom claimed she'd tried, but said Dad was unapproachable. Our lives became even more complicated as both Mom and Dad almost immediately had new partners and rallying, bullying, taking sides, and despondency settled into our lives.

On one of our last days in Vermont, I stood behind my little curtain-draped stand selling lemonade at the largest yard sale Randolph Road had ever seen. We sold everything. At nine years old, I looked out the back window of our light blue Volkswagen van as we pulled away from my enchanted childhood home and from my sisters—left behind with our father. A deep, bleak, confused hole swallowed everything thereafter. I had become an only child. My cultivated response to life meant I either over-did or under-did everything, which left me emotionally exhausted and unsatisfied. My life became a tortuous balancing act as I realized I was on my own. My sisters were gone. We rarely visited, and correspondence dwindled to nil as the discordance between our parents seeded itself in us.

The move out west helped push all of that away. It disappeared deep within my subconscious, and I became an introspective, quiet child who learned to please. Mom, Sam (her new boyfriend), and I eventually landed in Jackson Hole, Wyoming, where our new life came together. Well, sort of. I missed my sisters, cats, friends, and the security of the Tinker House with its incredible gardens, fruit trees, and berry bushes. Wyoming was lonely, dry, windy, and new. Memories of the old barn across the street where my best friend and I had spent hours happily playing, bike rides up the hill to the river, and more berry bushes re-played in my head like grainy home movies.

The divorce left me with a legacy of abandonment. Whenever other girls were talking together in school, I assumed it was about me and was nothing nice. My insecurity made me feel everything was my fault.

ONE THING ABOUT NEPAL: no matter where my mind meandered, the intense smell of cumin, curry, and chili, mixed with urine and dust, always brought me back. Clouds of steam drifted up from a table on Dilli Bazaar Road, enveloping a Nepali man bent over an open steamer, feverishly and expertly turning little things over— momos (dumplings) served with a yellow hot sauce. I devoured the steamy morsels in a matter of minutes, and headed down the crowded street into the fervor: honking, swerving, yelling. I was on my own. No one knew who I was, and no one cared. Life was before me, its raucous, chaotic beauty. My tears, unseen, could drop onto the street as reminiscence, and deja vu happened spontaneously . . .

A fine dust and unregulated exhaust mingled at the edge of worn pavement in suffocating clouds. Dirt settled everywhere, its ambivalence authenticating every crease and surface, an integral ingredient along with cow manure, a substance smeared onto the floors of every house. It seemed repugnant, but amazingly had no smell when it dried, and looked like beautiful, smooth adobe. Urine was another familiar smell that curled the hairs in my nose much like lemon activates saliva in the mouth. Its astringent power was undeniable, yet strangely masked by the amount of dried and tangy sweat that coated the airborne dust, and, on occasion, mingled with the scent of burnt flesh. Completed with the scent of curry and incense, pungent and oppressive, the atmosphere of Kathmandu was extremely distinct. The intense bouquet made my lower throat push down and upper chest compress as those scents rearranged my cellular makeup. My whole body breathed, not because the olfactory nerves were overloaded, but the pores of my skin opened and closed like anemones, and I was born again into an exotic realm.

My eyes, too, adjusted to change, deciphering stares from glares, depth of perception enhanced by the warm, earthy colors of brown skin, brown hair, brown eyes against colorful saris, the Nepali traditional dress for women. Saris are wrapped expertly around both thin and plump bodies, whose money and other important things were hidden in its folds, while bangles of thin, glassy churas on women's wrists and arms jangled in tinkling unison with their pierced ears and noses.

I could never look like one of them in a sari, but the punjabi was my style—light, narrow pants with a long tunic, comfortable and customary. The bindi seemed to be a necessary accoutrement, as I was often fixed with one by my host family—a little red or black sticker dot, made of thick, felt-like material, worn between the eyes on the forehead, to act like a beauty spot and for good luck.

Everything moved together—warm bodies on overly crowded buses with no handholds, leaning with the turns, held secure by the commonalty of people and the pulse of a primitive-looking—yet spiritually aware—city; prayer flags snapping vigorously before the lofty Himalayas. Their massive countenance venerated change, excitement, age. The rugged brown prisms of the Nepali eyes reflected life, culture, do's and don'ts, an aggressive discipline, and ingrained compassionate teachings tinged with desire for what I had —or was it merely the reflection of me wanting what they had?

I sat on my bed, shared with bugs that bit me every night, and I wrote. I was just a white ant stuck in a brown anthill.

7

THE MAJORITY OF PEOPLE WORKED LONG, HARD HOURS TO GET simple tasks done—different from the United States, where pushing buttons and talking on phones did the same thing. When exposed mainly to that, the act of actual physical labor was one of beauty. In America, the body alone was often lost to volumes of flesh, cosmetic surgery, and makeup.

It was intriguing to see hardcore manual labor. Of course, it also happened back home, but not on the same scale. I'd seen and worked with enough carpenters, landscapers, dirt movers, and builders to know that the manual labor population existed in every country, but in Nepal, it was a way of life. People worked for pennies. I was not discounting the abuse, prejudice, and lack of hygiene, but simply acknowledging a population who used their body for hard work and ate simple peasant food, the best for health, daily. Most things were not done for looks, but for cleanliness and necessity. People swept the streets to keep the dust down rather than using a leaf blower!

With all my admiration for Nepal, I was not blind to its faults. Every year, thousands of children were sold into slavery and prostitution. Dubbed "Nepal's Stolen Children", young girls were taken and sold, their families persuaded to let them go into the hands of smooth talkers, merely lies told by ruthless traitors, who promised jobs or school opportunities.

Lack of experience and knowledge, something I suffered from as well, as what young, naïve, girl shouldn't have a safe and happy life? Why was it ripped away from some? And why, in the cruelest ways, were girls and children raped, abused, sold, and beaten? Every country has a dark and brutal underside, but the contrast of Nepal's beauty and spiritual history made it seem all the worse.

As a student, studying Nepali culture and life, I could taste the acidic images that arose in my psyche from such aberrations. In my imagination, Nepal was an idyllic utopia. In reality, I felt anchored by a sadness, heavy and ubiquitous as black ink that forever stained certain memories and emotions. Seeing girls in the streets, I wondered—were they free, or trapped? What were those imploring eyes really asking?

An informal dinner at the home of one of our teachers in Kathmandu

We had gathered at the home of one of our teachers for an informal dinner. Sitting on the floor around a square, stout table loaded with plates of delicious, spicy foods, eating with our hands, we shared thoughts of Third World life. The house was simple. I had assumed that with such a great job, money would have been spent on more comforts. The traditional household displayed the bare minimum, which I loved. The teacher's gentle and engaging way portrayed a confident woman, able to lead a conversation with recognition of the undercurrent of Nepal's dark side. Hesitant yet purposeful words in hard-learned English flowed from her unpainted lips, posing questions to make us consider the obvious and the less evident situations in Nepal as well as in America.

"We just hide better in America," one of the students said in English.

"It is not as simple as that," our teacher said in Nepali, encouraging us to practice in her native language. "Look around you. Poverty is everywhere. We are no different being a Third World country."

We asked her to repeat that a number of times until we understood.

"But there is a difference," I added. "Poverty is more accepted here."

And it was true. Consumerism was at a whole different level in Nepal, I thought as I leaned against a wall, having eaten a delicious array of traditional foods including delectable samosas (fried, cone shaped pastries filled with potato, spices, and vegetables). When Nepali people smiled, I felt it came from a deep place of compassion. Their primitive level of living appeared to be only surface, as their humanity, grace, and sufferance embodied a deeper sense of existence. I was enamored by their incredibly enlightened and eclectic culture. Of course, the depth of its reality would hit me later. The being-here-now was a fast injection, and came with a slow consciousness of understanding.

Her little boy peeked from behind a curtain, chanted, "America, America, America," giggled, then ran off.

"Are you teaching him English?" I asked.

"Yes. Lucky for him, it will be easy." Her tired smile indicated how hard learning English had been for her.

8

In Kathmandu, skies were blue, roads were narrow, and the valley was big. Intense colors always made me momentarily breathless: brown skin, red tika, turquoise sari, black eye liner, gold nose ring. Sometimes everything became very still—the tree outside the porch, just beyond the clothesline I had strung from a beam; a flute's lyrical voice, mystical and free.

Back at the Manaslu hotel, away from the smoky remnants of cooking in the kitchen, I sat alone and wrote, far from everything and yet in a space that seemed familiar and wonderful, even though I was nervous about the pending family stay.

The college agenda sounded good on paper, but the reality, though exciting, was daunting. Now past the challenges of traveling, visas, and logistics, I wished to be on my own.

A haze descended, eyes closed, my soul melting into a puddle on the floor. Stepping into it, the stillness broke, asserting the need for this experience to shake things up and so I could gain objectivity to my life. The exposure of living with families was necessary because I would never push myself to do it.

Carl peered into the room. His blue eyes, shaggy brown hair, partial beard, thin-set mouth, and small teeth did not dissuade his clear and resolute voice. He was insightful, unwavering, and strong, always with a hint of comedic relief that was true and cutting, yet forgiving.

"Bhok lagyo?" ("Hungry?")

"Ho." ("Yes.")

I looked up as he entered and sat on the bed, emptying a bag full of bananas.

"What are you doing, Sobha?" he asked suspiciously.

"Writing."

"Ho Didi [meaning older sister, or a friendly term for female friend], but what are you *doing*?" He knew I often wrapped myself up and barely came up for air while pondering in my journal. It sometimes made me feel spacey.

Closing my book, I peeled a banana. "These are perfectly ripe," I said with a smile. The bananas cut through my contemplation with their delicious sweetness.

"What are you brooding about?" Carl asked, grinning.

"The family stay," I said.

"What about it?"

"Just nervous, I guess. I'm totally looking forward to it. In fact, I can't wait. I can't wait for the initial weirdness to be over, and... I don't know Carl, it's just—"

"Sobha, Sobha. You think too much."

"I don't want to disappoint them, and at the same time I want to be real, not pretend that everything is okay, and just get it over with."

"Maybe you don't want to be disappointed?" he asked, raising his eyebrows.

"Are my expectations that high?"

"Oh yes. Oh yes, yes, yes, Sobha."

9

A FIELD TRIP WAS PLANNED TO PASHUPATINATH, THE SACRED Hindu temple on the banks of the holy Bagmati River, where people went to worship. We sat above the ancient site on a ledge and watched an old man wash his body and scrub his head down in the river by the temple, rubbing himself up and down over and over. A look of complete devotion and duty was relinquished to the mechanism of his limbs. Then he rinsed over and over again, as if he couldn't tell he was clean. He would likely be reciting the verse from the ancient Vedas, or answering someone as they, too, scrubbed and rinsed until dirt that hadn't arrived yet on their bodies was cleansed away.

From the Shivapuri Hills, the river ran northeast of Kathmandu, wide and swift, sand and silt giving it a brownish grey color. The river turned ten or so kilometers southwest through the Kathmandu valley—through the city, where it was used by millions of people for washing, cleaning, and transport. Foreigners, and anyone who was not Hindu, were not allowed to participate. We watched from the opposite bank, intrigued by the procedure of purification. I was not brought up religiously, and a ritual of that nature baffled me. How could people care so deeply for their bodies, but then be unequal in gender and caste? The oppressive poverty constantly reminded me that I had nothing to complain about. And though the streets were unclean and water quality questionable, obviously every culture had its weakness, and humans are hypocritical in one way or another. America may be hyper-vigilant about using anti-bacterial soap, but largely ignorant of excessively polluting its oceans with to-go containers and cheap plastic beverage bottles—only one of the many atrocities we turn our backs on.

The metaphor of a river cleansing the soul was that old man scrubbing his body in service to his spirit. Karma was tempered, duty substantiated, and being "clean" took on a new dimension, one that I had read about and discussed in classes with teachers. The body was sacred—news to me. I didn't regard mine as anything more than something to clothe and get me places, not something to worship!

I sat on those uneven rocks near the Bagmati River, contemplating the washing ritual, young and old expertly getting every crease. Women, while washing, wore a wrap called a lungi that tied under their arms and hung to below their knees (the men wore one too, but only covered their hip area), and dunked their children amidst crying protests. If poverty was so terrible, how could there be such deep laugh lines on their cheeks? Or were those lines from tobacco, or the lack of cosmetic surgery? Or did they come from life in general? Sooner or later, we all get them. Evidence of aging was everywhere, but in the western world, we strived to hide it.

There was so much to think about.

I wrote in my journal while sitting on the rocks above the Bagmati, observing the scene below. Carl sat down next to me, picking at the rutted rocks with his finger, probably wishing he had that ornate knife the airport officials had taken away. He asked what I was writing.

"Poverty is a disease, chronic and debilitating if not dealt with," I read from my journal. "It's woven into the fabric of life here, and sanctioned in the codes of reincarnation."

"Is that a line you just fabricated from the depths of your soul?" he asked, looking at me carefully.

"It's one of the paths to spiritual liberation," I said. "You've seen the holy men and monks in the streets in their robes with long dreadlocks, bare feet, and an uninhabited look in their eyes."

He made a wide-eyed, crazy look.

"It serves a purpose," I said seriously. "For some, it's not just a means of measuring wealth, and not necessarily always a bad thing."

"But the degree here is different. It's more pervasive among the population."

"That's partly why I chose Nepal, you know. To live in poverty."

"I know," Carl said, nodding.

"To be forced to see it and feel it. Even then, because it's my choice, I'll never *actually* experience that reality. Is poverty a *choice*? Is disease a *choice*?"

Platforms, emerging from stone steps, line the right bank of the Bagmati, and are used as funeral pyres. A bustle of people down by the water caught our attention as they gently moved a man dressed in flowing white fabric closer to the river. His wrinkled face, closed eyes, slightly opened mouth, and frail body lay on a bamboo litter. I got out my binoculars. Someone placed his thin, bent toes in the flowing water. Immediately his body shook, and then relaxed. He nodded slightly. Everyone settled for a few moments.

He died with his feet in the sacred waters. They had brought him here to die so he could first relax and completely let go. The suffering endured in his life presumably leads to spiritual growth, and possibly a better rebirth.

"I think he just died," I said to Carl. "Moments before his death, they brought him to the water. How crazy is that, to be so in tune? Can you imagine knowing the *exact* moment you'll go?"

I had never seen such a happening. When I was in high school, I had thought about suicide. How easy it would have been to pull the steering wheel of my parents' car as they drove and send us all over a cliff. I knew I could never actually do that, but it disturbed me to have even considered it, and I wondered if something was wrong with me. Was I more depressed than I thought? Did others think about it, too? Why didn't I want to live?

Being close to death in Nepal made the anomaly of it less fore-boding. Talking about it as a stage of life rather than an ending was not new to me. It was the candidness that I liked.

"This is rare to see," one of our teachers said calmly, sitting down with us. "Death is part of daily life, and everyone partakes in its ritual with flowers, food, and prayer. That man's last journey will be with the sacred waters. After his body is burnt, the ashes are collected and swept into the river, which will eventually join the holy Ganges."

Chanting and singing floated up to us, diminishing into angelic murmurs. My own words I had written in my journal fit the chant-ing: Death, always within reach, sometimes uncomfortable in its transportation or acceptance. Death, a natural cycle of life, never gone forever. Death, the greatest escape, the ultimate reconciliation.

"Even for one born into a lower caste," our teacher continued, "death is a noble passage. It accounts for no reasoning, only sanctity. It meant a life lived, for better or worse, and once finished, the next step would be dependent upon how good or bad one had been."

"And who is to judge?" I asked, rhetorically. "Had humanity been served, had arrogance, ego, and greed been kept in check?"

"Yes," my teacher answered thoughtfully. "A combination of cosmic influences, moral consequence that crossed lifetimes, and lessons learned for spiritual advancement."

"Neatly fit under the term *karma*," I added.

"What goes around comes around," another student said, joining us.

"Reincarnation affords the dying and their family peace amidst the grief and struggle, since they believe it isn't really over—"

"What about pain? Is that just part of one's karma, too?" Carl interrupted.

"Death ceremonies help with every stage, but it is understood. Each must walk the path," our teacher finished as he got up to talk to other students.

As a foreigner, I was beginning to see the culture before me, discern its strengths and weaknesses, and compare. I had long revered Asian culture, feeling it to be wiser and more beautiful than mine. Dipping my toes into that Third World had already given me a taste of reality—the dogma, the lies, the magnanimous situation of a populace and its impact on the earth. How we carried on individually mattered more than I had imagined. Everything was dependent on everything, the great mobile shifting when any change, ever so slight, occurred. American culture was just as consequential. Ultimately, we are all the same, just different degrees of progress not all reliant on bigger and better.

10

Bicycles, strapped with towering loads, staggered along on road-weary tires all but flattened from the weight. Buses carved grooves, leaving dust clouds as they careened on the narrow, chipped, broken roads with top-heavy, scary-to-look-at, loads of goods, people, animals, and who knew what else. The human spirit dangled precariously on that edge where life and death met.

One after the other, scenes like these completely took me through horror, comical abandon, and sadness. And even though I came to experience the barrenness of a people and their country, the reality of poverty was always crushing.

Children's desperate hands reached out on the street, pushing and grabbing. Westerners had infiltrated their homeland and freely gave rupees. I had experienced the truly despondent who barely had the energy to ask, to the brazen, vicious demands for something they did not have. It appeared cruel in the face of what Nepal was coming to, what it was, and what I thought it should be. Progress was a savage beast, ultimately destructive, but with its perks.

And it was inevitable.

LIFE WAS DISCLOSED in every ripple and deed. Nothing was covered up: the stench, thick and grotesque, as I squatted close to the gravity-driven drains, susceptible to leakage, which flowed alongside water pipes and created anxiety since water-born contaminants were rampant. How was sewage dealt with? A lack of coordination existed among certain organizations who worked in the field, but not much was being done. Most personal homes had out-houses, but many, including mine, as well as most hotels, offered the squat toilet, or charpi, which I actually preferred, a more natural way for humans to relieve themselves.

The charpi consisted of two pads of flat tile on either side of a hole in the floor or ground. Squatting was the best way to defecate, urinate, give birth, eat, keep the joints lubricated and flexible, the anorectal muscle could straighten, and thus lessened pressure on the whole system, making evacuation easier—which was also said to relieve hemorrhoids and constipation. I'd done it thousands of times in the woods since I was a kid, as my mom and I were seasoned backpackers, but some of the students were having a hard time. Not necessarily because of the position, but it got to the grit of personal hygiene in a very intimate way.

I must say, using my left hand to actually wipe my ass and get it clean was humbling. Plus, we had no hot water and soap. Cold water did clean and freshen the genitals, but being wet, along with a slight odor of urine, added to the discomfort of living in Nepal. I didn't think toilets and toilet paper were necessarily the answer either. Washing sewage down with a small amount of water was economical and energy efficient. Imagine how much water could be saved each minute in the United States if that method was applied—and without adding toilet paper! Could the western world actually adopt the habit of using their left hand? Think of the millions of trees that would save!

Granted, the Third World suffered hygiene problems, but couldn't some kind of middle ground be met? Defecating is a very basic need, but, ironically, chronic intestinal stagnation had become a silent epidemic in Western civilization. Partly because we packed it all in and pushed it all down—an accumulation of decades of old, stuck stuff. Maybe we needed to change our position, and Asia needed to get soap. I don't know, but some better method could be invented.

The left hand, in general, in Nepal, was jutho, or "polluted". The right hand was used for eating—and not with utensils. The two were kept separate. (Keep that in mind when visiting.)

I also recognized Nepal's practice of Ayurveda, a Sanskrit word meaning "the science of life." It is a system of natural healing based on the balance of health between the mind, body, and spirit. Tibetan and traditional Chinese medicine both had their roots in it. The neti pot for nasal irrigation, oil-pulling to help the dental-mouth cavity, as well as cleaning the blood in the entire system, tongue-scraping, colonics, fasting, and other methods of hygiene were commonplace, and done daily. The awareness and diligence to purity within one's body strangely juxtaposed the lack of outward organization in certain aspects of hygiene. In Western cultures, cleanliness was at a high level on the outside, but inside, chronic disease and laziness were rampant, especially in children, where type 2 diabetes had nearly doubled from 1990 to 2010.

COMING BACK in the late afternoon from Thamel, I saw a child squat on the sidewalk of a busy street, defecate, then pull up her pants and run off as cars whizzed by. No one seemed to notice or care. What dropped onto the edge of the sidewalk was almost bright yellow. I felt sick—not because I just saw first-hand what I didn't want to believe, but for the livelihood of the people. I wanted them to be safe, for everyone to have the basics of life taken care of: a safe place to relieve oneself, food, shelter, and water. That image was so striking—the color of her stool, the smell of urine, urine, urine! Who was I to complain about anything!?

No matter how much I loved the culture, that act disturbed me. Did the poor child have parents? Was anyone looking after her? What had she eaten to produce such a color? I later found out it was possibly Hepatitis A. How many children and people defecated in the streets? The problem was chaotic, and the awareness of it made me diligent about rinsing my left hand better and keeping my fingernails short. Travel taught responsibility, as well as the necessary reliance on one's own awareness.

I continued through the streets, past stacks of rubble picked clean and left in forgotten corners—not really trash, but fossils of debris that would disintegrate into the ground with the next monsoon season . . . or not. The weak and old were a part of the scene, not in retirement homes, but working—sweeping, cutting vegetables, holding a baby. Children were cared for by their families, if lucky enough to have them, and slept side-by-side with their grandparents.

Mini-skirts flashed every once in a while, but I thought the Nepali cropped shirt, skirt, and wrap were far superior in looks and functionality to western wear. I understood, though, how Nepali girls wanted to be free to wear what was advertised in movies and magazines from other countries. Locals, however, were offended by showing too much skin. I bought a hand-tailored tunic that had been sewn within a day for only a few rupees. It fit perfectly, better than any store-bought shirt.

JOURNAL ENTRY: September 1987, Kathmandu, Nepal.

The slow moving beast of Nepal is gaining speed and recognition, what will the impending consequences be? I want to think of this hamlet as the pristine, spiritual, lofty place I have always thought it to be. Sometimes reality is no fun, and I might crumble with it. The old Roanne, fragile and unknown, is starting to breathe in life fully. Swallowing this nitty-gritty serum, the bottom falls out, familiarity gauged on life disintegrates, and what am I left with? I don't know— to feel, deeply sad, anger, hurt, shame—have I not connected the lost and disconnected shards of despondency, unattached wandering—no. I have experienced them all cuttingly, flesh driven and wounded. Will I find out that I have nothing to find out? Have I avoided disclosing myself, or just putting it off? But I have time. It takes time. La. Everybody's back, I must stop.

11

Meeting our Kathmandu families at the tea party, at left is me, then Muni, and Tara

A TEA PARTY WAS HELD THE FOLLOWING WEEK. A MEMBER OF THE Nepali families we were to live with would meet us at the Manaslu, hear more about the program, and then escort us to our new homes. I braided my naturally frizzy hair, dressed in the Punjabi I had purchased, and wore simple flip-flops.

Tara, the woman who came for me, sat several chairs away. We stole glances at each other, but our eyes never met. Her hair was a bit frizzy, pulled back loosely, but tighter than mine. She looked tired and reserved, with a subdued excitement, not for me necessarily, but of being included in this cross-cultural tea party with lots of tasty snacks. We made small talk with the group, then awkwardly gathered our things, and off we went. I was excited, despite my apprehension of that particular home.

Maya Bhandary's house, where Tara also lived, would be home for three months. The urban portion of my adventure began in an upstairs corner room of a relatively big house. My space included a bed, a night table, and a small window with a view of rooftops. A curtain separated my part of the room from Maya's.

Eleven family members lived in the house. They were of the Chhetri caste, part of Nepal's largest group, Indo-Aryan hill Nepalis. In India, where the diversity is much less in the western Himalaya, they are called Pahari ("hill people"). In Nepal they are often called Hill Brahmins and Chhetris. There are over one hundred ethnic groups in Nepal, speaking more than ninety-two dialects. Originally archaic Nepali was called Khas kura, and still far west Nepalis say they are and speak Khas—considered more like a dialect, which is difficult to understand. The Brahmins and Chhetris also call themselves Gorkhalis, identifying with the unification of Nepal in 1769, the rise of the House of Gorkha and the royal line descending from there. The differences between groups depended on the population, where they lived, cultural traditions, and ancestry. Chhetris, from the Sanskrit "Kshatriya," hereditary warriors and rulers, are mostly Hindu, and speak Nepali, the country's official language. Maya Bhandary's family can be traced via the Khas in western Nepal (they still wear turbans and smoke the hookah) and to the lowlands of northern and north western India, being forced from that area into the lower Himalayas by consecutive invaders from the time of Alexander the Great, to the Persians, the Mongols (Chhingis and the other Khans), and following that, the Islamic wave that established Mughal India and dissolved into a Mughal Empire that was more of a local, accommodating, or watered-down, version of Islam. The Rana (also Chhetris) claim with some right they are descendants of the Rajhastani Rajputs (born ruler caste), and to this day the high families of the Rana caste try to find brides from Rajhastan.

Maya's house sat off a busy side street in Chabahil, a town on the northeastern side of Kathmandu. It took twenty minutes to bike through crowded streets to our school. Nima, kanchhi bahini (youngest sister), talked and sang sweetly while brushing my hair. She was eight years old, and made me feel more at ease than the others. Mero arko bahini (my other younger sister), Muni, was sixteen, wispy thin with short, wavy, ebony hair, and large, pensive eyes. Whenever we were in the same room together, which was often, she did not stop talking in Nepali and some English.

I took to Maya-didi easily, the head of the household, who hugged me right away. Her eyes reflected age and experience. There were many to meet—two brothers, an uncle, a grandmother, sister-in-law, and Tara, who had come to get me. The situation felt awkward. *With time, things will get easier*, I repeated to myself.

Why was I there? For the first time it really hit me—six months in a foreign country was a *long* time. I'd already projected ahead, my usual suffocated feelings of abiding by rules I rebelled against: college rules, Nepali rules, household rules. Their rigidness and protection shielded me from that naked feeling—as scary as naked-ness is, I knew that was how I had to experience Nepal. Fiercely aware of what lay ahead, I didn't know then that that raw exposure unveiled a quintessential truth for me: how immersion—into anything I was interested in—was how I learned.

THAT NIGHT, Maya looked at me occasionally, and I back at her, shyly. Her eyes were deep and slightly guarded, full of wisdom, kind-ness, and gentleness. They sparkled, something many Nepali people had, as if their eyes glowed with light, laughter, and life, which made me think of a book we read for class, "Beyond Culture." It talked about mono-time (western culture) versus poly-time (Nepal, Third

World). Anything goes in Nepal, but in America so much is scheduled and compartmentalized. I saw calmness in Maya's eyes. I had no problem waiting for a bus, but internally, I had no patience. I hoped Maya and the ancient Nepali culture would give me a sense of self, to help me be in the present.

While Maya hummed and got ready for bed, I wrote in my journal my Nepali name, *Sobha*, and my new family's names. Outside, darkness crept into the street and courtyard. A cat fight, loud and vicious, started and stopped abruptly. I settled into bed like an orphan, a fledgling, and pulled the cotton comforter up to my chest. Maya smoked a small, hand-rolled cigarette, its smoke twirling into my space and out the open window. She was a widow, and head of that household, the aama (mother), but she liked to be called didi (older sister) because she looked so young.

She worked for World Neighbors, an international development organization that aided in the elimination of hunger, poverty, and disease in the poorest, most isolated rural villages. I wish I had taken more interest in her work, and would have liked to visit the site, but she never offered, and I didn't ask. That was the reason I chose Nepal, because I thought I needed to be immersed in not just the language and customs that came with the territory, but the poor, rawness of life when shelter and food were not a given. I wondered if Maya thought it would have been too much for me to see. I learned that letting go came from maturity, an evolved, emotionally charged experience that surpassed logic and caution. Am I prepared for that kind of struggle? Is that what I wanted? Am I being merely romantic and naïve to want to live in poverty and be exposed to the brutalities of selfless devotion to humanity? To find and follow my bliss? To be happy with nothing?

I lay back in the narrow, firm bed. It was dark. I fell asleep to new sounds.

I AWOKE HEARING Maya brush her hair, the radio crackling melodic Hindi songs, men hacking from balconies, kukurs (dogs) barking, scurrying little feet, and soft voices speaking my second language. I smiled, filled with a sense of belonging. I lay listening. My own watch was ticking; I had slept well.

The second day, one of the two male language instructors, always with a crafty glint in his eyes, led us down narrow alleyways in and out of archways and broken down walls and finally through a low doorway into a crowded, bustling room. Bicycles were everywhere. Inquiring eyes and beguiling little brown faces surreptitiously searched our pockets. Shiny, new, red, classic-style bikes were picked out for the white American students. My heart sank. In the face of those tenacious, artful people, something in me needed to be like them.

"New bikes are not necessary," I whispered to our teacher.

"You want something that works and does not need to be repaired often," he insisted.

"But we are only here for a short time. Couldn't I get one that I see most of the Nepalese riding?" I pleaded, trying not to draw attention. The streets were filled with old English bikes—dark metal, simple and not flashy. I wanted to meld into that place, not stand out. I pointed to the iron workhorses along the wall of that shop.

"You need good equipment, and here in Kathmandu, we can provide," his clipped words warned that the conversation was over. The difference between white and brown grew wider. He continued, "Sobha, you need a *new* bike. It is good. Do not worry. And you can sell it afterwards and get a good price." He smiled, thinking he had me pegged.

I let it go, paid for it, grasped the handlebars, and took off. The freedom was contagious. It didn't matter what I was sitting on, I was free on the streets of Kathmandu, cycling to all the places I loved and wanted to visit.

Ring Road, a twenty-seven kilometer highway that circled Kathmandu, connecting all its various townships, had double the clamor and danger of the inner city streets, and it was inescapable. Traffic police wore white masks to cover their mouths, but they were infrequent, and found only at certain busy intersections. Traffic lights and stop signs didn't exist, and if lines on the roads were painted, they were largely faded. The streets were not designed to hold what they did, completely congested with people, cars, rickshaws, bicycles, motorcycles, and trucks, everyone speeding up, slowing down, cutting in and out, honking and yelling incessantly. It was crazy. There was no method to navigate the lawlessness, especially to one not born there.

Parking my new red-hot flyer at Swayambhunath became a weekly ritual, even paying a young boy a few rupees to watch the bike—a steady business for many little ones in the area. Early morning trips to Bodhnath, another famous shrine near Chabahil (where Maya's house was), spending hours in the sun, conversing with travelers, and working on school papers became part of my daily routine.

"Where are you from?" I asked a couple sitting near me, looking in a travel book atop the majestic Bodhnath stupa.

"Canada," they said. "Ontario, you?"

"I'm from Canada, too, Montreal, but living here right now for school."

"Really?" both said at once. "What program?"

"World College West in northern California. The second year we choose a country and live with families. Are you here for a while, or traveling through?"

"Lucky you. We're here only for a couple of weeks, traveling with a group. Next is Hong Kong."

"Enjoy your time," I said, turning back to my book as a few others of their group joined them.

Escaping for fresh momos (dumplings) or coconut cookies at lunch hour developed into an addiction. Pedaling past shops of colorful clothes, strings of glassy beads, going slow enough to take in the array of people—their faces barely discernible—I could detach and float. City life unfolded as a clandestine labyrinth. Breaks at cafés for tea or soup, writing in my journal or reading a book interrupted hours of cycling. Stops in Thamel, then onto Durbar (palace) Square in Lalitpur, where the city's kings were once crowned, Hanuman (Hindu monkey god) Dhoka (gate), Dharahara Tower, and unending temples, squares, parks, and places to simply people-watch. The menace of scents and sounds charged every pore, and fleas made their way into my oiled braids. I rarely brushed my frizzy hair, but a fine-toothed comb had to be purchased and daily combing done very slowly and patiently, serving as another meditation, smashing between thumb fingernail any live critter that wriggled in the teeth of the comb. Inevitably, parasites also nested in my intestines.

I was Nepali. In my heart and in my legs, I was brown and poor, aching for release into a new world when, suddenly, my newfound liberation came crashing down with a thunk, a pop, and a flat tire. While inspecting it, my seat mistakenly wound up in cow dung—or holy excrement, since bovines were considered sacred animals. Cows freely roamed the streets, were given food, covered in colored powder, and traffic often backed up while drivers calmly waited for a beast to move its sainted body to the side of the street. It was a hysterical scene. My bike had been officially initiated into the streets of Nepal: a nail is a nail anywhere, easily finding its way through rubber. I knew enough about bikes to pick out another one for half the price, but my teacher would not hear it from me.

"Ah, Sobha, drop it. Just drop it. Pick up the bike and move on."

I pushed the bike a long ways before finding a family who could help me, another gentle and humbling encounter with those delightful people. Their questions were not "Where are you from?" since they knew it was some white country far away, but "Come inside and have tea." And because I could speak Nepali well enough for basic exchange, it was mostly giggling, touching material, and remarks on origin as they helped me fix my bike.

12

When I awoke the next morning, I heard hushed voices in Nepali.

"Is she up?"

"Ho bahini? I am up, come in," I said to them. Birds sang sweetly outside the small, open window above my bed where a cool breeze refreshed the insulated warmth of the comforter. The chortle from my bahinis (younger sisters) and kukurs (dogs)—the constant moving of Kathmandu—made me smile. Maya brushed her hair on the other side of the curtain, as she did every morning, and told the girls to get ready for school. The youngest peeked into my room. We giggled, then Maya's command sounded again.

Life was exposed, whereas we westerners were more hidden and secluded. They did not show their skin as we did. Women did not wear tank tops or shorts. But Nepalis hacked, practiced religion, picked for fleas in each other's hair, shared rooms, lived with all family members old and young, and burned their dead in public as ritual. Nepal didn't have the luxury to allow privacy. People were not separated by long driveways, large houses, far commutes, or even disease. They lived in close proximity, even in the outlying areas. The population was enmeshed; ceremonies, festivals, and rituals linked them together. They were a tribe, much like our ancestors.

The sky was grey on the first day of school, a puppy yelped, dal bhat (rice and lentils) was served, heaped as high as Annapurna! What to do?

"I cannot eat all of that, Maya," I said in Nepali.

"It is okay," she said, disappointed. "Leftovers go to the dogs."

Classes went well at the base house; lectures and conversations on the Nepali language, history, and culture slowly developed as we sat informally around circular tables. Our two-story school building sat on top of a small hill off the quaint road of Purano Baneshwor, with a lopsided wooden gate, small yard, and flat roof. The caretaker was a middle-aged man who had a droopy eye, thick lips, and slow speech, and reminded me of the Elephant Man, but not in a deformed way. This gentle soul had a huge heart, smiled timidly, and was easily manipulated, but we didn't take advantage of him. He loved it when we made popcorn, or included him in a homemade meal.

Both our female teachers dressed in beautiful saris. One was married to a Nepali businessman, and she always appeared especially elegant. Those slender, kindly women always arrived with tika, painted eyes, bangles up their arms, and starchy saris. Our two male teachers dressed in dusty suits, and asked about our new families as we went around the group. I had mixed feelings about my family.

I quietly told one of the male teachers my family had fed me in my room by myself. He talked to them, and that evening I ate in the kitchen with hajur aama (grandmother), Tara, bahini (younger sister), and bhai (younger brother). But something felt missing, other than not meeting all my family members yet. The ones I had were reserved except for Maya and the youngest, Nima, whereas the other students it seemed had already bonded. It didn't take much to stir the already tenuous insecure soup I swam in. How did they feel about me?

JOURNAL ENTRY: September 1987, Chabahil, Nepal.

Living here with them is so new. I want it to work, easily and quickly. The strangeness is the same for them. I have disrupted their house, their life. Do I really think they don't care about me? Isn't that presumptuous? Do I have any sense of the impact I have on them? I don't know whose daughter is whose, are they all Maya's children? Or does Tara have any? Will I ever meet all the family members? Am I interested enough to ask? Do they sense that? I am not sure.

I WAS INTERESTED, but could not speak Nepali well enough to convey those feelings. Already an inhibited misfit, instead of taking the leap to talk about things, I became a polite observer, waiting for the right time. Unfortunately, being overly sensitive about every little thing—a wrong look, something not done right, a harsh tone—didn't help the situation. The effort of questioning everything left me depleted and raw, always double-checking, making sure I remembered what I'd learned and had done to get it right. I wanted to blend in without creating a ripple—funny! This white girl with gold hair caused a ripple without having to do anything. Just being there had already created a stir. Did I want to be one of them? One of what? I wanted to be noticed, be someone special, but I didn't want it to be a big deal. Such contradictions.

Indulging in food eased my anxiety and filled the cracks of inse-curity. In Nepal, snacks were plentiful, such as the dried coconut, delicious and greasy, bread, soup, curries, biscuits in little packages, samosas, and dal bhat (lentils and rice). Eating became a problem, filling the cavernous hole—the hungry ghost Buddhists refer to. This neurotic tendency toward obsessive compulsiveness had its roots in some kind of childhood darkness that had crept into my adult life. Some handled it better than others. I hid from it.

JOURNAL ENTRY: September 1987, Chabahil, Nepal.

I actually don't want to be noticed, and at the same time, desperately want notoriety. Even though I have thought about suicide, I could never do it. Life is work, and earning that right to take my life was not what I wanted to do. I would rather be miserable and in the dark long enough to figure it out. Youth gets

*in the way of understanding what the hell is going on and travel has a way of
undoing everything comfortable and reliable, to stand on the edge of an abyss,
both horrific and beautiful.*

I AWOKE the next morning with a blocked nose and a full stomach.
My family still tried to get me to eat too much late at night. I wanted
to be thin. Plump was much more accepted in Nepal, preferring a
more natural woman's body. Curves did not interest me. I longed to
be svelte, and I was slowly losing my incessant desire to eat, for it
had always been my comfort. America liked the lanky, cadaverous
look—sexy, "in," and desirous. I wanted to feel light, unencum-
bered, but the weight I carried felt heavier than the few extra
pounds I wanted to lose.

That day I decided not to eat dal bhat. I wanted a break, but
had to lie about it. In the kitchen hajur aama (grandmother) pointed
to a full plate, but I responded quickly, "Hoina Aama, mero pet
dukheko chha, tara dhanyabad." ("No mother, I have a stom-
achache, but thank you.") I pressed my hands together and bowed.
She raised her voice in a squeaky shrill and called Muni, who
rushed in, looked at me and the plate, then at hajur aama. They
spoke heatedly. I sighed, and my heart sank. I interrupted them,
"Muni, no khane aja, tara dhanyabad." ("No eating today, but
thank you.") I went on in English and Nepali about how I got a
break at school and would eat there. I had to eat less. "I am pugyo,"
(full) and patted my stomach, "naramro." (bad) I looked into her
worried eyes, trying to make me obey the commands, probably from
Tara or maybe even Maya. I smiled quickly, waved goodbye, and
left.

When I got home from school and told my family that I did not
want tea. They brought it anyway with two pieces of roti (bread)
and some crackers. At dinner they said if I didn't eat another piece
of roti I would be malnourished. After dinner I was in bed, almost
asleep, when Muni came in with a tray of tea and snacks. I barely
opened my eyes when she turned on the light, put the tray down in

a tight gesture, and said, "Sobha," in an intimidating tone, "khane Didi." ("Eat, sister.") She tapped my shoulder, and without an answer from me, turned abruptly and left. I didn't touch it and went to sleep. It was gone in the morning.

I knew they were concerned, but it was more than just too much eating. Constipation had plagued me since the first week. Something more than too much food was stuck inside and had been there long before Nepal. The two younger girls, my bahinis, were skinny and hollow-looking, probably going with less to give me more. Maya was worldly and amazingly conscious, though she could also be swayed by cultural demands. They did not understand me, nor I them. I told them so many times in a day that I don't want so much food, why didn't they get it?

The next few days I ate what I could and politely stopped when full, but not before praising their food, which was always delicious. It wasn't a matter of taste, and I tried again and again to talk with them, make analogies, and hear them out. I just sat there, similar to how Maya was in so many situations I had seen her—gentle, calm, and sure of herself. The disappointment in their eyes matched the grievance inside myself. The reserve between us was understood, and though unsettling, silently agreed upon . . . eventually.

Nepal was a journey of self-realization. I had to travel far away from everything I knew to start the awareness of seeing myself. Only then could a change of habit be possible. Nepal is the birthplace of one of the greatest teachers, Shakyamuni Gautam Buddha, who says that we are responsible for our own lives. It's a good lesson, one that will probably stay with me my whole life.

I had already taken the leap by getting on the plane. I was beginning to unlock my past, and what better template but a writhing, colorful, intense world such as Asia? Nepal was beautiful, alive, pulsating, every move watched by the Buddha's eyes, that painted gaze on the stupa temples—fascinating, lazy, beguiling, wise . . . and tika. How could I not unfold and change, grow, break free?

I HAD many occasions to meander through my thoughts while sitting on my bed at Maya's house or in the kitchen at night near hajur aama, at Bhodhanath, in cafés, or on my bike. Often I reflected about being taken away from my sisters and father after the divorce. Since then, I had not been able to fit in anywhere. Now, living with a family that I didn't know how to be a part of pushed the edges, and I questioned everything. Were they nice to me because they *had* to be?

I didn't really believe that. I was not out to exploit, in any way, and neither were they. I just wanted to slip in unnoticed and experience Nepali life, to write, become someone—or at least understand who I was—then escape back to the mountains where I could be a recluse, an old maid (I never expected to marry), or become a famous writer and speak at huge events. As much as I wanted change, I think I fought it.

Maya's hum broke my reverie, her voice sailing through the curtain in Nepali.

"Sobha? Kasto cha?" ("How are you?")

"Takai lagio Didi, ra tapai?" ("I am tired, and you?")

"Maile tapailai sapana ma dekhen," ("You were in my dream,") Maya said, parting the curtain, tilting her head, smiling as she handed me a small plate of dried pounded rice and roasted soybeans.

"Ho?" I said, and shook my head. "Hoina, I already had something, tara dhanyabad." ("No, but thank you.") I often ate something with friends at Pumperknickels after school, one of our favorite cafés downtown.

"Ho." She frowned and went on about her dream. I think she left something out, I could tell by her lingering gaze. Nima, my bahini, ran in, panting, and took my hand.

"Ma sanga aunu huss!" ("Come with me now!") she said. I looked at Maya.

"La," she said, waving us off. Excited, Nima led me up to the roof and pointed to the sun, melting in a lavender sky. We sat huddled on the edge of the concrete wall, watching the beautiful sky, talking in Nepali and a little English.

"Nima, what do you want to do when you grow up?" I asked.

"Sing." Her little lyrical voice said, looking at me with wildness in her eyes. She stood in front of me and sang the sweetest Nepali song and danced. I clapped heartily.

"Teach me?" I asked, getting up and standing next to her. She giggled and took both my hands in hers.

"Do this." She tilted her head and sang a few words.

"Pheri bhannos, tara dherai—" ("Say it again but very—") "—dherai bistaarai!" ("—very slowly!")

She laughed, interrupting me, and repeated it many more times as she did little dance steps. I followed until a chill overtook us. She looked at me, wrapped her little arms around herself, and shivered. We ran down to dal bhat.

Dinner was late, around nine p.m. I was allowed to cut vegetables and handed over bowls of them to hajur aama, then prepared spices according to her instruction. When I finished, I gave them to Muni, who placed them on a flat, thick slab of rock (khal), and ground them with a round rock pestle (batta). Muni's action with that ancient-looking mortar and pestle blurred as she pulled and pushed back and forth, the separate ingredients transforming into an aromatic chutney. She smiled, barked little commands at hajur aama, who just rocked on her heels, wrinkled her nose, acquiesced in uncertain grunts, and waved Muni off with a face of fallen dignity. Hajur aama once was an enigmatic woman of prestige, no doubt. Now her life, filled with smoke and forgotten days, crumpled in humble and misgiving attitudes, was mostly hidden from everyone around her. I didn't know if she ever slept, or got up from that dirt floor.

A FEW DAYS LATER, I biked home through the dark streets, riding fast, eager to get to my journal, the solitude, privacy, and sanctuary that resided in its pages. I had been writing in diaries since the age of six, initiated by a family trip out West. At the time we lived in Vermont when my two older sisters and I were taken out of school for a trip across the country. Keeping a journal of our experience was part of our homework, and since then, I had written volumes. I felt an obligation to record my life. Unfortunately, much of my writing was censored by an alter ego who thought it would be found and read. Much later, I finally overcame that fear.

Journal writing allowed me to express my feelings, no matter how dumb, repetitive, or immature. I loved the blank page, preferring hardcover, un-lined art books. Lines on a page resembled the first step into fresh snow—the page had been used, it appeared chaotic to me. I also liked a black, ultra-thin, felt-tip pen. The first words on crisp white or flimsy newsprint paper, a pliable and earthy feel, were like biting into chocolate cake, overwhelmingly addictive and satiating. My journal was my best friend. The look of the words on the page made me feel accomplished. The expression and scenes portrayed objectivity. I recorded life. I could move on. Even if the emotion or situation was not resolved, at least it was *out*.

Me on Boudhanath stupa, near where I lived at Maya's in Chabahil, Kathmandu

On a sunny afternoon I sat on Boudhanath, one of the largest Buddhist stupas in the world, just a few kilometers from where I lived. I'd peruse my journal as monks, nuns, and local Nepalese walked around in a clockwise direction, chanting *Om Mani Padme Hum*. An episode from another day had helped break the ice with my family.

JOURNAL ENTRY: September 1987, Chabahil, Nepal.

I washed my hair in our yard today. Something as simple as that turned out to be a big thing. Eventually both bahinis (younger sisters, Muni and Nima) helped while neighboring families watched. "Hah! How does white girl with gold hair wash hair?" The first words I've heard out of my uncle's mouth, and then, also in broken English, "What color after? Gold wash off?"

It was funny, I must admit—that bulky lungi (large wrap of material wrapped under the arms to below the knees) clinging to my body while I tried to wash under the wet material, every movement cinching it tighter around me. I looked up, water dripping down my face, soap everywhere, and just smiled. In return, more laughter and comments from a bunch of old crows with crooked mouths, wrinkled skin, loose flabby bellies, squinting eyes with tears of jubilance and guileful abandon.

I still am treated like a guest and don't like it, but ultimately, I am. They don't know what to do either. I splashed Nima, she giggled and splashed me back. I chased her and Muni laughed, her hand holding her mouth. Nima ran and ran, and because I was getting too cold, I had to finish. Nima came up again ready to splash, but Muni warned her to stop. We all giggled. And my uncle just sat on the balcony, drunk on raaksi (rice liquor) and toasted to us. I wonder where he got all that stuff? I don't think he worked. Did Maya give him an allowance?

THE HAIR-WASHING EVENT had eased tensions. I closed my journal and looked up. Boudhanath was a hub of Tibetan culture, with many Gompas, or monasteries, around its serene, symbolic presence. I loved to sit on its large, rounded sides, open and free like a beach.

Time passed quickly. Dusk crept in. I gathered my things and biked home. That evening, Maya and I talked about education.

"I learn better through experience than repetitive lessons in 'writing and arithmetic.'" I said in English. "I have the privilege of choosing how I want to learn, and having the time and freedom to pursue it. Our cultures differ in this respect. It's who I am, and how I was brought up."

"There is no time. You must study," she said slowly in Nepali.

"Ho Didi, I must study, I know," I said in Nepali. "But also some of my study is done with your family, helping out, learning how you wash clothes, doing things as you do them. I like that best."

She understood my words, if maybe not so much my meaning. Education was very important in that country. I was privileged to receive it. Her eyes admonished, hard and relentless, but she kept silent. I knew what she was thinking: '*Be grateful, you have no idea how easy you have it.*'

I needed to let go and allow things to happen without trying to control every move anyone made, wanting it to fit into my picture of the perfect cultural experience. Why were my expectations so high? I wasn't brought up in a household of never getting enough . . . or was I? Maybe in my childhood the necessities of survival were at a low. Love? Consistency? The split in our family had happened at a delicate age for me. I was too young to comprehend what was really going on. All that fear, trapped inside—repressed.

Maya and Tara were arguing about something. I heard my name. Uh-oh, that made me uneasy. Tara left. Maya was quiet. She lit a cigarette and inhaled deeply. During the long silence, I knew not to ask, but let her work it out as she had done for decades. I blew out my candle, lay down on the hard, familiar bed, and fell asleep quickly.

13

OUR TEACHERS WERE ALWAYS POSITIVE AND SEEMED HAPPY TO BE with us. Our base house was a regular Nepali house, its rooms converted into classrooms with all the typical trappings of school—chairs, tables, chalk boards, and lockers. We often worked in a comfortable sitting area with windows, a casual scene that lent an ease of attention and distraction. Learning different languages frustrated me only because I thought they were hard. In class I grew tired quickly, and struggled to be attentive.

I enjoyed the field projects, similar to my high school education, which had been very diverse. I had spent two years attending a conservative public school in Wyoming, and then my parents, determined to expose me to an alternative education, found the Mendocino Community School on the northern California coast. It changed my life by rekindling my love for learning. I discovered school did not necessarily have to be in a classroom, but rather in the world. We progressed at our own speed and we had understanding, yet firm teachers who gave us choices and listened to us. The school was based on Evergreen State College in Washington state, a progressive liberal arts and sciences college whose tag line fit me perfectly—*Go beyond majors, classes, and grades and experience your education the way you imagine*. The head of the community school had a magic touch with teenagers. He spoke our language and made me feel comfortable and included.

For my senior year project (in high school), I chose to construct a Navajo loom and weave a rug as close to the traditional method as I could. A local weaver who had transformed an old water tower at the edge of the headlands in Mendocino into a studio made my already-rich experience into an artisan's dream. She created colors from natural ingredients—mushrooms, plants, and seaweed—that were beautiful. Something about the feel of the wool, the earthy colors, and slowly seeing a weft of handmade material emerge from the antiquated-looking loom was exalting. I helped to fill orders at her small business in tie-dyeing t-shirts as well. I was not sure what piqued my interest in weaving, but the attraction continued in college, one of the reasons I chose to live in Tangting (the village I stayed in after Kathmandu), known for its hand-woven garments (or bhakhus). Weaving was my project during my stay at the village.

The first two years of high school in Wyoming I learned to write and do geometry (well, sort of—the teacher was mean and impatient, and I had to cheat my way through his class). High school was high school. If you were plain-looking, shy, and a late bloomer, that was tough. Lessons were hammered in, and as long as my homework was on time, everything was okay. Intimidation—now referred to as bullying—was ever present. Asking questions brought on stress and horrible feelings of humiliation. I knew I'd be criticized for my "stupid" questions and weird lunches (miso soup, rice cakes, and sprouts), so I waited until the end of class to ask. Once I got to the alternative school, my self-esteem improved, but the damage had been done.

Even on the other side of the world, during class in Kathmandu, I waited until a break to ask a question. Our teachers patiently answered my inquiries. Their kindness made me feel accepted, and, finally, I relaxed.

Biking in Thamel, I'm on the right

Carl, the student whose knife I had tried to carry through customs, was always ready to skip a class or go for a bike ride through convoluted streets in some corner of Kathmandu. His positive, light-hearted nature came out in conversations where he'd skillfully take off from where I'd stopped, and then turn the topic into a shockingly funny and bitingly true joke. I could be crazy with him, say things I wasn't sure of, but get it out and muddle through until the deeper meaning appeared.

He and I biked into Thamel after classes for chiyaa (tea) and bread. Pumperknickels, our favorite café, made dense, chewy rolls studded with salt and seeds. In the back, away from the busy street, a funky, comfortable gravel courtyard held small tables, plants, and hangings. Being mostly outside, that spot was the best in nice weather.

"Alternative education works for me," I said as we locked our bikes. "Even though the early years in Jackson made me afraid of geometry and history."

Carl laughed knowingly.

"I always felt inadequate. I just didn't get it," I continued with a sigh. "Maybe that's the crux of the matter. I had a block against math, and maybe it's the same for language. High school French was a joke, but I loved Algebra last year! So is it the subject, or the teacher?"

"Depends. Most often the teacher, I think. And me, too, about language," he said. "But I took Spanish, didn't learn much, it was a study-take-test-and-then forget everything type of class . . . It's just high school in general. Who remembers Spanish from high school?"

We got our snacks and went out back to our favorite table near a large tree-like plant that offered us some privacy.

"Any language is hard to learn," I said, "and I've never really had the brain for it. I guess I was, and still am, a typical teenager."

"Sure, Sobha," he said. "Though, a little on the odd side of typical. But the excuse has worked for a long time." He laughed, pulled his roll apart, and chewed on it.

"I didn't put the work into something because I was already unusual, which I figured accounted for something," I said, raising my eyebrows to accentuate the point. "I had the knack for things, you know. A tinker of all trades." I dipped my roll in the hot tea.

"Youth is wasted on the young, anyway. You just need to grow up," he said, smiling.

"Grow up? Then I'll have to figure out what I want to do. I actually like the concept of education. I want to be smart and find my passion, but I don't understand it in those terms. The ones that are taught in school and parroted by teachers, parents, therapists—no matter what they say, even if it's, 'Do what you love, the money will follow.' *When?* I don't have time to wait for it."

"So impatient, Sobha! It doesn't matter now, just pick something and you'll eventually figure it out."

I scoffed. "That's a waste of time. Mozart knew what he wanted to do."

"Mozart didn't necessarily choose, but he got good at it because he did it—"

"My parents hated each other when I was five," I interrupted.

"What's that got to do with anything?" he said skeptically.

"I was swept into that craziness, but I didn't escape into the piano or something, even though I took lessons then."

"Right, you hid. You had to protect yourself, and that's where your energy went."

"I'm so insecure, Carl, I can barely breathe sometimes."

"I hadn't noticed," Carl said, leaning back in his chair.

"And confused, and I don't know what to *do*. Anyway, I hear too many renditions of what people say and read into their thoughts, assuming what they said wasn't really what they *meant*, or maybe what *I* say isn't what *I* meant?"

"You're a mess. You think it's because of your parents' divorce?"

"I don't know. . . It's always a number of things, right? I worked as a baker and ate too much junk in my teens, which added to the scattered thinking, too. Making decisions creates anxiety, so I avoid them and rely on the wind to push me onto a path—at least for the time being, until its course changes." I finished the last of my tea.

"How can you avoid making decisions? You *decided* to come here, right?"

"It's been a life-long dream."

"To come to Nepal?"

"Yes, you know that."

"How did you know about it?"

"It's the Himalayas, Carl! I love mountains. Everyone knows about the Himalayas, and most people want to see them."

"So obviously you *can* make a decision."

"The easy ones, yes. The tougher ones, like career, relationships —I get caught up in what I *should* do, and then what I *want* to do gets buried and I can't feel it."

I was frustrated because the big knot inside me was bruised and angry. We fell silent for a moment.

"What are you thinking?" I asked Carl.

"My parents never divorced, but they should have. It was brutal growing up with them. I'm sure it's what made my dad sicker." He finished his tea. "Ready to go?"

"I guess we should." I knew a little about Carl's home life. He did not have much love.

We parted outside of Thamel as the sun set and dusk brought on an urgency to get home, about twenty-five minutes of pedaling.

I did have an inner-agenda that worked on me throughout adolescence: *Do what you want to do!* One thing I knew for sure, I wanted to see the Himalayas and live like a poor peasant—so why not fulfill college credits at the same time?

14

For a day trip to Changu Narayan, the oldest temple in the Kathmandu valley, taxis dropped us at the base of rice fields, where we followed a winding path until we came to the Manohara River. Everyone removed their shoes and socks, waded across the cold water, laced back up, and hiked through beautiful Champ trees with their thick, oily green leaves and peachy colored flowers. Finally, a long courtyard of chiseled rock slabs placed in jagged lines welcomed us at the entrance to Changu Narayan.

The temple had been built for Lord Vishnu, a Hindu deity. There were conflicting versions as to why, but it had something to do with Lord Vishnu unknowingly committing an awful crime, being cursed for it, then freed by a Brahmin (part of a caste group of Nepal) who had caught a young boy stealing milk from his cow.

I marveled at the pagoda style temple, Hindu in origin. The slow, old pace to its countenance resonated like an old coin, something I wanted to keep.

We enjoyed a simple picnic on the grounds while listening to the ancient legend colorfully told by a skilled raconteur. The scene lulled me, along with a slight breeze and tinkling sounds of the daily rituals around Changu Narayan. The place was remote, and visitors were infrequent, making it feel more authentic, like a recollection of what Nepal was like decades ago, before the modern world. Antiquated sculptures, deeply embossed stone structures, ornate handiwork, worn out areas where thousands of years of devotion touched the stone. We explored the sacred site in hushed groups and silently alone, then returned down the terraced path to the river.

I decided to walk the five or six miles back to the base house (our school) instead of taking the bus. A couple of friends joined me, as well as ten local kids, lured by the sweet melody I played on my penny whistle. The children giggled every time I turned to see if they were still following us. A few times I raised the little tin flute up high and brayed it loudly. They would turn and hide. I took a few steps back towards them and they would come out of hiding, laughing and looking back.

School was far enough away, and the landscape strangely unpopulated, that we got lost a few times, yet managed to find our way again. I thought of the legend of Changu Narayan and how complex humans were. . .

Studying and experiencing Nepal's customs, religions, and culture tugged at my provincial roots. These people were connected to a greater wisdom, a source deeper and richer than I ever imagined. Its power was so great, and so right for them, that the ceremonies, body decoration, and daily rituals kept the human mind, in all its distractions, tamed and focused. This humbling encounter could only be understood in momentary glimpses. Living under the Buddha eyes, painted on so many stupas across the country, was a constant sign to remember.

Upon entering the Community High School in Mendocino, California, a plaque of painted wood hung on the wall, containing one simple word: *Remember*. The head teacher pointed to it during *Circle*, where we gathered every morning to talk about plans for the day or week, important events going on in the world, and vent on the unjust, cruel, unfair, wonderful, altruistic, positive state of life on the planet. We were teenagers, and had a lot of angst and energy to get out. That forum allowed us to speak our mind, be listened to, and answered in honest, heart-felt, intellectual rapport.

Remember, take a breath. *Remember*, you have as much to do with everything as anyone else. *Remember*, look at yourself and why you do things, be aware of the consequences of your thoughts, your actions. R*emember*, it takes work. *Remember*, listen, *remember*, listen, *remember*, listen . . .

———

THE DIRECTOR of Asian Studies at Tribhuvan University in Kathmandu talked to us about ancient Nepali history. After class, I rode past him on my bike as he was walking home, and noticed a different side to him. Something in the way he held himself had changed after he'd left the school.

On the street, that dynamic man became thoughtful, sensitive and strong, yet small or shorter from when I had just seen him talking to our group, as if a shell coveted his body like a genius entourage of imaginary conversations between this world and the ancient. Slightly curved, his thin body seemed to master the narrow line of the sidewalk in reverence to the soul-serving nature innate in most people there. Maybe he was not as confident on the streets? I almost saw his thoughts above his head, circling around, encompassed in deep reflection. He seemed a very patient and interesting man—he *was* ancient history.

Do we become what we are interested in? Can we choose *exactly* what we want? What if I didn't know what I wanted? What if I wanted too many things? What path would I choose? What if I was too scared to do what I *really* wanted? Some of the people in front of me were doing what their parents did. Others had chosen their own paths.

As I biked home, my eyes felt tired in the air, thick with dust. Scarves wrapped around mouths and noses, a good idea and a partial solution for a huge problem. Cars did not go through emission testing in Nepal. Toxic black smoke billowed from many vehicles, and with it, Kathmandu and I melted together into a mirage of colors, making all moving things into something called culture—a rich, deep organism always striving to repair itself when an organ was lost or the natural order of things went astray.

It was dark when I parked my bike inside the courtyard of Maya's home. Hajur aama called me inside the little building where the kitchen was. I peeked in, greeted her with hands-pressed-together, namaste, and cocked my head slightly to one side. "La, Aama?" (I often dropped the hajur with her, as I heard Muni and Nima do).

She pointed to a knife and a pile of vegetables. I motioned to my things as I went up to drop them off in my room, then raced back down to sit on the mud floor recently spread with cow dung, which they believed kept bad omens and spirits away. Hajur aama smoked her pipe, rocked back and forth, smiled weakly, and stirred the pot of cooking rice. The crackling fire threw shadows across the room, bringing it to life. She said something, laughed, pointed to my mouth (in reference to my language abilities), and said in Nepali, "So Nepali now."

"Dhanyabad (thank you) Aama. It must be something in your delicious food!"

I never heard her laugh so much, and I had to join her.

15

I AWOKE EARLY THE NEXT MORNING IN DARKNESS. I DREAMED I was biking with Carl when we came to a place that had old, broken down stores. We stopped and, strangely, gave away our sleeping bags, as well as some of our clothes. A small child bought me a book from one of the shops. On the way back, Carl fell off his bike. Bunches of bananas and tufts of grass also fell off. He was mad at me, saying this wouldn't have happened if we hadn't lied to each other. I didn't know what he meant. Later in the dream, at a monastery, children were taking confession. I overheard them and decided to do my school project on proxemics. Inside the monastery, I found a wand with a picture of a priest or deity who wove a Jewish-looking symbol on its cloak.

I tried to analyze my dream. My bike may have represented freedom and independence. While riding, I easily made decisions—where to turn, which road to take, what to explore. Whereas life decisions, even about what to wear, were intimidating and stressful. Giving away sleeping bags and clothes could be signs of waking up, becoming conscious of my health and/or lack of awareness about what was going on in my waking life. I didn't connect opposing situations, how they could mirror each other and offer insight into everyday stressful events or feelings. Bananas and grass, possibly good stuff already innate to my character and psyche, but they'd fallen off. Was this because I put too much weight onto other people, hoping that transference would fulfill my lack of identity? What had I lied about to Carl?

It all became too heady, and I got lost in the transcription, but it was fun to try to see where a deeper part of myself was going. I had studied dream interpretation a little, I was an avid dreamer and loved symbology, but ultimately the work was beyond me, even though I yearned to unlock my secrets.

People in dreams often represented aspects of one's self. If that's the case, who was Carl, and why was he so important in my life? He was a good listener, like the brother I had always wanted. His naïve sense was similar to mine and, like children, we resonated in a playful way. We were good friends. Even so, I sensed something unsettling about him. It would be years later before my intuition was confirmed.

A YEAR after our return from Nepal, Carl and I had met again on my way through California for a backpacking trip into the Marble Mountains. He was staying with his paraplegic father in a rundown, cluttered house that seemed to be full of ghosts. It felt like a dark psychic presence infiltrated the room, and I couldn't wait to get out of there.

Carl was emotionally removed, his playful nature heightened to hide an impatient disregard toward his father, who didn't say much. He baked bread to take on our five-day hike, and once it was in the oven, we packed up.

The Marble Mountains were a beautiful area of open rocky alpine bowls colored with speckled boulders and studded shrubby bushes. The days rolled into one another, sweetly spiced with the reminiscence of our time in Nepal and cold nights sipping tea.

The walk out to the car finally came. I was impatient to get on the road. Carl had wanted to stay in the mountains for a few more days. I could tell he wanted to be together. The difference created a silent chasm between us.

We lost touch after that. A year or two went by, and he found me in Washington state, where I was checking out another college option. He arrived, seemingly fine, but the first evening I caught him in my bathroom, talking to himself in the mirror and making strange clucking sounds with his tongue and movements with his hands.

The next few days were awful. He lost touch and tried to force himself on me. A friend helped put him on a bus after buying him a ticket to send him back to his father's town. The bus pulled away with Carl standing up in the aisle, eating one of the sandwiches we'd packed for him. I worried that he would eat them all too soon, or be forced into sitting down by other passengers and get violent. We had heard from a friend of ours in Portland, Oregon that he got off there and wandered for days, looking for me. It was incredibly sad and disturbing. I was at a loss as to what to do.

Eventually, I just went on with my life. Years later, we spoke again and mended our ragged friendship.

Where did the line cross? Why did we break down to such degrees of loss? I didn't love him in that way, and even if I had, I was not emotionally stable, due largely to the opening and raw vicissitudes of my Nepal experience.

THAT CRISP MORNING IN NEPAL, needles of light splintered in through the window. I was in bed, staring at the ceiling, trying to understand that dream. I thought our friendship might be too much for Carl to handle. I was sure of where I stood, and didn't have a problem with it. The dream also brought up religion—interesting, because I had no religious training.

Hinduism was the dominant religion of Nepal, but Buddhism was followed as well, which I leaned more towards with its Eightfold path, a premise of understanding and practice. The Buddhist dharma path was about the disclosure of truth and liberation from suffering so that one could learn to live authentically, taking responsibility for their choices. That path suggested the root of all problems as attachment to desires that could be eliminated by following the Eightfold path: the right views, right intent, right speech, right conduct, right livelihood, right effort, right mindfulness, and right meditation.

I really didn't have a full understanding of either of them. Hinduism was similar to Buddhism in the law of cause and effect, or *karma*, and that the soul reincarnates. Devotees of both were guided by enlightened gurus, or teachers (Buddha in Buddhism, the three gods in Hinduism), and to lead their lives under the influence of personal discipline, self-inquiry, meditation, and good conduct. Both were a way of life, to live by certain ideals that I believed in and could strive for, I thought, when I was older. I always felt an affinity toward Buddhism, a mystique of meditation in high mountain monasteries, a non-violent nature. Books about its teachings helped demystify its lessons.

Hinduism was the world's oldest religion, supposedly having no beginnings, so its mystical nativity supported the individual to find his or her own truth within. Living in a culture whose sole purpose was abiding by a complex tapestry of faith, festivals, and traditions was groundbreaking for me. Those rituals were the fabric of the Nepali society, and guided every move no matter which religion it served. Nepali people lived together in a melting pot of tradition, but civil unrest was brewing into an explosion of political change which didn't break through until years after I had left. But the first undercurrent could already be felt.

GREY, damp clouds hung low. Hajur aama pointed to my scarf and bulky clothes, mumbled something, smiled sheepishly, moving her lips over missing teeth, and pointed to dal bhat. I finished every bite, gathered my things, and biked off to school.

Are we basically instinctual? I wondered, weaving through the crowded streets. I saw it as a razor's edge between what we know to be right, what we don't care about, and then what we do.

School started with a talk on local government. Nepal was a Hindu monarchy ruled by King Birendra. How strange, I thought, a land ruled by a king! The current Panchayat system was cracking; a discord among the population promulgated into the Nepalese Civil War (long after I left, lasting ten years), then democracy brought its own set of problems. The people of Nepal largely didn't seem to care about that as much as inflation and nepotism. The new government also brought freedom of religion and disintegration of the caste system. People converted from Hinduism and their untouchable or low caste status, to Christianity, thus the proliferation of missionaries.

What a mess it seemed, all this attention on class differentiation and segregation. Religion never had been important to me, it just caused a lot of war and dissension. My father was Jewish, but didn't practice it. My mother was adopted and never knew her real past, but she'd been raised Jewish. I was brought up liberal, and practiced no religion. Thanksgiving, Christmas, and birthdays were fun because they were just big parties with food. In my dream, the Jewish symbol could simply have reflected that part of my life etched in my blueprint, paired with this Nepal immersion and how extreme change could unearth deep-seated mores.

MAYA SEEMED to have a progressive attitude toward religion in her country. Though petite and soft, her solid outlook rivaled her name—popular in Nepal, meaning *love*. Maya was also the name of Siddartha's mother. She eased her floral sari gently into the side of my room, smoked her salvation daintily, as the only reprieve of a fantastically burdened family life, closed her eyes briefly, then smiled, saying in Nepali, "Tomorrow we will go to the monkey temple."

Maya, me, and Tara outside the base house, Kathmandu

I awoke to Maya singing my name in a made up song. I looked forward to salty dal bhat and saag—cooked greens of some kind—with Maya. We ate together, rare to have her company in the mornings since she usually worked very early. Stepping onto a bus with her on that Saturday (or Holy day, similar to Sunday in the States) was like being carried in a dream by an invisible hand. The thick air of separateness parted, lightness and intrigue took its place. People who were shy or contentious became inquisitive, and I was included in conversations. Though my Nepali was rough, I could understand and converse in basic terms. However, the cold, ulterior energy was still there from some locals who were suspicious of a white girl in the company of Maya, an enigmatic angel who worked for peace and communication between villages. She was known in some small way by most inner circles.

The slow, bumpy ride moved along to the sound of raucous local music as I viewed toothy smiles, vacant stares, clutching hands around baskets, bundles, bags, and little ones through half drawn windows. As our ride carried us forward, I stared back, never looking at one person for very long. Women I could out-stare, and often received a smile. But the men, whose steely black orb-like eyes in almond slits penetrated a desire, an aggression, in an otherworldly unease that disassembled judgment and safety to the point that anger and disgust overtook reason and caution. They thought they had that kind of power over me simply because I was a woman. I stared them down, too, even though I was told not to, but being white had some power. I didn't use it often, and I was prone to hide it. (Hide I was white? Impossible, I stuck out like a bruise.) Indian men were the worst with their stares, whereas the Nepali men seemed not as intrusive. Without trying, I was finally popular, foreign style.

Everybody was touching because we were crammed together like sardines in the bus. Men held hands, women too, but a man and a woman did not show affection for one another or hold hands in public. Strangers said namaste to each other, a beautiful sounding word meaning, in general, 'I bow to the divine in you,' often accompanied with palms pressed together, fingers pointing upwards. That gesture was different than a wave or a handshake. It felt like more was at stake. If I took a moment to greet someone in such a graceful way, an automatic receptive connection formed, instant and fleeting, soft, structural, and complete.

When encountering a white person, it usually brought an abundance of smiles and giggles. People laughed, and why not? I looked odd in a traditional Punjabi or shalwar kameez, hair braided, glass bangles, chatting in Nepali with a Nepali woman. I wondered what they were thinking.

Before Nepal, I had always seen brown people as the minority, and it bothered me. I grew up partly in Jackson Hole, Wyoming, where only two or three black people lived, and one, on his way cycling to work, was roped off his bike by a couple of inebriated cowboys in their pickup. Jackson wasn't a despondent, middle-of-nowhere kind of town. It was an affluent artist community, swashbuckling working rodeo and western life, as well as an intense climbing, hiking, and skiing hotspot.

I couldn't imagine being lassoed and thrown into the sagebrush, then left with a mangled bike run-over by rednecks. That sickened me. Deep down, were altruistic people really racist? I felt racism was learned, not innate in human beings. Now I was in the opposite situation. I was the minority, finally, and being it was different than seeing it.

We arrived at the base of Swayambhu and made our way up the steps into the sun. Our talk, in English and Nepali—but mostly in Nepali, with Maya helping me along—cascaded over many topics, including marriage and companionship, a subject highly coveted in Nepal.

"Sobha, why have you not married? Don't your parents want that?" Maya asked, stopping to look in my eyes.

"No, Didi, they want me to do what *I* want to do. In America, marriage is not the same as it is here."

"Yes, I know, but it is still something you want?" She was concerned.

"No, Didi, I do not want to get married." I smiled at her, and pointed to the monkeys all over the trees.

"Oh, they are terrible." She shook her head and shivered, squinting her eyes toward the dangling rascals who yipped loudly. "Never Sobha? Never marry? Oh, that is not good. A man is good."

"But Maya," I stopped her, "you are not with anyone, and have not been for a long time."

We stood for a moment to catch our breath. The three hundred and sixty-five steps to the top were etched, rocky slabs, stepped on by millions, their smooth, cracked surface imprinted with every walk of life, the thin dust beneath our feet further polishing them. We chuckled at a group of Oriental ladies cringing and squealing at the monkeys who grabbed at them.

"It is their perfume and colorful material that they like so much," she said. "Sobha, my story is a different song. Do not follow my life. I had a wonderful life, but now, it is not so bad either."

"Didi, my parents had a rough break-up when I was little. I am not ready to choose a man to spend my life with. Maybe one day . . ."

We turned back to the stairs and finished the ascent. Once at the top, Maya showed me around, then hurried off to do puja (worship), teeming with locals doing the same thing. I floated free, dodged tourists, and sought lonely corners where monkeys wouldn't bother me. A young, dark-skinned boy with shaggy black hair and a dirt-crevassed face interrupted my silence. In broken English, he offered his help for rupees. I did not give money often, not because I had very little—an American dollar was an incredible amount to that little guy—but I believed people needed to work and earn money. Perhaps if I were wealthy, I'd hand it out, but I preferred sharing food, or offering a ride, or giving a piece of clothing. More often money would be spent on alcohol or drugs, at least in the States, though I did not think this kid would do that.

I struggled with what to do since he might be punished for not bringing home enough money. Maya came over and asked if I was all right. There was a long line for puja, she said. I assured her I was fine and to take her time.

"My name is Shiam," he said in English, and sat next to me. "What is yours?"

"You speak good English! I am Sobha."

"Is that your real name?" he asked with a twisted smile.

"Hoina, my teachers here gave it to me. Mero nam Roanne ho." ("My name is Roanne.")

"Ho Didi!" he exclaimed. "You talk Nepali, I talk English."

He went on to explain how he had no home, or money, or food—at least that was what he told me. His eyes exuded with disclosure, but not in a pleading way. Nepali children were conscious of the responsibility to beg, to bring in enough to feed the family, or care for siblings, or take on chores that were above and beyond what any child would be subjected to in the western world. Nepali kids were soft and sweet, yet tough. Shiam, a street diplomat, conversed unabashedly in Nepali and English in a sensitive, charming way. He was good at what he did, and though I offered no money, I shared the last dried fruit I had. He tried to finagle his way in by asking if he could watch my bike while I shopped or sat up on Swayambhu. His lighthearted tone accepted a poverty-stricken life, which was everywhere. But in Nepal, the religious notion of it leads to enlightenment—or at least that's what the philosophy implied.

To some degree, poverty happens in every corner of the world. Who was to blame—the people, the government, the educational system? Why can't people get themselves out of it? Did it have to do with extreme malnourishment? The food in Nepal, primarily rice and lentils, seemed to nourish the soul far better than western food, where alcohol, drugs, and junk food threatened lives more than starvation. What really *was* poverty? A state of mind? A degree of health? A physical manifestation of not having enough? Poverty was deeper than any of that. It was like a disease, a degenerative condition of the soul.

I told Shiam that when I come to Swayambhu, if he is there, I would pay him to watch my bike. He pressed his hands together, nodded, and moved on, throwing one last lingering, sad, but hopeful look in my direction before disappearing into the prayer wheels and robes.

Kathmandu was beautiful from Swayambhunath. It seemed very still, yet moved with lively, colorful people. The sun was warm and eased the tightness in my gut. I felt good, actually, but something bothered me that I couldn't pinpoint. Perhaps I never would. Perhaps it was all in the little box that held my personal things—not the material ones, but rather the intangible, true thoughts and feelings, the ones that came out when exposed to a different culture.

Centuries of devotion and ritual infused Swayambhu, its vibration grounded, so compact and fixed that even my dreams could not give symbols to reach down into the ancient realm and know why that all manifested. Life was a funny thing, and changed constantly. The amount of history right there, under my feet, was mesmerizing. A legendary story is told of a great lake that filled the Kathmandu valley over two thousand years ago, although the lake must be considerably older. Archeologists have made finds of Neolithic peoples (tools mostly) in the Valley dated back eleven thousand years. Then an enlightened being drained it, and soon, the perfect lotus flower grew in the center, later perching itself on top of the hill that transformed into what is called Swayambhunath—the Self-Created Stupa.

Feelings of safety and freedom, a desire to pursue Nepal and not answer to anyone, emerged. Nepal churned in childishness where a choice could mean one thing or another; neither wrong, but each very different. Perhaps the whole world functioned like that, and I had just started to become really involved. Conversing with people where language was a barrier made me rely on everything else to communicate, liberating funny antics and creating instant friendships with a smile. Swayambhu, a melting pot of locals and foreigners, its lineage reaching back to creation itself, was one part of a grander scheme of things.

Nepali people were rich with culture and deep in tradition, but both were strange and unknown to me. I barely knew my grandparents, an entire side of my family sliced away by adoption (my mom's side) and the other side by divorce. I didn't grow up with my ancestors.

The roads vibrated with the essence of people. Years of walking, talking, worshipping, and fighting pounded the earth below the infinite heights of the Himalayas. America was young, but here I could feel the layers, so deep and as magical as a massive redwood tree whose presence awed. Swayambhu needed to be experienced over and over again, and I visited it often.

I found Maya still in line to do puja. She handed me her bag to hold, and I looked for another spot to wait. There were so many people, all colors and sizes, receiving tika and worshipping. A little time went by before Maya returned. She put tika on my forehead and a flower in my hair. We moved to some steps in the shade and ate crackers, noodles, and the rest of my dried fruit. The noodles were raw out of the package, strange, I thought, yet a frequent treat that was remarkably tasty and probably laced with MSG. She rattled off in Nepali, then smiled and repeated the same words slower, still in Nepali, so I could understand.

"I do not come here much Sobha. I do puja at home. But it is good. Thank you." Hungry dogs and monkeys snapped delicately at her fingers as she threw crackers. "I cannot enjoy food unless everybody else around has some too," she said with a tired smile.

I agreed, still learning so much from her about giving and sharing. "Thank you for what, Didi?"

"For coming into my life."

She patted my hand, looked warmly into my eyes, then, "Tut

tut." She waved off a monkey who was determined to get the rest of her package of crackers.

When I met a sad person, I felt sad. Or with a sick person, I felt their sickness. I had always been like that. To many it might sound simplistic, but I truly believed that if more people got in touch with their emotions and showed empathy, we could lessen the disastrous antagonisms of the world. If all the soldiers in the world stopped fighting, then there would be no war. If they, and everyone else, refused to fight, then other means would have to be conceived to deal with societal and political strife. Non-communication and violence between countries is terrifying. Wasn't it easier to talk about problems or make affiliations happen that served the best for everyone?

Why could we not live in peace? Where did all the fighting and hatred come from? Were we born with such distrust? I didn't understand where the vicious cycle of abuse and prejudice stemmed from. Were we really *that* detached from our hearts? Ah, such questions.

But Maya felt the same way. She couldn't eat a cracker without feeding the monkeys.

Carl saw us and came to say hello. He sat down and my didi offered him crackers. She was animated, excited to see one of my friends from school. She invited him to come over several times, and though it never happened, it was a kindly gesture. Then she asked Carl to take our picture.

Later, when looking at that photo, I was shocked at how large I appeared compared to her! My five feet four inches and one hundred and twenty pounds seemed Amazonian, bulky and unnatural next to her smaller frame of at least five inches shorter and thirty pounds lighter. Her physical delicacy struck me because I'd seen her as tall, strong, and wise. She had smiled softly, open and confident for the camera, whereas I smiled modestly, awkward in my body, but I did lean slightly towards her.

Me and Maya on Swayambhunath, Kathmandu

On the way home, she held my hand as we made our way through the crowd. I thought about my life there, settling into a rhythm, biking back and forth to school, learning Kathmandu and Nepali, sitting at stupas with my journal, and warming to Maya and her family.

After Maya and I left Swayambhu that day, we suddenly came upon a flaming pyre of crisscross logs. I stopped, my hand pulling away from hers. Two feet stuck out, the toes gnarled in red and black flames. I involuntarily inhaled the smell of burning flesh. The fumes were surprisingly similar to barbecue. Maya put a hand over her mouth and nose and shook her head. Burning flesh filled the air, and it smelled good. What a strange thought. I stood transfixed, fascinated.

Maya conversed with an old lady nearby, and then told me in Nepali, "His toes had just been in the Bagmati River. That's when he passed over."

His body melted in the flames near the sacred water. The energy was active in the invisible space around us, as if that man's soul was alive, his body spent and released, now giving thanks. Is he dancing? Rejoicing? Spreading his wings? I was consumed by the smoke, the smell, the colors. The scene made me feel alive. Around the site, everyday life carried on: rickshaws passed, cows meandered, splotches of colored dust and ribbons sailed in the smoky breeze. Children scurried, bearing heavy loads with goats, babies, or food as people washed in the river. Maya wrinkled her nose and told me in Nepali to come quickly.

I said to her in Nepali, "Death is very natural here, Maya, different than where I come from."

"Oh Sobha, it is natural everywhere, but here, we celebrate it. If we do good and live kindly, then we will move on." She took my hand to hurry me along.

"What about fighting and war here?"

"Yes, some do, many do. Change must happen. We must learn to love each other." She did not want to talk about it. The street was insanely busy, and we were trying to get to her friend's house quickly.

Her friend greeted us at her door and looked at Maya comfortably. She pointed for us to sit down amidst their exchange in rapid Nepali about the burning body, the busy traffic, and the day in general. Maya knew I couldn't understand too much of what they said, but rather than explain and interpret, she leaned on me or stroked my hair, held my hand, and sometimes patted it. I sat in the company of adults, obediently relaxed into the lull of conversation, sometimes hearing my name in soothing tones. I might be the center of attention, but did not have to be, and that was exactly how I wished to be treated.

Maya was like the sister I had lost so long ago. Her tender patience, even with a hint of fatigue, made me feel equal, as if I was meant to happen. That morning she had come in and had spoken to me slowly, in Nepali, making sure I followed her. The bond between us was sincere; she told me she loved me. I looked at her, squinted my eyes, and smiled. I thanked her for being so tolerant and for taking me in. I knew she got paid for it. She interrupted, "It is good for us, too. We need to experience another culture. It is easy this way."

Maya had high cheekbones and smooth brown skin. She felt deeply about her country. "I wish more people would work. They are lazy here." Schooled by her own desire, Maya had forged through the working class arena and carved a path to get beyond what many normal girls of Nepal didn't fight for. She supported her family and kept her frustration in check, but it couldn't have been easy with so many to care for, including the alcoholic, unemployed, free-loading uncle. An innate calmness, gentle perseverance, and amazing patience portrayed the overall picture of her graceful everyday moves. I was amazed at how she continued to push through, no matter what.

That evening, I still had the image of burning flesh in my mind, and asked Maya about it.

"Do most try to get to the Bagmati River to die?" I asked in English.

"Speak Nepali, Sobha," she said in Nepali, so I asked again in Nepali.

"Many do," she began. "It is a hard journey. Most die in their sleep or in accident. Disease also, especially children." She stopped brushing her hair, looking at me. "It is why my work is so important." She sighed and continued brushing.

"Is that why you chose it?"

"Ho Sobha, my bahini died from sickness, in my arms, when I was young." Her eyes deepened, then creased into a painful smile.

"I am sorry, Didi. I have never had anyone close to me die."

"One day Sobha, you will. You will. La, it is late."

In Nepal, death was as common as a child growing into adolescence. The transitional stages were learned naturally as part of their rich, religious life, so when it was time . . . I didn't know, really. Perhaps they fought it as much as westerners did. But how could that be? Death was seen and experienced: ritual, public cremations, family's young and old living together. Birth and death were major events the whole family took part in. Yet, I saw into their lives, where inequality reigned, outdated tradition prevailed, and reticence to change was covered over with arrogance and habit. All came out at odd times, like Maya wanting to feed me more food. Was it driven by fear of not being able to provide? Was it upholding a belief or practice that served an outdated notion rather than the individual? Or was it simply making sure their guest was well fed? I learned to recognize the conflict between tradition and progress in Nepal.

I realized that change only happened within an individual, and occurred as a very unique and personal passage—not necessarily attached to a god or religion, but more like an inevitable awakening from a disease, accident, or trauma. Those were the forces that made us come out of ourselves and see the larger picture. Even then, some of us just didn't get it.

I wondered if I would.

AGE WAS REVERED IN ASIA, so different than in western culture. Karma, too, played an important role—when the effect of a person's actions and thoughts had a direct consequence to that person's destiny—and kept the smiles ever glowing. That was an interesting notion. Whatever you did in life was checked in some realm and would come back around so the lesson could be learned. I believed in it, but repeated so many mistakes not because they appeared in different packages, but once in the middle of something, I would forget and fall into an old rut where insecurities and inexperience shined and the repetitive action ensued.

While sitting up on Swayambhu, waiting for Maya that day, my thoughts had come up in a relaxing litany—such humble people, such rich experiences, such heavy consequences. I was an adventurous young woman leaning on a handrail a thousand feet high on a temple over-looking the land. The view blurred into an indistinct cloud of mindfulness. My breath and thoughts were cool and clear as sounds from behind were muffled. In awareness, I felt I'd stepped into the dimension frequented by the chanting monks.

Ah, but that instant dropped, the land materialized. A monkey sat near, its hunched, furry shoulders twitching. Cows strolled the streets with tika, red powder, and a holier-than-thou saunter. My thoughts merged with the differences of back home and here in Nepal. What a contrast to where I came from where brutal slaughterhouses killed those gentle beasts in massive lots, but Nepal worshipped them. Nepal, where angry teens targeted foreigners with water balloons and wads of paint on a traditional festival day, a public venting of cross-generational and cultural frustrations. The images unraveled, each one in sequence, yet in no apparent order. Their vivid detail and sharp colors flooded my mind as I sat on the roof of Maya's house early that evening.

A little girl's face surfaced again in my mind, one I had seen in a dream or passed in a crowd. A few days ago near a busy street amid the normal humdrum of traffic, horns, and chatter, she cried a piercing bawl while sitting alone on the edge of the road. Her wailing was lost in the cadence of people, hectic and alive. Her tears smattered dirty cheeks. She sobbed, heavy and uncontrollable, pulled at her shirt, and wildly looked around. Was she hurt? I waited at the curb. Ten minutes went by, but no one stopped to help. After a few more minutes, I went towards her, but stopped suddenly when a young Nepali girl ran over and picked her up. She yanked the child's wrist, roughly told her to be quiet, and the child's body crumpled under the weight of her emotion. The girl held her tight and walked off.

What if the girl hadn't come and the child was left? I looked around, taking in the craziness of saris and punjabis, half-naked men, foreigners in a motley mix of scarves and jeans, all bustling about, the smell of charpis (squat toilets), spicy dal, and a constant upheaval of dust that never settled.

Moments like those happened everywhere, all the time—children left crying, and some never picked up. It broke my heart. I couldn't shake that image as I sat on the roof, gazing into the dark night sky. I had continued on through the crowd that day, jostled by others in a hurry. My feet moved, one after the other, until pellets of rain suddenly seized the city. People scattered, crossing the street into buildings, under awnings, huddled together, peering and pointing and waving arms. It poured hard, then turned to hail in huge balls. The scene was blurred and dirty white.

It stopped abruptly, an instant of quiet abandon. We smiled and shook our heads, realizing how small we were in the midst of that great land. On with life, loud noises, people talking, laughing, and shaking their clothes. One man in rags and bare feet ran down the middle of the road, his arms waving high, singing.

Nepali dust was different than anywhere I had ever been—a spice in itself. But dust was dust, and when it settled long enough, it broke down its host and softened it. Nepal was doing just that. I was nineteen, completely impressionable. I shivered in the night air, got up, and went down to my bed.

16

ONE AFTERNOON I STOPPED AT THE BASE HOUSE TO PICK UP SOME books before going home. A few students were sitting outside, talking. Juni was speaking in her typically animated fashion.

"Human need and survival pull at every angle. You can see that here in Nepal better than anywhere." Her cheerful demeanor turned serious. "People's faces reveal the work and hardship, and it's incredibly beautiful to see." Juni was short, her shiny, black, shoulder length hair framing smooth, olive brown skin. She smiled like she knew something secret about you, or maybe it was just her carefree attitude and positive outlook on life.

"I know what you mean. It's amazing to see," I said.

"In the West, we curse age," Juni continued as she acknowledged me with a smile. "Why do we do that? When did we learn to be ashamed of growing old?" As her fingers made invisible quotation marks, she added, "Everything is fine."

"Right," I said. "We cover up the ugly, the bad, the taboo—in one form by washing volumes of chemical hair color down the drains just to erase the grey. Women have to color their hair every three weeks to keep up with it! Don't we have more *important* things to do?"

"We've certainly come far from the truth of what America is, or once was," Juni said as she bit into a banana.

"Which is?" Carl asked, leaning forward. He was a good debater, and liked playing the devil's advocate, always with a thought-provoking angle.

"A long time ago, we were thinner, ate less, and ate simpler," she replied, reaching for more bananas.

"Yeah, we weren't so concerned with getting somewhere fast and with having more," I said. "We were content with relatively little. More like here." I waved my arm to include the entire country. "At some point, didn't our grandparents mean more to us than the latest, greatest gadget?"

"Communication was once honest and deep," Juni added. "Can you imagine?"

"And it's not now?" Carl interrupted, provoked by our generalization.

"It's different," Juni said. "When did materialism, fear, and shallowness move in?"

"Materialism, fear, and shallowness?" Carl echoed, shaking his head. "It's always been here. It just seems different because Nepal is such a unique backdrop."

"No, it's not that simple," I said before Juni could respond. "The shift happened with such force and so completely that we've forgotten how truly good we can feel in life without stimulants."

"What shift?" Carl asked.

"When life changed from being simple and authentic to something very busy," I said. "Too many cars, too much garbage, too much sugar, too much coffee, too much electrical crap—too much everything!"

"It's a state of mind, really," Juni said. "Of course, there is too much. Unfortunately, it's the direction the planet is headed."

"And this fast-track has got to get to the extreme," I said, "before it swings back into some kind of balance. There are places where people live simply, surviving off the land. There are many who are not buying into the craziness."

"Like here," Carl said. "Life feels easier here."

"That's because we've been physically removed from all that craziness. Isn't that why you came?" I asked, looking from Carl to Juni.

"It's part of why," Juni responded. "The parody of western culture isn't so comical. It's sad."

"And the parody of Nepal," Carl added. "Its poverty and compassionate teachings infused in every deity, stupa, ritual, and person is unforgettable."

"Because its people are so humble," Juni said, now munching on crackers.

"What about you?" Carl asked, looking at me, smiling knowingly. Something was missing in his subdued, hidden demeanor, which made his dreamy smile and easy way even more curious. "Why did you come?"

"It's easy to see character traits both good and bad in someone other than yourself," I said. "It's as if everything is a reflection, don't you think?" I didn't wait for a response. "My own weaknesses and strengths come to the surface through these challenging experiences. It's all about moderation." I laughed. "Which is something I struggle with constantly—it's either all or nothing." I reached for some crackers.

"Yeah, maybe," Carl said, stuffing a whole peeled banana in his mouth. "When the information gushes and everything gets choked—"

"It's really *us* who need to change," Juni interrupted. "Life is the same. Is that why you're here, at the base house now?" she asked me.

"What do you mean choked?" I looked at Carl stuffing that banana in his mouth. He smiled wide, looking like Jack Nicholson in *One Flew Over the Cuckoo's Nest*.

"Too much coming in at once." He reached for another banana as he nodded and waved it. "Too much of a good thing isn't always good."

"Yeah. I can be silent," I said to Juni after a long pause. "Sometimes gravity wins out and the 'fairy tale' of Nepal is exposed in such intense colors that I have to squint . . . and then I peek into its beauty like I never did before."

"Gravity wins out?" Juni asked.

"The heaviness of my thoughts, of Third World living."

"It's a force of attraction. We're all here for a reason, this is all happening for a reason," Juni said.

I left the conversation to get home to my "busy" house in Chabahil. Juni, Carl, all of us students, were reacting to living in close quarters, tired of language translation, and a powerful awakening of thought. The aliveness of instinct was bittersweet. It punctured my system in joy and responsibility so heavily I couldn't taste anything else. I felt profoundly linked with the suffering on the outside by what I felt inside. Validated by the likeness, Nepal allowed me to breathe. I wrote about those feelings often.

JOURNAL ENTRY: October 1987, Kathmandu, Nepal.

The grueling non-communication within my biological family and the angst that I've held inside since childhood has a voice. But this is happening on such a visceral, sub-conscious level, that even though I appear to myself and others as fiercely independent and needing to be free—it's from myself that I need emancipation in an urgent way—an objectivity or a fisheye's view. But even if I had that kind of sight, would it solve my problems? Would it help me to see clear, could I avoid the constant questioning and self-doubting?

WEEKS BEFORE STEPPING onto that plane for Nepal, while still a college student in California, I had dropped acid for the first, and only, time. That seemed an appropriate initiation—just take it once, since I'd heard of people going crazy on the stuff, and that the effects could return, unannounced, even decades later. Doing it once should be okay, right? I wanted to experience something beyond what I was capable of consciously doing, something bigger than myself. I hoped to be exposed to a different realm, maybe even develop extra-sensory abilities.

None of that came to be. But something *did* happen.

I took it sitting straight and nervous on a sunny weekend afternoon in Linda's psychedelic poster laden room with her and Juni. Then we walked into the golden northern California hills above campus, waiting for it to take effect. The dry, stalky grass undulated and my heart pounded frantically. I reached out with my hand as the stoic eucalyptus trees slowly transformed into swaying shades of digital colors melting into each other. I had been scared to do it, but Linda had taken it more than a hundred times, and was the quintessential guide through the trip.

We stretched out on the dry, rough grass and looked up into an endless, deep blue sky. A mirage narrowed in front of me and the sky turned into a large ornate corroded stone or metal gate. Little brown-skinned children with wide brown eyes peered through the openings, like animals secure of their place, looking in at me as if I was in a cage. The children seemed curious, silent, unobtrusive, and sensitive, yet not on purpose. They looked at me, I looked at them. We watched each other. Their hair moved in the breeze and their hands grasped the sides of the gate tightly, then let go. They pushed at one another for a better look.

I was in Nepal, where I had yet to go.

The image of the children was frighteningly real, their gaze inquisitive and intense. Voices from their moving lips, inaudible, shimmered like cicada song on a rainy night. I stayed with them for a long time until they faded away. I sat up as the undulating trees slowed. Hours had passed when my college friends returned from walking the hills to check on me. Acid was exhausting, but different from mushrooms and marijuana—which was like incense to me, as the smoke had always been in the house as I grew up. I didn't need to hide or be infatuated by it, and only smoked when wanting to get "out there" creatively or on occasion with friends. Pot affected me deeply, emotionally, but nothing like even the *thought* of acid. I didn't like the uncontrollable aspect of drugs. I tried different ones for the experience, but I found they weren't for me.

After about ten hours of constantly being pulled out of the "real" world into other images, moving shapes, and circumstances, I finally started to come off the trip. At dusk, a wind picked up and a chill made us smile at each other. We made our way back to Linda's room, where we talked nonstop and laughed uncontrollably. She always got ravenous after trips, and voraciously ate Kraft cheese slices on dry, cold bagels. I was not hungry—felt very full, in fact—but watched in awe. How could she pack it away like that? Her huge mouth and red tongue, ogling eyes and sloppy nature amused me in my post-acid haze. She had me rolling with laughter until we finally said goodnight.

I retreated to the sanctuary of my college room. The acid trip filled every corner of my skin, its energy consuming, truly a foresight into the journey on which I was about to embark. I couldn't read much more into that image other than I would be there soon. Those large, brown eyes and persistent fingers around that ancient, ornate gate continued to play in my mind. Those eyes. They penetrated softly, seriously. Those eyes. They stared. I had never been the center of such focus. What did they see?

Nepal was as far away as I could go to find out who I was. Trying to escape or discover through drugs, as the acid trip showed, didn't get me there. They were artificial, and drugs didn't allow me to totally let go. I could smoke a lot of pot and still hold a conversation, but eventually it made me ultra-paranoid, so I could only smoke alone. On those occasions, I wrote. I was afraid to be around people, for they might see me fall apart, lose it, crumble. I stopped smoking.

To relax, I ate, rode my bike, played guitar, or wrote in my journal. Sometimes I just lay under the sky or in a dark room and let my mind go to feel an intense expansion, detached from my body, just floating. I came back refreshed and strangely grounded, yet still with that feeling of being far away.

I knew drugs were not the road to awakening. No magic pill could make it happen. But choosing what to do confused me. I was so practical that I didn't venture too far from Jackson Hole, Wyoming, the town where I partly grew up.

Far from home, tasting the bitter and the sweet of the world, unleashed a potential of possibilities. Those eyes peering through that ornate gate during that acid trip further dismantled my shell. I felt that familiar expansion when bicycling through the shadowy streets of Kathmandu, or sipping chiyaa (sweet, milky tea) while rickshaws loped by, or discovering ancient pieces of sculpture masterfully chiseled into the side of a building. Stepping into a foreign land made me move forward, even though I knew what I was looking for was always within me.

MAYA HELPED me with Nepali lessons—reading and pronunciation. I was like a child, and the poor woman had already brought up so many. I put my books away and did some yoga on the bed while she had a cigarette. She asked in Nepali, "What will you do with your life, Sobha?"

"I want to help people," I responded in Nepali. "I want to see the world." I looked her straight in the eye. "I don't know, Didi. I don't really know."

She smiled, took a long drag from the cigarette. "You will, Sobha. One day you will know what it is that means something more than eating, sleeping, travel even. And you will walk to that light." She looked down.

"Did you find that?" I asked her.

"Ho bahini, ho, but Sobha, it was different for me here."

She went on about the differences of our countries, the beauty of the mountains, how strange that foreigners came to climb them. Her weak English and my weak Nepali prevented a deeper exchange, but it didn't stop us from trying.

She continued, "Even though skin is different and languages are not understood, we are still all people." Her tone saddened, and though I missed many words and meanings, I got the gist. "We have the same feelings, same thoughts. All over the world babies need their mothers—we all need food and share basic necessities to live." She folded some clothes, said "La," smiled, and left the room. She returned shortly without losing a beat. "We may look different, but we all get hungry." She offered tea and little crunchy things that were salty but tasty.

I continued where she left off. "There are two kinds of people—a person who is materialistic, and one who is not. The first one needs money, clothes, cars, you know, to be happy. The other needs nothing. That person is happy with a smile, with a meal, with less." That was how I saw Maya. I knew that was basic, but there was a difference we all understood, and to talk about it with someone like her was exciting. To connect with someone so far away from what I knew and had experienced, to reach out and communicate—that's how it was supposed to be, a global connection.

"Nepal is very poor, much poverty," Maya said.

"I know," I replied, "but it is more accepted here. Whenever I am in the streets, I say namaste to people and they smile and say namaste back—sometimes asking me where I am going, or what I am doing. America is more unfriendly and untrusting. One cannot do that as easily in many of the cities."

Maya spoke slowly to make sure I understood. "Yes, the people in Nepal are very friendly and open. But they should spend less time in the street talking and do something for their country, help in the offices, teach people, learn something about the world, and try to help others. In a way, people here are very selfish."

I said eagerly, "But in America, it is the same. There are many people who have enough money to live in rich neighborhoods and only be around rich people. They never see poverty or starving people. Maybe once in a while they drop money in the 'save the children' pot at the grocery store. And there are many poor and in-between people who are lazy and do nothing. It's all degrees of the same thing. There needs to be a balance where wealth and opportunity are more evenly distributed and people are educated."

Maya's auburn eyes sparkled. Gracefully, she held the cigarette between steady fingers. "I wish more people would work." She shook her head. I smirked, looked at my schoolbooks, then at her. We laughed. "La." She put out her cigarette. "Bok lagyo?" ("Hungry?")

I was getting to know my family better, even though I still had not talked with my uncle or two brothers, and hadn't even met a few of the others. But I had Maya, and that was enough.

17

I AWOKE ONE MORNING IN A HAZE, IMPATIENT AND IRRITABLE. I decided to take the day off from school and hike. I'd left my bike at the base house locked up outside, but once there, after a twenty-minute bus ride, realized the damn key was back in my room! Maybe it was sign not to go, and in fact, the day at school turned out to be wonderful. In the afternoon, instead of language class, we talked about Dasain and Tihar, the Nepali holidays coming up, while sharing biscuits, tea, and singing Nepali folk songs.

After school, a few of us decided this was the day to get a phuli (nose ring). It was a big deal. My mom was adamantly against *ear* piercing, a major drama when, at seven years old, my dad's girl-friend brought me back home with a little purse, lipstick, and freshly pierced ears. My mom was livid. I loved the earrings, and couldn't wait to replace the first ones with little gold apples, but the holes closed up before new ones could be poked through. I didn't tell anyone, since I had already done something I shouldn't have.

Inevitably, my mom got what she wanted; my ears literally sealed. The nose ring, though, had purpose in Nepal. I wanted to be Nepali, to meld in as much as possible, and, anyway, it didn't have to be permanent. When two female school friends heard I was getting one, one of the girls said, "I can't picture you having one." Her words crushed me. I couldn't understand why she'd said that. Why couldn't she see *me* with one? She didn't say that to anyone else, but I'd never been one of the bunch, and she made sure I knew it.

I pretended to ignore her comment and rode behind the rest of them as doubt coursed through my already unsure self. Maybe I shouldn't, maybe it wouldn't look good on me, maybe my guilt came from knowing my parents would not like it. I exhausted myself questioning the consequences. But I knew *I* wanted a *phuli*.

Thamel had become a frequent hangout for us. We were told about a little shop on its narrow, convoluted streets where nose piercing was done, and a few of us headed there, including the mean girls. On the way, piles of beautiful, wooly-smelling, soft and coarse fabrics caught our eye. In the Nepali shawl, which I had completely adopted, abandoning my coat, I felt swaddled, yet free and, with its swinging tassels, strangely feminine.

In the small, crowded shop, we were shown nose rings. Everyone was nervous, no one wanted to go first, so I stepped forward. Confidence was not a strength of mine, but proving my decision had to be verified. The sure hands of a large Nepali man covered my face; they were dry and smelled faintly of turpentine and dust. He pushed something through my nose, then secured a small phuli, and it was done! I was initiated into that culture by mere body mutilation—punctured and triumphant. Just a drop of blood, and I emerged a different person.

Upon leaving the sacrificial ground and re-entering the street, a sense of false belonging veiled my impressionable eyes. The narrow road teemed with small-framed, short, brown people. I was tall, and now a phuli had been added to this white girl with gold hair. Although Nepali rolled from my lips, enough to get by, I must have looked like a freak—or perhaps not. Nepal may have appeared simple and antiquated, but it was 1987; movies and media had already infiltrated the masses, and they were savvy to the new world.

But I was so *happy* with my phuli, as if I'd been finally immersed in Nepali culture, fit into a society I did not really feel a part of. My needs were great and insecurities so pervasive that I believed what anyone said about me—even a dumb schoolgirl who got a nose ring the same time I did!

That night I dreamed about being in some sort of school at graduation time, and I was getting pictures taken with my nose ring. My parents showed up, and I tried to take off my bra under my shirt. I succeeded, then went into the bathroom. They kept trying to see me as I went. Then I put on a frumpy dress that they liked, but I did not.

Getting the nose ring was an act of independence, but with obvious repercussions. I felt strong and free. I'd broken away from my mom's persona of how to be and how to look, stepped out on my own without anyone's influence. Although Nepal was a heavy force in that direction, I got the phuli partly to be like the Nepali people, trying on characters and feeling out territory like a child learning to walk. My parents were enmeshed in my past and too involved in my future. What kind of maturity did it take to be my own thinker and not attached to the deeply held emotions of my past?

My mom was against me shaving my legs and wearing a bra in high school. She probably would have been fine if I had asked her, but I couldn't talk to her about anything she was against for fear of hurting her. I tried to keep it a secret and shaved a few inches up from my ankles, but she found out. At such times, my mom projected an energy that meant there would be no arguing. I couldn't stand up to her. I wished I could talk, honestly and openly, wished I could express pent-up feelings towards her, her rules, and her desire for me to fit into her view of the world. She didn't understand what it was like to be a teenage girl in the eighties, going to a very hip, alternative school in northern California.

My mom thought I wanted to be like her, a hippy with hairy legs and no bra. She was forced to conform when she was growing up, and had decided to keep me free of it. It didn't work that way. I wanted normal things to offset—or balance—my unusual upbringing. I turned off emotionally because deep down I felt it was *her* fault for laying such stupid rules on a teenage girl. She needed to deal with me growing up, to accept what I wanted to experience—

becoming a woman in my own way—which might be normal and conventional, if that was what I chose.

As a teen, she had shaved her legs, wore a bra, and married early "to get out of her house." She came of age during the late 50's. Back then, there wasn't much choice, and it took hard lessons to change. However, she *did* change, in a remarkable way. The price was total upheaval to her immediate family. I learned from her through all of it. Transformation was a necessary shift, not what it appeared to be on the outside. My mom couldn't have passed on that information better. She did it through showing, not telling. But *I* wanted to shave my legs, wear a bra, and bring a normal sandwich for lunch.

Being in Nepal freed me from my mom. I could do what I wanted, sort of, but because of my upbringing, I still struggled against being a good girl and following the rules. The dream of watching me in the bathroom portrayed the frustrations I lived under, habits taken on from my parents who were brought up a certain way, who had also struggled with rules set by their parents and their generation. I wondered, were my dreams just movies of my life portraying a picture of who I was and where I came from?

I loved my parents. We had a good relationship, and talked deeply until we got to the underlying issues that prompted over-reactions in everyday situations. They taught me to express my emotions as a way to avoid physical ailments such as colds, sore throats, and even more serious illnesses. They gave me the groundwork to handle the storms of life, and I was grateful, but sometimes they didn't see their own hang-ups about what they thought was right and how it should be handled. They thought they knew more, as most parents do, but they were not conscious of their own shortcomings, antiquated ways, and hypocrisy. I was the new generation, brought up freely in a household that did not necessarily push higher education or marriage. Our generation demanded the chance to discover what we wanted, to go out and do it. I felt torn between doing what I thought *they* wanted me to do, and doing what *I* wanted.

18

In late September, our teachers took us to different areas in Kathmandu to experience Dasain, a fifteen day long annual celebration of the god's victory over wicked demons, extolling good over evil. The focus surrounded the goddess Durga—after she was evoked, Lord Ram could triumph in the battle. People traveled from far away to visit each other and take part in puja. Across the country, the ceremonies included numerous bloody sacrifices of animals, signifying glory and death through bloodshed. Nepali men, holding huge khukuris (knives), would bring their blade down with all their might on an animal's neck while its head and body were held by others, slicing it off with a single, clean blow. The animal would then be dragged around in a circle, blood spilling, staining the faded, rutted pavement.

This outrageous scene gripped me in fantastic surrealism. I entered the arena as if it were a Salvador Dali amusement park at night. Jagged, tempestuous lights of fires spitted from hot grease as the constant feeding of wood rendered shadows of people larger than life moving chaotically, syncopated with music. Their dance-like steps were triumphant and quick, as if everything was rehearsed. It had been this way for centuries. Many households practiced fasting until the killings, when fresh meat roasted over open fires brought forth a fury of salivating hunger and wildness, since meat was not a daily staple. The roasting smell, smoke, and the aura of it all was paganistic and incredible. Energy swelled in satiating, greasy smiles, heated conversation, and deeply felt gratitude.

I had never tasted goat meat. It is chewy, lusty, and richly juxtaposed with odd bites of cooked vegetables and spicy pickle, complimented and enhanced with raaksi (a grain alcohol made from rice) or kodo (a different alcohol made from millet, potent and distinct). The earthy shreds of roasted meat were served on thick green leaves and washed down with a healthy serving of that homemade firewater. The evening turned black with night and smoke, a frenzy of fires around the city blazing beneath a waxing moon as Dasain, the madness of blood and puja, family reunion, and the ultimate sanction of truth, ended with the night of a full moon. The somewhat tantric undertone, as it honored Durga, the divine mother goddess, and her fierce aspect, Kali, were seriously worshipped. She was seen as a source of life to the Nepali people, and if she were neglected, misfortune befell. Many workers and laborers took the entire time off, and since it came right after monsoon and the harvest, feasting was at a high.

I arrived home late. My family had finished their celebrating and the quiet courtyard felt expectant. Maya's dim light awaited me. Our eyes met in a namaste with a light exchange while changing into night clothes, and then a pat on her bed for me to join her. I relayed the day as best as I could. She hugged covers around her as she listened intently, and then asked in Nepali, "Is there anything like this at your home?"

"Ho," I answered. "Thanksgiving is similar, a big feast, family visits, but different."

"How?" Her eyes blinked as she sat up, lighting a cigarette, then leaned back, ready for a story.

"Animals are not killed in the streets, and meat is bought in stores. I am vegetarian, mostly."

She cocked her head. "Ke?"

"Na ma masu khanna." ("I don't eat meat.") But I couldn't explain the difference very well, so just simplified it. I repeated it and shook my hand.

She raised her eyebrows. "Hoina?" ("No?")

"Tara," ("But,") I continued, "when I travel, I try things." I smiled. "It is a time we give thanks for the year for an abundance, or lots of harvest of food, and to be with family." I motioned with my toothbrush.

She questioned me further. "We do not eat it a lot here, but when we do, you have eaten it too."

"Ho Didi, I like to try."

"La," she said, "takai laagyo." ("I am tired.") We brushed our teeth outside under the stars by the spigot. I rinsed my face, hearing a tinkle in the kitchen, and peeked in. Hajur aama smoked a pipe (hookah?) while crumpled in a little ball in the corner. I said, "Subha ratri." ("Good night.")

She barely responded with, "La, Sobha."

Being with Maya relaxed me. Her helpful and generous way with time, and listening without getting angry or opinionated, was sincere. She didn't try to fix everything. Instead, she laughed or chuckled with a soft undertone of surrender. I think that kept her young, with eyes so bright.

Day by day, my Nepal stay got better, even with its difficulties.

I WANTED to get into the land, the people, and away from the car exhaust and familiarity westerners already had there. Our head teacher's lazy attitude and disinterest in us and in the program was reflected in his frequent absence. I was in a beautiful country, diverse and enigmatic, but spent most of my time in a sedentary classroom with other white students. I had to get *out* of there.

My quiet disposition steadied a pressure below my surface that had nothing to do with Nepal or my family there. I didn't know what I was feeling most: angst, anger, or frustration. Then it hit me as I unlocked my bike: I realized I had to *finish* the program, even though the boundaries were not my own, but pre-set to someone else's standards—of safety, of experience, of how to behave in a foreign country. I wanted to learn discipline, something I always fought, but knew it was part of any path chosen, as this experience was making me adhere to a certain set of rules and responsibilities.

I pushed my bike through the lopsided gate and onto the dusty road. I argued that I could be on my own, that age couldn't stop me. I was considered an adult, free to go. But I felt locked into a prison of schedules.

Living under rules of home, parents, and society had been my life, and I knew no other way. I chose college and Nepal because I wanted to go as far away as possible so I could do and be what I wanted. How could I do that when I had to report to a class daily and then to a house of strangers whose main purpose was to keep me safe and fed?

A busy intersection flooded with cars honking rhapsodically tore me away from thoughts of wanting something sweet in Thamel. Waiting for an opening took timing, precision, and concentration. I had to live through that breadth of space to learn commitment, patience, and—an opening. I darted into the mess of noise and exhaust and cycled crazily to gain speed. I was not being tortured, abused, or abandoned, just existing in normalcy, skimming the edge of a desire to go. And why? Was I afraid?

In that instant, the power and independence in the pedals of my bike captivated my mind in pleasure and exercise. The need to satiate a sweet craving turned into an idea. I changed direction. I biked to Chabahil and planned a trek. A jaunt into the mountains always helped me get a bigger picture. It enabled me to let go of the menial and destructive nature life sometimes spiraled into and relaxed the boundary between me and the outside world, for then deeper thoughts would come out.

The next day, our head teacher obligingly acquiesced, exasperated by me—a daydreamer unable to concentrate. He granted my request for Juni and I to go on a backpacking trip for a few days. He made it clear that my restlessness, my mockery of the necessity of mainstream learning in a classroom setting, and my yearning to be a part of the life that teemed just outside that wooden gate, had exhausted him. Too much time spent in a city with its constant noise and action had rattled my country girl spirit. I was sure the Himalayas would help to extinguish my cripplingly defensive attitude.

19

I QUICKLY BIKED HOME AFTER SCHOOL THAT DAY TO LET MAYA know of my plan and to pick up a few things. She wasn't there, so I left a detailed note with Tara (written mostly in Nepali) and hoped it would be passed on. Tara didn't care whether I died in the mountains or not; her twisted smirk and listless wave set me off. I could see an urge to like me in the pause before she turned away, a desire to soften and understand. But angry, invisible scars marked her sour expression of whatever wrongdoing prevented her from being able to love and be loved—from letting go of her past. Respect for anyone I met was innate in my nature; I just wished we could have found some warmth between us, and hoped maybe we still would.

I returned to the base house in the evening, packed my backpack, made noodles and broth, read an old mountaineering book on relatively easy treks in the area, and fell asleep. It was cold and damp when Juni and I met the next morning at dawn. My stomach was restless, so we purchased a few packages of biscuits, and each had one bottle of water.

Juni and I went on a trek in the Helambu/Langtang region

With no destination other than the foothills of the Helambu valley in mind, we caught a taxi toward the northeast side of Kathmandu, where the road eventually ended, then climbed into the rugged, gorge-like lower Langtang Region. Cresting a ridge, the valley opened, and the distant Himalayas captured our beating hearts. Continuing on through an oak forest, we found ourselves in the village of Mulkharka and stopped for a chiyaa break. What a wonderful area, as there were very few people on the trail, no foreigners, and only some locals carrying heavy loads. The quiet breadth and beauty lauded an immense expansion of the landscape as an unending number of steep ups and downs brought us deeper into the verdant country.

It had seemed easy and adventuresome to leave the monotony of the classroom and get out into the wilderness, but Nepal was not a national park, and there were no roads to high mountain villages. Trails were how people got around, but they weren't *just* a backpacking trail into the lofty Himalayas. They were the connection, the means of transport, the line of communication—a common ground conduit, populated all the time. That wild land had been cultivated for centuries; it was their yard, their life. Trekking in Nepal posed a delicate balance between high mountain solitude and sharing the views with the people who lived and worked there. I didn't pay a fee to hike, but assumed I could go anywhere I wanted.

Being out of the grips of school and Kathmandu and feeling the deep breathing of my body, the fresh air and solitude, made me stop for a moment. I didn't want to explain the instant emancipation and happiness I felt at being back in the mountains to my friend when she caught up, it seemed trivial. She sat next to me, and we shared some biscuits.

"It feels so good to be up here, away from all of that," I said, waving my hand down toward the valley and wiping away a tear. "I get so frustrated in the city and at the base house."

She nodded. "I know what you mean. Sometimes it feels like I'm missing something, like we're not experiencing what we should be. I mean, I'm here, but . . ." She shrugged. We both stared at the valley far below.

"It's true," I said, tears dropping again. "I can't seem to take things in stride. It's either all or nothing."

She looked at me. "What do you think is the worst thing about the program?"

"I just feel trapped. I want to be doing the program, but I also want to be free."

"Yeah, I get it. I've experienced it, and now I'm ready for it to be done." She kicked her foot in the dirt. "I love my Nepali family. They're great, but it isn't easy to talk with them, so it's the same thing over and over."

"Yeah, I don't know what I'm searching for," I said, "I just get overwhelmed and want to live in the mountains and not see anyone." After a long pause I sighed and smiled. "Maybe we should get going?"

"Those biscuits are good." She grabbed a few more. "Why don't you go to a monastery for a while and just meditate until something breaks and you can see clearly?"

I laughed. "It might take decades."

"No, I'm serious. I mean, why did you *really* come to Nepal?"

I pointed to the Himalayas. "To see those. To be *in* them. Maybe for that freedom, or to find my strength. I just wanted to come. I needed to experience something much bigger than myself."

We continued along forested ridges until the wide, worn trail eventually descended, leading to the small village of Chisopani (meaning cold water). Along the way, we met a Tamang family heavily laden with baskets, their bright, wrinkled faces anchored in mixed Tibetan and Mongolian ancestry. We chatted about the trail ahead and a place to stay. The father spoke Nepali, since their village dialect was hard for us to understand. We thought he told us about a nearby guesthouse where we could stay the night, but weren't sure. Before they went on, we thanked them and nodded in agreement to whatever they said, not really understanding, but assuming it was just parting words.

It turned out to be a lucky encounter. Surrounded by mountains, terraced rice fields, and little grass and mud huts, the rapidly darkening hour and seemingly isolated area didn't reveal any campsites or guesthouses as far as we could see. *What were we thinking?*

Suddenly we arrived at the Tamang's family house, which was close to the trail. We tried to slip by unnoticed, but were caught by the children. They led us in with joyous eyes, grasping our hands, to the smiles of their parents, who seemed happy to see us. Obviously we had misunderstood earlier that they had meant *their* house. A lonesome wisp of smoke rose from their little hut. We helped to clean and cut vegetables, then had a snack of churi (pounded dried rice) and raaksi (local liquor). The dal bhat was so spicy my mouth burned and eyes teared, both of which embarrassed me, but amused them to rolling laughter. The low lighting of a single butter lamp, tight quarters, somewhat drunken company, and our limited vocabulary made for the best reality game of charades. That crazy, slapstick-fun turned into a memorable evening.

One of the older daughters showed us where to relieve ourselves outside behind the house. She handed over a glass bottle filled with water for washing our left hand, and waited until we were done. Back inside, hot tea awaited. The smell was unfamiliar, its bitter, salty flavor a surprise. I swallowed and nodded. The father asked where we were going. Pati Bhanjyang, I said, pulling out a map. The butter lamp was set in the middle and the whole family gathered round, pointing, giggling, and questioning. It was mostly in Nepali, so the father interpreted, explaining to them where we were and where we were going.

Yawns all around. The map was folded and put away, the dishes gathered and washed. I said slowly, in Nepali, "Dhanyabad (thank you) for the food and your kindness," and, not wanting to be more of a bother, "We'll leave early in the morning, before dal bhat." And then asked, also in Nepali, while pointing toward the door, "Can we roll out our bags on your porch for the night?" I put my hands together, put my cheek on them, pretending to sleep, then looked up and smiled.

"Hoina," (no) the father said immediately and kindly. I tried again, but he refused. "You sleep upstairs with the women," he said in Nepali.

No matter what we said, he would not change his mind. So up we went with our packs into a room that measured approximately six by six feet. There were eight of us squashed in with the door and window bolted shut. Before bed they smoked cigarettes, filling the already dark, claustrophobic room with smoke. I thought I was going to die. I did mention again in sleepy words that we would be leaving before the morning meal.

Sleep came easy, though. I awoke in the morning to giggles and wide eyes. Stuffing our bags away, the women pointed curiously to the strange looking packs, and we let them open and inspect every piece of clothing and equipment we had. Emerging from that whimsical scene, we said dhanyabad (thank you) and namaste to the family, leaving the map, a chocolate bar and a few dollars in rupees as a thank you (the father adamantly refused the rupees, and made sure we understood that we were welcome on our way back).

The rugged trail went either straight up or straight down toward

Suryijang and then Pati Bhanjyang. Two young boys and two Nepali men fell in step with us along the way, talked about the hill people, named the mountains (Annapurna, Dhaulagiri, Nagarkot), and mentioned tea shops and lodges to stay at in Pati Bhanjyang.

When we arrived, my heart saddened at my first impression of the small, dismal, trekking-leftover town, offering not the picturesque, high mountain village I'd hoped to see. Garbage lay off the trail, children pulled at our hands and packs, asking for rupees, pens, anything, and the sense of the place disillusioned me. Climbers were not known for tact or tidiness, and the place reflected an uncaring attitude of "peak bagging."

We hadn't eaten anything, so I bought wai wai noodles (similar to ramen) and asked a woman in a tea hut to cook them for us. She seemed tired and uninterested in my Nepali small talk. She had obviously heard and seen everything before. After the noodles and tea we thanked her and quickly left to trudge back up the long, steep hill we had just come down. Little villages were tucked away in creases and folds, with the trail going through the people's yards. It felt strange, as if we were trespassing, but no one seemed to mind.

We exchanged a few words with workers in the field or families by their houses. Initially, they appeared aloof. However, once they heard our Nepali, their smiles and interest brought them closer. Many others took no notice, being used to frequent trekkers along the well-known route. Never were we really out there in the woods hiking along precarious ledges. Instead, the wilds were the *villages* and the *people*, and trekking was what I knew backpacking to be and what exploration into a foreign culture became. It was about inter-action with those wonderful people—bridging the gap between my internal world of needing to be alone and, at the same time, wanting to be part of something bigger, as well as being in the mountains.

Large piles of rocks I thought to be cairns (trail markers) were actually graves—or at least some of them were. We stopped by one, inspected the layering as it spiraled around to a cone-shaped top about four feet high. Leaning very near to it, pressing my ear close, I heard a hollow and raspy sound, as if from a large seashell. Its rocky pockets held imagined mournful cries, echoed and distant. A fresh, silent breeze carried us further along the expansion of those hinterlands, flanked by terraces and pastures. I could relax, think, and just let go into the earth beneath my feet, one step after another, in slow, methodic, deliverance.

It bothered me that I may have been perceived as a rich, white westerner with nice clothes, a fancy pack, and time to just walk around the mountains, whereas the villagers worked constantly, ate little, and were barely educated. I wondered if they ever got the chance to travel? I lived simply, ate health foods, and worked hard for every penny, but the degrees were staggeringly different and impossible to compare. I knew I had the chance to go to college, buy a car, and have the freedom to do what I wanted. Their freedom came in a different form—a non-materialistic world built on thousands of years of culture and the support system of village life.

I labored up the steep hill. The weight on my back kept me present, and both dispelled unsettling thoughts from taking over. The joy of being in the mountains offset the inertia of school and family life in Kathmandu. I started to feel light and happy and alive again.

We skirted a short rock wall, endless in length, that separated Gokarna Forest from the terraced hills. The afternoon descended into a magic, silvery dusk. Tired and hungry, we found a private spot behind the wall about a hundred feet from the trail to stay the night, taking a chance no one would notice us. Under the stars, surrounded by high, rolling, grassy hills and an expanse that rivaled the wind, we tucked ourselves inside our warm bags. Eating dried wai wai noodles, we gazed out over rippled ledges, magnificently structured, that went on forever. A pink sky flowed over the hills. The Himalayas nestled in a thick blanket of mist, daring me to go further into them. I made up a song of deep canyons taking my soul into endless hiking and time-warped dimensions. I sighed.

Juni asked, "You okay?"

I nodded. "I'm good. I feel peaceful. There's nothing like natural beauty to fill in the cracks of ambivalence and smooth over anxiety."

"M&M's usually take care of that for me, but of course, other than withdrawals, I've never felt better, here and now." Her voice trailed off, pointing to a tiny rainbow between two clouds.

A cold, wet wind slowly moved in—dampening my clothes and settling into my bones. It thickened into a fog that swallowed the shaggy grass and everything around, making the once enormous territory into a virtual sound studio. I picked up my penny whistle. Its piercing, clear tone was almost visually sucked into the vortex of calm, and my body shivered.

I laughed. "Do you feel this?"

"Yes. Weird, isn't it?"

"The fog is so thick I can chew it."

It disintegrated slowly as we heard drums pulsating in some distant village, doing puja or something. Peeing in the grass, brushing teeth, and securing our packs, which served as back rests against the rock wall, wrapped up our peaceful evening, and we settled into sleep. At the very brink of slumber we heard a horrible belching, a loud grunt, heavy breath in spurts, and the quick, pelting steps of something running. We climbed to the top of the wall.

Even though it was only four or five feet high, it offered some protection from the dark streak that ran through the mist and disappeared. A wild boar? We cautiously walked along the wall and saw a bhaisi (buffalo)! It seemed stranded, maybe hurt or being chased by something else—we couldn't tell.

"What if that beast sees us and attacks?" Juni asked. We huddled on the wall and pulled our wool shawls tightly around our bodies.

"What about all of our stuff?" I asked, looking at our abandoned belongings below.

"He can have it," she answered weakly.

We talked into the night, vigilantly keeping eyes open, quivering at any grunt or rustle in the grass. It might not be safe up on the wall, but it definitely wasn't down on the ground. We tried to stay awake, but, at some point, exhaustion took over.

We awoke with a start. Our legs stiff and sore from keeping them cramped in the light wraps while squeezed together for warmth. We'd survived, and the dangerous monster had gone.

If it were wet enough to rain, it would have come down as snow. I loved the chill, the bareness of our belongings, the exhilarating night—especially after it was over. It left us giddy from fatigue. The day unfolded slowly, freezing rain moved out with a breeze as we jogged in place and then stretched in the wet grass.

"Can you imagine just doing this and not going back?" I said while packing up.

My friend chuckled. "It's what you'd like, huh?"

"Yes. But I couldn't imagine it without speaking Nepali."

"School isn't so bad." She breathed deeply. "This has been really good."

We hoisted our packs and moved on. Tea and noodles in the next village, and then we hiked far enough to find a hidden place in a shaggy grove of trees to camp. The night was quiet and safe; no wild beasts or fog, just calm and quiet, comfortable in our bags under the stars. The next day we felt sheltered enough to stay another night, so we lounged, talked, read, dozed. I played my flute, sang, watched the weather go by, and we wrote in our journals.

JOURNAL ENTRY: October 1987, Helambu Valley, Nepal.
I can't always run away from what I don't like, and toward something

seemingly grander. It's only that way because I haven't reached there yet. Where am I trying to go? Am I running from or toward something? I love it here. I love the mountains. I can think easily. There are no boundaries and no harsh words, except my own . . . except my own Sobha.

WE DIDN'T HAVE any means with which to cook, so we existed on biscuits, which were easily purchased along the way from locals who sold a few provisions from their houses, and then chiyaa, soup, and dal bhat in the small villages. I slept lightly on our last night beneath the dancing sky, where stars and clouds wove a shimmering weft, surely a sign that the strings of my life were coming together in spite of my slow evolution—a *thread* at a time—and alas, the choice of weaving for my village project metaphorically revealed its true nature. I turned on my flashlight and scribbled in my journal:

I AM LIKE A WEAVER, living life in lyrical, haphazard, and unstructured moments following an impromptu pattern set down long before I could be conscious of it. Isn't that where dreams come from? Some place of unfinished scenes and karmic fate? I feel different, like something has been cleared away.

WE PACKED EARLY the next morning and started back to Kathmandu. It would take most of the day to reach the base house.

Watching my feet walk, feeling the load on my back, hearing wind in the midst of a grassy knoll, I stopped. Juni was far behind me. A warming in my throat, like I needed to cry or yell, and my thoughts arranged themselves into lucid perception. Nepal was one big trek. Every minute of it—the flight, Manaslu Hotel, Tara, Maya, Nima, our head teacher, the parasites inside my intestines, the mountains, the tears, the angst, the dreams, the daily grind, the monotony of study, and then those great Himalayas. Every image, experience, hardship, and joy passed through my mind. Threads of a grand tapestry came together on this *trek*. I dropped my pack and sat down in the dirt. Juni caught up and joined me.

"Snack time?" she asked.

"Yes," I said, then sighed heavily.

"What's up?" she asked, poking me with her elbow.

"I'm okay. *Good*, actually. It's really nothing." I laughed easily, holding emotion back. Tears come so easily for me, I thought, and I didn't want to show them or explain that it really is nothing, just another epiphany of Nepal's beauty and how it unleashes a softening and understanding.

"I'm starving," she said. I had a package of biscuits, completely broken, and handed them over.

She smiled. "All for me?"

"All for you," I said, taking the last sips of water I had.

After, we hoisted our packs and walked in silence. She exclaimed every so often on the beauty around us and chatted about home. I was deep in thought. Instead of getting caught up in the low places, why not treat them as part of the journey, yet another step along the path I so want to take? I knew every experience happened for a reason. I had chosen it. It was part of the greater plan of my destiny. At least that's what Siddhartha and other metaphysical texts implied. After all, complex situations, once grievances and hardships were over, turned into simple realizations and life went on.

On Friday afternoon we got into Kathmandu, dropped our packs at the base house, and biked into Thamel for hot soup. That night all the students, as well as two other invited school groups, celebrated Halloween at the base house late into the night with momos (steamed dumplings), popcorn, fruit, dried coconut, singing, and dancing. I felt a light abandon, like I had passed a test, and talked to the other students with interest. Their stories were intriguing since I could feel what they talked about on their various reasons for coming to Nepal, their mishaps, how they dealt with the frustration of being a minority and the lack of understanding countries had with each other.

We had so much stuff to deal with; the feeling of being very small and inconsequential took a certain amount of passion to overcome in order to follow one's path no matter the consequences. In between such heavy banter, we danced. That freedom of body movement was an incredible release. After the other groups left, we collapsed into exhausted slumber. In the morning, a breakfast of eggs, potatoes, garlic, and tomatoes was a delicious break from dal bhat, as was being away from school. It did not satiate the thirst for freedom, however, just whetted my appetite.

Upon returning to Chabahil and my room in Maya's house, Tara brought khaja (snack) of a biscuit and persimmon. In a stern voice she asked how the trip went. Her eyes seemed to show disapproval. She didn't like me, or maybe she didn't like what I represented—a rich white girl who had it easy. Nevertheless, I described the trek as best I could in Nepali—she spoke no English. With a short smile, turned to leave, but I caught her, and praised in Nepali the delicious snack she had brought.

"A persimmon!" I remarked. I smiled sincerely, hoping she'd fall into it. "What a treat, dhanyabad." ("Thank you.")

"Ho bahini." She stopped, turned, and actually smiled, but it disappeared quickly as she left.

Later in the kitchen, hajur aama stirred a pot of cooking dal while I sat against the dark wall with a knife and bowl and joined in the simple task of helping cut vegetables.

Nima ran in breathlessly, squeezing in close to me. Hajur aama said something to her, she retorted back, and they quarreled. Nima ignored her to sing to me. Hajur aama interrupted a few times. Nima waved her off and finished the song, staring into my eyes, an inch from my face, holding my cheeks in her hands, and then said, "Bhannos." ("Please speak.") Hajur aama said something. Nima spit nasty words, then looked at me. I smiled briefly, but with a disapproving look about being mean towards hajur aama.

"Ke bhannos?" ("Speak what?") I asked.

"Your thoughts," she said seriously (in Nepali), blinking her long lashes slowly.

"I love when you sing, but I don't like when you are mean to hajur aama," I said in Nepali, staring softly into her eyes, in different verb tenses and mispronounced words for sure—as I did every exchange in Nepali, which they loved. It cracked them up.

Nima rattled off fast, looking to hajur aama and back at me, but I couldn't follow her.

"Pheri bhannos, tara dherai bistaarai," ("Say it again, but speak slowly,") I asked.

They looked at each other as if the arguing earlier hadn't happened, and laughed. Nima repeated slowly, still in Nepali, to me. "Hajur aama wants me to go get greens, but I said I'll get them later, but she wants them now . . ."

"Ho Bahini, listen and go," I said, then I smiled at hajur aama and thanked her. Greens were my favorite, especially the way she cooked them in spices and ghee (clarified butter made from bhaisi milk).

"La," Nima said, and ran off. Hajur aama and I continued with dinner.

20

I awoke again to a tight feeling in my abdomen. I had been constipated throughout my stay, with each week getting progressively worse. I hated to think about it, talk about it, admit it—and didn't, to *anyone*. I felt ashamed that my body wouldn't function normally, especially since Nepal usually had the opposite effect on most people. I also awoke with red pimples on my nose that portended something bad, since I never got them. A week after the trek with Juni, I decided to take a laxative for a stool test, which came back positive for intestinal worms. Antibiotics followed, leaving me spacey and sick. Uncontrollable tears spilled down my cheeks as I looked into a little pocket mirror, inspecting the blemishes. I worried about what might really be going on inside, thoughts of the months before flying to Nepal surfacing.

My father had called me at college, our first contact in ten years. It stunned me. His sure tone and righteous plea for wanting a relationship with me twisted a knot in my gut. Tears welled, hot with anguish. I could barely get the words out.

"I don't want anything to do with you, please don't call me again," I stammered.

Though miles away, I could sense the angry tension on the other end of the phone as his silence cut through me, acidic and ragged. I hung up, feeling old emotions whipping through in a violent storm of tears. He was the bane of my silent, constant malaise. The call left me anxious. What does he want? What will I tell mom? Why am I so scared? The tragic irony was that finally being away from home and on my own, I hoped to feel the freedom to respond honestly.

But you did, I thought as I sat on my narrow bed in Nepal. Even *if* I wanted him to try again, I had said what I felt in that moment. The magnitude of feeling imprisoned in my body, and in Maya's house in a Third World country, exposed the fragility of life. The familiar words '*You are who you are no matter where you are,*' played in my head. I understood the message—Nepal won't change me. Nepal *won't* change me.

Then what will?

The trek helped. Laxatives helped. My journal helped. Sleeping in that shared room with Maya, separated by a curtain, helped.

Nima ran by, yelling something at Muni, who yelled back in agitated Nepali. They argued like siblings as Nima cried through gasping words. Muni softened.

I thought of my sisters living in Canada. Sadly, we hadn't communicated very much since the divorce. I looked down into the courtyard where Muni hugged Nima and talked softly to her. My body stiffened rather than softened, and, strangely, my tears stopped. I wanted to cry more, but the scene tapped into personal, sisterly memories, and I automatically disengaged. My feelings were blocked. Numb. Frozen. Muni and Nima came back and I ducked into my room.

Being in Nepal *did* help.

Many who traveled to Asia often became sick in some way, but easy precautions could be taken. I had brought an herbal tincture to help against parasites and other potential invaders which I took a few times a week—obviously not often enough. The parasites only added to an overwhelming assortment of problems that went much deeper. Though I appeared independent, tending to the personal aspects of growing up and taking responsibility for my health and wellbeing had been slow in coming.

The morning sun warmed the small room. Living *simply* felt right. I dressed and went to the bathroom with its grey cement walls and bare floor, except for a squat toilet in the middle, a jar of water, and an open window with a light, a ragged curtain blowing in a pleasant breeze. The door didn't lock, but no one came in when it was closed. I squatted, trying to relax. My thoughts flowed, why wouldn't my intestines? The reality of Third World travel was intimidating, and I didn't want to experience the negative aspects of it. I was still a kid. Nineteen and no boyfriend, only kissed a few times and never even close to going all the way. A late bloomer, just interested in getting "it" over with, but I knew it wouldn't happen in Nepal. I wanted to understand, release the turmoil on my own, and grow up.

Suddenly, the bathroom door burst open. I looked up, shocked, but barely got a glimpse of Muni running out, wildly yelling about the broken lock on the door. I finished and left the room. Moments later, gripping my shoulders, Muni rambled in Nepali about the state of things in that house. I reassured her in Nepali and smiled. "Ho Bahini, it's okay. Really, it's okay."

"Don't worry, be happy," she said in English, with her hands up and a goofy look on her face.

"What? How do you know that?" I said in Nepali.

"Didi, it is a song," she said in Nepali.

"I know," and then I sang it in English and asked her, "Can you in Nepali?"

"Ke garne." ("What to do.") She raised her eyebrows. We both chuckled, then her tone turned serious. "The door Didi, it will be fixed today." She trotted off down the stairs.

I returned to my room, thinking how life could overwhelm everyone. Youth had a way of undermining intuition and timing, and I ignored the signs of my health. My parents would remind me that I wasn't the only one and sometimes that helped, but I knew at some point the usual distractions of travel, eating, biking, hiking, or playing music would eventually cease to work, and I would not be able to deal with my feelings and symptomatic health issues affecting me. Later, I thought, next year, or when I'm thirty. I've got time.

"Drop it *Sobha!*" I said to myself. "You've got a case of parasites needling away at your energy, making you anxious and constipated, that's it!"

"*I was constipated* before *coming to Nepal*," I answered myself.

"Yes, but now you've got a great excuse."

"*And laxatives will fix it?*"

"For the time being. Does everything have to be analyzed and picked apart?"

"*Yes. I can't let go. I've got to question and prod until the deeper meaning reveals itself. Until I find* the *answer*."

"To what?"

"*To my problems.*"

"And you think the time and place is now? What makes this different?"

The banter went on in my head.

I took the parasitic antibiotic for a week, cheap pink pills bought at a Nepali pharmacy. I felt a burning sensation in my stomach thirty minutes after taking them, hopefully frying those little bastards so my system would get back to normal. Unfortunately, the pills did little to clear anything.

21

BHAI TIKA FELL ON THE FIFTH DAY OF THE FESTIVAL OF LIGHT, or Tihar, where not just gods were worshipped, but animals as well, since there was a divine attachment between us according to Hindu mythology. On the first day of the festival, the crow was honored and given offerings of food placed on the rooftops across the valley. The people's warmth toward the magical black "creator" was infectious, devotees talking to them while they landed and pecked away. The gesture helped people deal with grief and sadness, even to deflect it from their homes. (*Hmm, maybe I should pay closer attention.*) The next day kukurs (dogs) were celebrated and given delicious food. They had malas (flower garlands) dangling from their scruffy necks and red splashed foreheads. On cow day, symbolizing wealth and prosperity, their mournful expressions were deepened with smatterings of tika, which resembled a cheap whore with smeared "makeup" running down from goopy eyes. Extra patience was given to let the 'holy beasts' cross streets or stand on sidewalks.

Later in the evening, houses were cleaned and decorated with marigolds and chrysanthemums as oil lamps and candles were lit all around. The people visited, singing and dancing, while fireworks infused the misty dusk as the night wore on. The fourth day, I could not recall exactly, since my local family was not strictly religious, but more cleaning and preparation for the final day took place. I woke up feeling bloated. Maya brought hot water with lime, then scolded me for reading and playing cards.

"You shouldn't waste time with such things," she said in Nepali.

"Ho Didi, you are right." I didn't want to do anything. I needed a distraction—not thinking about school or work, especially the language, and not fitting in. I didn't know why many things were done there, nor was I supposed to. Disciplining myself to learn the Nepali language and culture was hard (yes, sprawled out on that bed, lost in Solitaire, listening to George Winston, whose music moved me, hot lime water brought to me—really ironic!).

"Dhanyabad Didi." I smiled. "I am sorry." I continued flipping the cards.

My family had to accept my ways as well. It was a give and take. Nima peeked in and smiled infectiously.

"Jaane?" (pronounced like "Johnny", meaning "let's go") she said.

"Ho." I got up, stepped into sandals, grabbed my bag, and followed her out. Her giddy, wide-eyed head shake and swishy little skirt took me out of my self-deprecating world. Her beaming, proud face was held high as she walked down a bustling Nepali street holding the hand of a white girl. People turned to look as her skinny little body flitted about, and I, also in high spirits, held her hand, feeling privileged to be in her company. Both of us, children of difficult circumstances, free to be totally different with each other, and yet completely understanding and happy.

A little stall on the side of the road sold strange, local treats. She looked at me, I nodded, and she picked out a few things while I paid. One in her mouth, one in mine—a red stained treat with a strangely sweet and spicy flavor that was pungent in a not too pleasing, but not awful sort of way. It was followed by a flat piece of possibly dried fruit that looked like old leather studded with salt, cayenne, and sugar—a favorite of Nima's. We walked around as she chatted with a few people, showing me off before returning to the house. The special camaraderie with Nima energized my spirit, helping me feel as though I fit in.

I went to tidy my room and finished a paper for school. Maya left to go tika her bhai (younger brother). Muni helped me into a sari she and Maya had set aside. She, too, put one on, and we gathered everything to perform tika on our bhai together: small leaf bowls filled with fruit, nuts, sweets, boiled eggs, meat, and a small tray holding different colored powders and dyed rice. The event ensures long life by honoring the protection given by the younger brothers. Her restrained but friendly manner did not hide a hint of weary duty toward me as she explained the procedures, telling me what to do, over-emphasizing cheerfulness. But it was not all an act. When our eyes met, a yielding companionship easily knit the space between us.

Muni and I sat on my bed playing cards while waiting for her brothers, who wouldn't get home until early that evening. We went up to the roof and took pictures of each other in the pretty saris. She looked paper-thin, with a languid, draping quality to her body, a relaxed demeanor with stars that glistened in her dark brown eyes. I wondered if she wanted to ask me things. We didn't talk about my life in America or the culture I came from. It's not that she wasn't interested, we were just in different worlds and knew it. The wide chasm was penetrable, yet it was unnecessary to spell out differences in the little time we had. Our small connection, delicately played with, was comforting—we didn't have to go beyond it. She was younger and didn't seem to acknowledge the greater aspect of life innate to her culture.

Maya returned, and I watched my uncle receive tika. He was always drunk and babbling nonsense, yelling at nothing. Maya sighed and rolled her eyes, but could not hide her anger. He was a friend of her late husband, who'd died ten or fifteen years earlier, and he had lived with them ever since. I didn't know the details, but was told to call him kaaka (uncle). His sisters did puja to him and gave me a boiled egg with bread, meat, and raaksi (homemade liquor).

I drank the cloudy liquid from a small cup, warmth penetrating every cell instantly. They filled it again, which I did not want, but tipped my head and drained it, only for it to be filled again, against my protests, all to no avail. I hid that one behind me on a shelf, and left for a moment to deposit the fried bread and other stuff I couldn't eat in a bag I had in my room to take with me to school.

The time came when we sisters had to do puja to our younger brothers. The intricate ritual began with us circling around them while we dripped oil onto the floor from a small copper cup, and then onto their hair, after which we placed multi-colored tika on their foreheads. Money and food were exchanged.

It must have been strange for the brothers to have me contribute to this service. I saw it in their eyes. I could imagine what their school friends said about them having a white girl in their house.

Maya and Tara wanted pictures, which I took, but the light faded quickly, and they came out too dark. When it was over, I retreated to my room, took off the sari, put George Winston on, and, with pen in hand, lost myself in the pages of my journal.

Tears spilled over again. Nostalgia? I don't know. A young woman whom I didn't know had joined us at the tika ritual with her very unhappy baby, wanting something. She tried to convey it to me while her baby screamed. I wiped my tears, which she noticed, and extended my arms. She started to hand him over, but he arched his back and wailed. She didn't know what to do.

"Maya? Tara? Muni?" I suggested, but no one seemed to be around, and then motioned to burp him, to really bounce him. "Maybe gas?" I said in Nepali, pointing to my stomach and then pretended to belch.

"Hoina Didi," she said, shaking her head, a frown on her delicate face.

"Joro aaunu, dukheko mal?" ("Fever, bad stomach?") I put my hand to my forehead then my stomach again.

"Dhanyabad, tara . . ." ("Thank you, but . . .") she said with a faint smile, shrugging her narrow shoulders, and then with an unspoken glance, but no words of, *Are you okay?*'

"Ho Didi, I hope your nani (baby) is okay, too?" I said with a nod, and she turned to leave. I stood outside the room, leaned against the wall, and looked down into the courtyard, where she walked in circles, trying to comfort her baby, bouncing him until he finally settled down. She looked up, I waved, we smiled. She was a young mom, nervous of the road ahead perhaps, or maybe she thought because I was from America I had something more to offer. We held each other's gaze for a moment.

What was it in me other than those damned parasites? Melancholic, lyrical piano music riled my emotions and filled me with turmoil that agitated my body. I wanted to get out of the house, to bike or do something to calm my emotional state, but night had fallen. Momentary emotional eruption fried my nerves as I sat on the edge of my bed, crying quietly, swallowing to push down feelings of inadequacy, hopelessness, and despair. In that moment of mishap, my system broke down, my cloistered life upended, and my pores pulsated from the nameless pressure. I shivered, my throat full and tight, tears billowing and dropping onto my hands. I wiped them on my skirt until it was finally over.

Maya would be back soon. Everyone seemed full of the festivities that afternoon—no dal bhat was offered, thank god! The house remained relatively quiet. I rinsed my face and changed into nightclothes, brushed my teeth, returned Muni's call of subha raatri (goodnight) from some distant room, and got into bed.

The ceiling was somewhere above in the darkness. I could hear the festivities still going on beyond the walls while images of the day's events passed through my mind. Maya arrived and got ready for bed. She said nothing, assuming I was asleep. When I heard her heavy breathing, I lit a candle, reached for my journal, and found solace again in the written word.

22

Halfway through the urban stay in Kathmandu, our group left for a mid-term retreat at Dhulikhel Lodge. The rustic resort huddled near a hill village southeast of Kathmandu—a gateway to Tibet with stunning views of the Himalayas. Langtang, Lirung in the east, Dorje Lakpa, Gauri Shankar, Melungtse, and Numbur flanked the drive, surrounding us with ethereal and magical views. I sat in the rickety old bus with my head out the window. No one could know the depth of emotion those magnanimous icons of strength held for me. The pointed mountain tops floated in a misty blue, detached from an unfathomable base—pure peace—as the whirling dervish of life stopped for a moment in lucid stillness. Mesmerizing!

I looked forward to four relaxing days in serene terraced landscapes with delicious food and a lot of free time. The rooms were simple, with no lights (just candles), two beds, a window with a view, and shared bathrooms. Lunch was a short walk to the Himalayan Horizon Restaurant, with scenic outdoor seating at tables with straw chairs—totally luxurious.

We shared dinner around a long, narrow table. The incredibly spicy hot tarkari (cooked vegetables) lightened my mood, and I saw undoubtedly the struggle of growth. To me, each of us looked different. Many were going through the difficult and joyous times of Nepali family life. I felt I could read their faces, a complacent tenure hesitantly revealed in smile lines, soft eyes, self-effacing words. A slight grasp of independence, a letting go, a query—I was not the only one questioning my existence, upbringing, and the long days still ahead.

That evening, I re-read some entries in my journal about Kathmandu being so alive. The constant movement and sound of people, cars, animals, lights, and Maya's busy compound were replaced by the light breeze at Dhulikhel and the slow mornings of chiyaa and conversation. The quiet stillness and reprieve bolstered a deep sense of renewal spreading through me despite my criticism of living in Kathmandu. Although I missed the serenity of the mountains, the constant bustle of city life had become normal. However, Nepal was not an ordinary place, and that made up for everything.

I roomed with Juni, who had returned from a shower wrapped in towels and sat on the bed.

"I *needed* that," she said emphatically. "I don't think I'll ever get used to washing in a lungi."

"I don't like it either," I said, "but cold water is invigorating. I've always wanted to get used to it, but never had to until now."

"Yeah, maybe, but I don't think so!" She laughed and sat back on the bed. "I love this place."

"I do, too." I left to take a shower, and when I returned, asked, "How do you think you've changed?"

She sat up, looked over at me seriously. "I'm not sure I'll really know for a while, but if I *had* to say something? I appreciate my life back home. My eyes have been opened. What about you?" She had changed into sweats and started doing sit-ups on the floor.

"My internal chatter is at an all-time high. So much is going on inside, I can barely hear anything else. I've never been so aware of my thoughts. This culture has turned me inside out. But I agree, it'll probably be decades before I understand what Nepal has done for me." I pulled at my hair, clearing the tangles with my fingers.

"I love the clothes," she said, getting up to show me a long, wool, Tibetan jacket, almost down to her ankles, and then a punjabi, billowy and brightly printed in white and blue designs. I liked the dignified, elegant look of the coat, and the punjabi, attractive and pretty on her, though it seemed showy instead of practical. I was jealous, actually, wishing I could pick out nice things, but I wasn't used to spending money on myself.

We changed and went down to meet the others for dinner. The dal bhat tasted different than any I had tried so far—the rice was speckled, meatier in texture and more delicious. Forks were offered, but we ate traditional style with our right hand, leaving our left hand neatly tucked into our laps.

The next morning, everyone took a simple, leisurely breakfast on our own time, followed by informal discussions in one of the hotel rooms. Our shoes were removed at the doorway, thick ornate rugs stretched wall to wall, pillows were scattered about along with small tables, and the room was low lit and warm. We talked about our family life in Kathmandu, and our complaints and suggestions for classes. In the afternoons we were free to explore, relax in the quiet hotel rooms, or hang out on the patio in the luxurious chairs amid the incredible scenery. We were given a stipend to spend on lunch at the Horizon Restaurant. Juni and I shared ours so we could order extravagantly, starting with a plate of pakauda, deep-fried vegetables served with a hot sauce, tarkari ra roti, vegetable and bean curry with small discs of unleavened bread, and other delicious delights. I relaxed. My internal questioning stopped for long periods. Another level of Nepal unfolded, and my rapt attention laughed in the freedom.

I took small hikes after lunch, one only part-way to Namo Buddha, an ancient holy site and legendary Buddhist Stupa where it was said Buddha gave his body to a tigress, which was engraved on the stone. The next day, a solo dip in a remote waterfall, drying off perched upon a smooth rock, filling journal pages. Each evening they served dal bhat, but on our last night they capped it off with delicious khir, a creamy, sweet rice pudding. Later, after the wrap-up talk, a few of us smoked some weed out of an apple. Pot grew wild around there, and one of the students had picked it from the side of a trail. It gave me a strange feeling—speeding up my heart, followed by a peace rippling through my body—not bad, just *different*, like Nepal. I didn't smoke much, since I spent most of my time in the clouds anyway, but I liked to try things.

The last morning, Juni and I got up before dawn, wrapped in pashminas, Nepali shawls, snugged tight against the cold and damp, and walked to a low stone wall. The horizon was deeply burnt in browns and blues, and slowly showed definition as the first rays of warmth rose in shards between the massive, snowy mountains. We just sat there and gazed at the beauty. I felt free at that moment. No pressure, just the blissful privilege to *be*. My thoughts drifted to what school and education were really about, and I found a renewed passion to learn.

As the sun rose slowly, my thoughts drifted to long ago, during my childhood, as memory established itself in worn, carved out ruts. We were marched into school, made to learn and memorize, withstand antagonisms, endure life at home (which had its own set of responsibilities and rules), and then we were let go, on our own, pressured to pursue a career. Did society teach an individual to feel deeply within, to find that search of happiness? What was life *truly* about? How did we make work fulfilling so that craft and mastery developed as well as getting paid for it?

Juni broke the silence, saying she had to pee, and disappeared into the bush for a moment. She returned, smiling.

"What?" I asked.

"Nothing," she said. "Just happy. This has been such a great break. I'd like to come back."

"It has been good," I agreed, and looked away.

"What's wrong?"

"Nothing."

"Come on," she pressed.

"I was brought up by two artists who made a living through their art. I experienced alternative schools and was even home-schooled, briefly," I began. "I have an underlying current to set my mind within certain boundaries and move in a straight line. Suffering is a part of life. To dream big and go for it is scary, unattainable—at least for me. Life comes with long hours and little pay, few vacations and inevitable disease. Even though I don't buy into *that* stereotype, something always presses inside that prevents me from taking a leap. I want to explore and create and be crazy, but the nest I cling to is home, where my parents are, and I'm pulled in two directions."

"So? What's the big deal? You're nineteen, right?" Juni said. "Your parents are artists? That's interesting, I don't hear that too much. Life is about risk, isn't it? How are you going to figure anything out if you don't get out there?"

The sun was full, warming our faces as my thoughts continued silently in my own heart. Beneath all the bravado and individuality I praised myself for, I feared not feeling safe in the world. So I tagged onto people and programs just enough to get by while I pushed life to its fullest—staying close within those boundaries.

"I want to make a lot of money," she said.

"Doing what?" I asked.

"I came to this school because I wanted to do Peace Corps type work, but not so much now. I think some kind of business management."

"Well, this experience will help in so many ways. Differently than any of us can imagine, you think?"

She nodded emphatically. "Absolutely. It's been a dream of mine to do something like this, so it doesn't matter if it connects into a career or not."

We jumped off the hard, cold, stone wall, breathed in one more view of the magnificent mountains, and slowly made our way back. She seemed comfortable in her life, knowing what she wanted and how she was going to go about doing it. She reminded me of my older sister in how she offered thoughtful answers in a self-assured way that made me feel relaxed. I, on the other hand, wanted many things, least of all money. In fact, I wanted to get by on very little.

Later that day, with our teachers, we discussed the reasons why we were in Nepal.

I began with a long-winded thought. "The black and white regimes of standard education only go so far to expand our mind, right? I mean, the gut feel, the smell, sight, and touch of the world is what moves me and opens me. How can you teach someone about Third World living, or any kind of living, without the experience?"

"That is true. Nepal will do that," one of our teachers said. "As would any country you go to that is not your own."

"But you have to *live* there," added another student. "Not just go and not just be in a school setting."

"The beauty and violence of this place has cracked me open," I said. "Hopefully, I'll remember it."

"Remember what?" the teacher asked.

"The feeling of that discovery, and then be brave enough to be there."

"You won't have to *remember*," our teacher emphasized. "It *is* there. You *have* changed. You have *been* changed, and can never go back to who you were before."

"Yeah, that tarkari last night certainly changed me," laughed another student.

I am pure experiential learning in a package, I thought to myself as the others commented around the room on their experiences. Each face held fleeting realizations or insights, softening the egotistical edge. We were humbled by the experience of living and studying in Nepal. I would have liked to fit in differently—to pump out the essays easily, learn grammar, understand geometry, and follow a chosen path—but, alas, I guess I had a different agenda in store for me.

My thoughts ended as someone brought tea into the room.

"And what about you, Sobha?" our leader, Dave, asked, all eyes on me.

"What?"

"What do you want most from this time?"

"To get lost in the Himalayas," Juni answered for me. We all laughed.

"It's true," I said. "But really, I just want to take it all in and be changed."

We had such a good time with Dave, all of us comfortable within our family life, candidly talking, but mostly laughing raucously about charpi (squat toilet) hazards, language miscommu-nications, and genuinely good times with the Nepali people.

Later that day, the bus took us back to Kathmandu. Once at the base house, I said goodbye to the others, then biked home to my family, dal bhat, and a restored sense of placement.

I THOUGHT AHEAD to the December break, a week off after fall semester ended, and then the spring semester beginning in the remote villages. I wanted to plan a trek into some magical hamlet, but I wasn't sure where yet. I had talked to Shankar, the Nepal program affiliate, and stressed the point of wanting to be as far away as the program would allow for the village stay. He'd chosen a Gurung family high in the mountains.

"Annapurna is just an arm's length away," he said with a sparkle in his eye. The family (actually the whole village) were known for their weaving, of which would be my village project. They made their own wool from their sheep. I'd be able to help in the fields, gather wood, collect water—it sounded ideal.

Although the late November weather brought mild temperatures and no snow in the valley, the mountains received a dusting overnight, making them appear even more exquisite, their presence calmly omnipotent. I was on my way to Pumpernickles, my favorite café, skillfully maneuvering my bicycle around a busy intersection in Thamel, when I heard my English name hollered through the cacophony. An unrecognizable man waved from an open door of a taxi, but I couldn't place him. He repeated my name, and then said, "Mendocino, yoga—"

"Oh, yeah," I shouted back, smiling in recognition. When I went to the alternative high school in Mendocino, California, years ago, I had rented a room from a woman who taught yoga in her home and had a business of making and selling Edgar Cayce's recipe of oily body lotions. He had been one of her teachers.

"Crazy eh?" he said. "I'm off to the airport. Good to see you! What are you doing?"

"Studying. You?"

"Just led a yoga retreat in the mountains. Heading back to Mendo."

"Oh wow, crazy is right. Say hi to Jackie. Safe travels!"

He bent into the taxi and took off. I continued toward Pumperknickels for a soda paani (mineral water) and reminisced on how small the world really was.

23

CLASSES ENDED FOR THE DAY. I MOUNTED MY BIKE AND RODE down the main road, took a left through Batisputali, and then on to Chabahil, where I lived, and hung a right toward Bhoudhnath, where I parked and locked my bike. I smiled at how well I knew my way around, at least in my "neighborhood," as I took a deep breath and walked to a favorite spot up on the smooth wall. The area relaxed me with its open feel. My system instantly settled, and I forgot about all the mishaps and discomforts of life.

Bhoudha Stupa was the largest in Nepal, and my favorite. From above, it looked like a huge mandala marked by five Buddhas representing the five elements (earth, water, fire, air, and ether) as well as other symbols of Tibetan culture. The base, three large platforms painted white and decreasing in size, symbolized earth, and two white circular columns, representing water, rose up to support the stupa. They were topped with a square tower showing painted Buddha eyes on all four sides. I loved the whiteness. Something about the feng shui of the place made me feel totally comfortable. A pyramid of "fire," built of steps, perched on top of the tower—a ladder to enlightenment—where prayer flags fluttered in the wind, constantly releasing prayers and mantras. Narrow streets, alive and colorful, lined with monasteries, street vendors, and homes, surrounded the incredible monolith. Bhouda or Bhoudnath's snow white spirit was mysterious and intriguing.

I climbed in roughly spackled white areas where a sense of freedom and devotion etched the air. This ancient Buddha stupa's pulse made journaling easy.

I felt the obliterated keenness of being alive, alone, and safe as the sun warmed my legs and the cool wind blew on my face and arms. People walked around the temple, spun prayer wheels, chanted, and mumbled prayers through dried lips and squinted eyes. Foreigners pointed and exclaimed, hippies and climbers at ease in the midst of the chaotic peace slumbered on the curved, low walls that surrounded the stupa. I saw rooftops, hills, Ganesh mountain in the distance, and the setting sun, sending its bright, heavy stripes into every crack and every face, as if each surface stood only for acceptance. I wrote journal pages and chatted with foreigners, a connection of home, far away, that reminded me of another me.

After months in this foreign country, long distance calls from family were strange. My mother and Sam (her partner after the divorce) had called yesterday at the base house. I had been immersed in another place and realm, and to concentrate time for the moments it took to connect over a wire was stressful. In the days before cell phones and emails, when talking long distance on a land-line phone was expensive, only added to the excitement and pres-sure. Not wanting my parents to worry, I tried hard to talk about my positive experiences. Hearing familiar, sweet voices who just wanted to hear my voice and hoped I was having a good time, warmed my heart. After, the evening chill forced me to wrap in a shawl, tight enough not to get caught in my bike, then weave through choked streets. My house and dal bhat were not far away.

Bhouda melted that weird feeling of displacement and loneliness which letters and phone calls often imparted. I liked fluctuating between Nepal and my dream of home. My head filled with thoughts of my parents, nestled in our Wyoming log cabin surrounded by piles of snow, doing their art while sitting on the edge of a chair, talking to me. We had never been separated for so long.

Mom had the hardest time, and the invisible energy between us fueled an unconscious strength. This bond had developed over years after the divorce, especially when my older sisters decided not to live with her. Her grief stitched our destiny tight.

While biking home to Chabahil amidst whizzing cars and people, I thought about the nature we shared. She and I breathed the same air, wore the same size, and loved each other. Our relationship bound all the unseen in heartfelt disclosure. A blazingly strong and independent woman, mom forged her life in marble as a sculptress and a mother. She imparted wisdom and a deep feminine spirit that withstood the test of changing times, but her overbearing hold on me heavily shadowed her ability to see me as a separate woman. It pained her when I was having trouble and could not express it. She had a difficult time letting me figure it out and just supporting me in a non-invasive way. The frustration generated from her trying too hard made me pull away, but our love and need to not get angry with each other drove stakes deeper into the soil of discontent, and though the pressure of that frustration accumulated, driving us apart, we eventually talked, generally on backpack trips in the mountains, going up a steep trail, bent under our heavy packs.

Many daughters were close with their mothers and were given keys to life, whether we used them or not. Mom had always been there, steadfast in my blood, rooted in the fever for that quest to unfold brilliantly, in all that she knew I could be. She supported me fully, and I knew I was lucky. Although competition innate to the mother/daughter relationship was known—its ungracious and scathing reality—she, being my greatest friend and most deceptively cutting foe, would be the strongest influence in my life. She prepped the ground I walked on, and it was her sweat that nourished my roots.

Nepal's culture was largely based in the sacred source of feminine power, and though I was brought up by a woman who helped me through those first stages of womanhood, I lacked a healthy self-image. Nepal's Third World culture beautifully evoked, through history and goddess worship, the divine feminine spirit to be amazingly real and worthy. But their paradox, the split between their religion and how women were actually treated in their society, troubled me. Those differences were classic anywhere. Nepal had color and richness, but Nepalese women seemed to have little choice in their lives, whereas men were free to be and do whatever they wanted. It didn't necessarily anger me, it just made me aware. The advantage of living in the United States may have been an incredible perk, but in some ways it felt like a burden, because existing under austere and rigid cultural mores might be the exact thing needed to force me to realize what I really wanted to do. And that would stir the fight in me to go out and do it. Or, would I be crushed beneath the weight of duty and not reach for anything? Were our cultures *really* so different? We all seemed tied up, pushed around, coerced, and generally at a loss.

Or was it just me?

I parked my bike in the usual spot inside Maya's courtyard, went upstairs to drop off my bag, then went back down to the kitchen. Muni held the lohoro (rectangular stone bar) and rapidly ground spices on the silauto (flat, thick stone slab) in feverish thrusts. She looked up at me, smiling.

"Sobha, kaasto cha?" ("How are you?") she said in staccato.

"Sanchai cha bahini, sanchai cha. Ra tapaai?" ("Happy, I am happy. And you?")

"Ho Didi," she said.

"La, Hajur Aama, ke garne?" ("What to do?")

That evening before bed, I pulled out my nose ring, cleaned it, put it back in, and looked in the mirror. My hair was braided in two coils, as usual, greased along the top to help deal with fleas and mites. I looked into my eyes while undoing the knotted curls, brushed out the tangles, then peeked out the window. Ribbons of indigo, dark grey, and white filled the sky, laced between a crescent moon. Roofs were silhouetted in soft shapes against a cautious spattering of rain. It felt ambiguous. I got into bed with no interest to write, closed my eyes, and sank into a restless sleep.

24

SOMETIME LATER I RECEIVED A LETTER FROM MOM AND SAM THAT said my last letter was strange and asked what was going on. Taken aback, piqued with guilt, I didn't know what to think. I wanted to communicate openly, but my need to censor every word so as not to worry them added to the already overbearing hold they had over me, and left me in a state of confusion. Being honest would have been easier and more helpful if I'd known what I was feeling, but not knowing how to talk about it only added to my uncertainty. All of it had built up within myself and began to disintegrate. Their letter took three weeks to reach me, so whatever they were referring to was long gone.

It didn't take much for me to fall into insecurity, which the letter initiated. I had met another student at Bhoudhnath. We had spent a lot of time together during our first year in college, but sometimes there was something unsettling between us. I was never sure if it came from me and my troubled energy, or from her, or from both of us.

That day at Bhoudhnath she acted cold. The reason for her distance wasn't clear, but was probably because I was basically a flawed person, and she was doing me a favor by being my friend.

(Why couldn't I just talk to her and voice my concerns? Because I was a mess!)

While we sat on the stupa, she recognized a guy from another group and went over to say hi. They talked for a while, without including me, and then left together. I felt left out, and figured they were probably commiserating about how plain and boring I was. That's where my mind immediately went. I didn't want to talk with them, but couldn't help feeling rejected.

What was going on? If I sounded strange toward mom and Sam, it was because everything wasn't wonderful. If I tried to talk about it, it would take hours. In Nepal, on my own, to not answer to their overly-sensitive energy, to not have to analyze and explain my every thought and feeling, was liberating. My parents smoked pot all the time and did their art. I had to be careful around mom. I didn't want to hurt her, and didn't feel I could blow up and have it out without censoring my feelings.

I had not been forthright in my letters to mom and Sam, but rather obediently judicious in my storytelling—somewhat truthful, but not complete. How could I? Everything was so different in Nepal. I saw myself as the same person as I was back at home, so what did that mean? The place (Nepal) didn't change me. The need to disclose this personality exhausted my ability in doing so, and went beyond wanting attention. I could not keep up with the psychological rhetoric to convince them "everything was fine" because it actually *was*—but I wouldn't come off sounding like it. I couldn't hide it, although it's precisely what I did for a long time, making sure my next letters were filled with wonderful events. Only my journal contained the evidence of the dark brew that held the inklings into my deeper self.

Left alone at Bhouda, I re-read mom's letter, then folded and tucked it away before leaving. Biking through the foggy sunlit streets of Ason Tole, a busy square in Kathmandu, people appeared ethereal, otherworldly in the lemon-light of the sun and riled up dust, and my eyes blurred with emotion. I wove through the lighted figures, letting me through as slots opened. It was after dusk when I pulled off a side street into the courtyard of my house. Immediately,

"Sobha," rang through the stillness. Spindly lamps and the salty-curry-smell of dinner greeted me, along with instant commotion in anxious Nepali.

"Sobha, where have you been? Why are you late!"

My Nepali was fluent enough to explain everything, at least enough to ease their sweet worry. Seated on the mud floor in the kitchen, a little room black with smoke, hajur aama stirred the fire and handed me a plate of dal bhat.

I loved it here. I loved the mystique, the hard times, these people who shared their house and life with me. I loved the freedom—yes, Sobha! I was living in Kathmandu, and I was *free*!

I ate alone in hajur aama's presence. The room was dark except for the light from the dying cooking fire, which cast shadows on the wall and danced on our faces. She bent down with a clay bowl in her hands and picked through the coals with her fingers. One by one, she quickly placed them carefully in a circle, piled others around to form a well in the middle of the hot, red, pulsating orbs. As she blew life into them, they glowed, quickly receding until another breath came upon them. She warmed her gnarled, old hands, chuckled, and tottered back and forth on old limbs which I imagined took her back to a life that was once very young. Her black, slitted eyes looked into mine with cautious inquiry.

Such an ancient gap between us, beautifully congealed in that moment of duty, hunger, and curiosity. She sucked on a hookah as if it were a lifeline—what did she smoke? She seemed to go in and out of consciousness, her mind off somewhere in the distance. Every few minutes I would look up, our eyes met, she crinkled into herself, cracked lips pressed into a sunken smile, then she closed her eyes and rocked on her heels. Did she ever leave that little room? She rarely talked. I licked my fingers, opened my journal, winked at her, then wrote down my thoughts.

JOURNAL ENTRY: November 1987, Chabahil, Nepal.

My problems are petty Sobha. So what if I'm a flawed person and can't get anything right. Let them go. Hajur aama is such a sweet soul.

Such a life we lead. So hard at times and when blind to the beauty, the repeated mistakes, the latent joy often repressed, someone may say, hey! —like hajur aama, with her wrinkled, childish, half-closed eyes, like an old cat—and help through the momentary strife. Life is much more simple than it appears. I'm not sure I'll ever really change just from being in Nepal. I may see things that hurt, surprise or amaze, but those are things passing by that affect me but don't really change me—then who is it inside that watches? Maybe my thoughts do change, and I need to look at those things, slow them down so I know what happened, and not let them totally take me away, and lose myself. Good luck Sobha! Can I actually have that kind of objective foresight?

I LOOKED up from my journal, barely distinguishable words written in the shadowed room. Hajur aama watched, and while her deft fingers tinkered with dried herbs, she cackled. What did she think about me writing in my book all the time? Time wasted on words, but not on dal bhat, something I loved. I lauded her delicious cooking. Her shy, bent body with her bowed head, and the most capricious smile with a barely audible, dhanyabad (thank you). I had opened to that family, and they to me, as much as we could.

I leaned back against the dirt wall and watched the coals glisten, a pulse slowly dying. I got up to rinse my hand and plate, but hajur aama stopped me and offered more.

"Hoina," ("No,") I said shaking my head, "tara mitho, dherai mitho!" ("but tasty, very tasty!") I kissed my fingers in exclamation. She was sad I didn't want more, and offered again with a crumpled, defeated look.

"Hoina Aama, tapai khane?" ("No aama, you eat?")

An unrecognizable sound, meaning no, she ate already, she was not hungry, or why didn't you eat more? You are so skinny, you must eat more. And then added, "Chiyaa?" ("Tea?")

"Ho, Aama, chiyaa, ho." I sat down again, she shrunk into her little cocoon and poured water into a pot to make tea.

"Tara, no chini." ("But, no sugar.")

"Ah, ah . . ." She nodded her head and rocked back and forth on her weary knees. She smiled wide, leaned over the fire, and patted my head.

"I wrote a kabita (poem), about you. You want to hear?" I said, pointing to my journal.

"Ho Bahini, ho Sobha, ho." She smiled quizzically and listened intently. I translated it as best I could.

> *The burning coals of a fire*
> *glowing with life from the breath*
> *of a soul withered from age*
> *and memories calls me from*
> *a distant land, a land that*
> *only she knows and looks*
> *for it in my eyes. Trying*
> *to find one of her kind—*
> *but her generation is gone.*
> *The times are changing. I*
> *comfort her though, and hold*
> *her hands, and gaze into*
> *her eyes with childlike*
> *curiosity, not being afraid*
> *of the old wisdom, dry cough,*
> *or bent figure.*

WHEN I FINISHED, she rocked on her bent knees, smiled with an open mouth and deeply saddened eyes.

"Are you okay?" I asked her, concerned.

"Ho Sobha, ho." She paused, still looking into my eyes. "No chini." ("No sugar.")

"Ho Aama, no chini."

We smiled at each other for a long moment, and then she looked down to stir the tea.

25

AFTER LANGUAGE CLASS, WE GATHERED IN THE BASE HOUSE kitchen for a Thanksgiving meal of mashed potatoes, hard boiled eggs, dark and dense rolls with ghee, an iodine-soaked salad of carrots, radish, and tomatoes, fruit, roasted cauliflower, and three hens—alive and nervously squawking around the back yard. I stood before them, not believing the end of their life would result from my own hands. A greater force existed—Hunger? Social formality?

The writhing animal jerked and kicked as I and another student, Linda, also from Wyoming—two cowgirls—held its body firmly. Immediately, the hen froze and went limp before I brought the knife down silent and quick. When I did, the head fell cleanly onto the dirt. Blood spattered, its beak opened and closed, the body oozed vital fluids onto my hands, warm and sticky. I let my breath out. The last one squawked, knowing where it was headed, and ran around in a panic. It took a few moments to catch it and put it out of its misery.

The base house caretaker had taught me how to kill and pluck feathers on the first one, then left us to finish the other two, but not before dabbing his finger in warm blood and placing tika on my forehead. His modest smile did not hide a self-assured man keen on his decision to let the students handle the killings. Or perhaps our leader suggested it. No one else wanted the gruesome job, so I had volunteered. I had a strange desire to be completely involved in that meal, and that was the only time I actually killed an animal. I didn't come from a hunting family, and I was vegetarian. That massacre defined new territory.

After the execution, we grasped the slim, spiritless bodies between our knees, and plucked the soft, wistful feathers from its stretchy, thick membrane. Each made a slight popping sound. Gutting the featherless bodies with bare hands, warm jelly-like liquid and innards spilled onto the ground in a bloody pile of purple, green, and red—shiny and smelly. A dot of blood for tika on my cohort, then we rinsed and placed the chickens into large pots, seared them in ghee, and boiled away the rest of any life they may have had with curry, salt, and onions.

We thanked the birds for giving their lives, then carved into their lean flesh with barbaric pleasure to feed our bodies while reminiscing about home. We laughed, talked, and sat back in drunken satiation. Nepal was a pagan country where deities were worshipped and animals sacrificed, where there was the daily routine of ritual, arranged marriages, "divine reverence" to a king and queen whose monarchy was as corrupt and backward as any in history—yet this country still had a strange and rich charm.

Homesick and lonely, together as a tribe, a pack of friends in it for the long run, our initiation passed, and our lives in a Third World country were well underway. It was a harmonious gathering of too many cooks spoiling the broth, not enough platters to hold the mounds of non-traditional dishes, and music from a visiting foreigner who had a guitar. Our bellies full, we relaxed in a circle, songs melting away any last vestiges of home. Later, we sat on the roof with keras (bananas) and suntalaas (tangerines), and felt very lucky to be in Nepal doing what we were doing, an experience we all knew would forever change us.

The urban stay was wrapping up. Preparatory meetings on the coming change of life and schedules for the villages were exciting: no daily school, no bicycles, no base house with its daily reprieve or its paperwork and chalkboard lectures. We were about to truly be immersed into Nepali life.

Muni and Nima, my two sisters at Maya's house, sat on my bed as I packed my few belongings. We shared chiyaa, sweeter than usual, and I furrowed my brow at Nima, who held her little hand over her mouth, laughing discreetly. She rarely brewed tea, so that time she made sure I remembered it. I made a face at her, which she loved, and pinched her when she put a mala (flower garland) around my neck. Even Tara leaned against the open doorway and listened. Nima cried sadly and openly. I held her hand as we sang Suntalaa Paani together, a traditional love song she had taught me, then Muni took her into her arms. I mounted my bike and rode off. Maya was at work; we had said our goodbyes the night before. One of my brothers yelled from the balcony and waved. I had one week on my own before leaving for the village.

THAT EVENING, a few of us students met at the Namaste Café in the heart of Thamel. The young, handsome Nepali man who owned the joint sat with us intermittently while serving other weary trekkers, foreigners, and hippies who came in for his milky chiyaa or strong coffee. His perfect English, charm, keen intelligence, and easy way, coupled with the place's local ambience, brought the world through his doors. His eyes were dark and deep, and I fell into them. I wondered who he really was, and wanted to find out.

Our eyes had met warmly the first time, so many months ago, and that spark never left our conversation. Whenever I visited, we conversed easily, chiyaa was freely filled, hours drifted by, and I imagined going upstairs with him. What would it be like to be with a Nepali man?

I was sure he had affairs—probably with students from our school—over the years. He had that air, not cocky or auspicious, but perceptive. I wanted to believe he chose his partners carefully. That evening, his lingering gaze on me was uncomfortable. Being a virgin, I didn't know what to do. I was ashamed of it and hid it. I didn't want to appear loose, an easy catch, so purposely avoided his soft touch on my back, and he seemed hurt. His eyes clouded, that sensitive, fiery look turning to a dejected silent query. We had an understanding between us, he thought, and he was right, but I was scared and couldn't talk to him about it. The next day I'd be gone on a trek to the Tibetan border, then the three month village stay, then back to the States. An affair for a night? I couldn't lead him on like that. Love and sex were different in Nepal, or so I thought. They were certainly different in my head.

His underlying gracious character and gentlemanly nature eventually glossed over the intrigue, chase, and failure, as he quickly opened himself again to our raucous crowd of free students. The evening turned into a late-night party, and his attention, too quickly, turned to Linda. (The rogue! Such a swift interest in someone else?) Confused and dejected, I made excuses to leave with a few others in rickshaws. I wondered if Linda would actually stay with him that night. Didn't he like *me*? Why wasn't he running down the street after *me*? Why wouldn't he grab *me*, pull *me* into his arms and kiss *me* passionately. Who was I fooling?

"Sobha, Sobha, Sobha! Dherai naramro, garib Sobha," (*"Very not good, poor Sobha,"*) I whispered to myself. I could have walked faster than that human-powered rickshaw, but instead slumped back and let the darkness envelope me. Pedal clinks and heavy breathing from the exertion, chain links needing oil, bumpy and slow, I looked forward to the mountains.

I curled up in my sleeping bag on the base house floor. *It could have been fun, Sobha.* I couldn't let it go, and got up to sit near the window. What had held me back?

"Sobha, are you okay?" Carl asked, leaning against the doorway. His expectant look, raised eyebrows, short brown hair cropped a chiseled, caring face. Serious in his inquiry, he sat next to me, waiting.

"Ho Dai, ho." I sighed and pressed my forehead to the cold pane of glass. A dog trotted by as a heavy mist settled around the low walls that surrounded the base house.

"Ke bayo?" ("What's wrong?") he asked again. "You seem off. Did something happen?"

"No," I lied. "Just thinking about Kathmandu. I love this city. I could live here."

Juni shuffled past on her way to the kitchen and returned with bananas and tangerines. We grabbed shawls and climbed to the roof. The fruit had skin that could be peeled, so it was safe to eat raw. The tangerines squirted, pungent and sweet. I breathed it in and exclaimed how good it smelled! The bananas were tiny, the size of a cigar—four or five, even ten could easily be eaten in one sitting.

I never answered Carl.

"I'll miss these times here," Juni said, eating a tangerine.

"Me too," Carl agreed. "Getting lost down endless streets, nothing you would find in any travel books, exploring and talking to these people. I'm in a fairy tale, an enchanted land. Nepal is still the old world. We're lucky to be here now."

We gazed toward the distant city skyline. Smoke rose in silhouetted spirals, faint noises of cars, people hacking as I leaned against Carl and he massaged my shoulders.

"I love Kathmandu," I said. "I can't wait to get to the village, but I love this Kathmandu craziness."

"You can say that again," Juni said, peeling a banana. "It'll be hard not having this freedom in the village." She waved out over Kathmandu. "But fun," she added, and we all agreed. We were more hopeful than sure.

Silence graced the three of us for a while until a rooster crowed. Sleep would probably be a good idea, and we retreated to our corners inside. My eyes closed for a short time, enough to have a disturbing dream: I walked up a hill outside Kathmandu with shops on either side. A man asked me what happened, what made me normal. He must be mistaken. A couple of years ago he said there was a girl here with blonde curly hair who was crazy. Strangely, an elephant walked by, and then I saw my sister through a shop window. I ran in and hugged her, cried, and laughed. She didn't talk, smile, or hug me back. Her hair was messy. She looked angry and unhappy. Then I was holding a little girl's hand who was very sick and could barely stand. We had to step over dead bodies. She couldn't handle it, so I carried her the rest of the way to a clinic, where they asked her questions. I tried to answer for her. Then I ran down a hill and awoke.

The dream encapsulated a merging of my old self—the supposedly crazy person in her total loss of reality from the inevitable situation of being young, naïve, and inexperienced—to connect to the one who had embarked upon a major journey of the soul. An elephant crossed—the Hindu sign of Ganesh (elephant god)—was represented in one way as the remover of obstacles, or in Tibetan symbology, mental strength—possibly a gentle reminder. My angry sister who didn't acknowledge me was just another aspect of myself that I was not dealing with. Death stood for a final closing, an ending where I carried a little girl (symbolically me) and helped her, obviously through the emotional rubble of her life. The dream was a bird's eye view of that personal sojourn in Nepal, and the transition to a wilder and solitary part of myself.

Preoccupied by last night's dream, I took a brisk bicycle ride through busy streets early the next morning. A quick stop for a lassi (traditional yogurt-based drink), its smooth sourness helping me clarify and ponder the meaning of the dream, trying to decipher what I was meant to learn.

The next couple of days were a bustle of finishing up term papers, packing for the trek, and preparing for village life.

26

DECEMBER BROUGHT COLDER EVENINGS AND MORNINGS HEAVY
with fog that dissipated into warm days. The urban stay in Kathmandu had ended. Our mixed feelings about leaving the city were
short-lived as the distant peaks called ahead. Carl and Linda
decided to come along on a four-day trek to Tatopaani, a little town
near the border of Tibet.

I wanted to get into the high mountains quickly, and had asked
the base house caretaker for some ideas of where to go as well as
suggestions from a few hikers at Pumperknickels. At four in the
morning, we quietly donned our packs and slipped out the squeaky
base house door. We kept a good pace in the cold morning on foot
to Ring Road, where Gorkha soldiers, dressed in utilitarian fatigues,
guns slung over their shoulders, patrolled the route. Known for their
speed, bravery, slight build, and fierce look, they approached us in
clipped strides. One of them discarded the smoky end of his rolled
cigarette and nodded. We were sitting on the curb, waiting for the
bus, but got up immediately at their approach, a little nervous. I
smoothed my wrinkled skirt as the soldiers looked us over. Their
name came from Gorkha, a small town north of Kathmandu,
where once the king of that region had united all of Nepal through

military operations (Nepal was unified in 1769 by the house of Gorkha, and that's when the Shah dynasty started ruling). Their origin is mandated by the legendary history of Nepal.

"Where are you going?" one of them asked in English.

"Tatopaani. We're waiting for the bus," I said.

"You go to the mountains?" he asked, eyeing our packs.

"Ho." I smiled.

His curiosity was piqued by that one simple word. "You speak Nepali?"

"Ho, tapaai angreji kasto ramro!" I responded in Nepali. They laughed. We conversed in Nepali until the 4:45 a.m. bus pulled up. The soldiers picked up our packs, handed them up to the boy on top of the bus, and, stepping inside, told the driver who we were and where we wanted to go. We thanked them—a jolly crew, it turned out—found seats, and waved as the bus took off.

The buses in Nepal were old, painted colorfully and amazingly capable compared to their rough look. They bumped along, broke down often, only to be wired back together by the streetwise hack who drove the stinky beast. We were the only white people on board, but were seasoned residents, and just stared back as we conversed with the surprised Nepalese in their language while sharing food.

The Araniko Highway, named after a 13th century Nepalese architect, connected Kathmandu to Kodari about seventy miles northeast on the Nepal-China border. The bus stopped in little towns along the way as people got off and on. The outside air cooled as the hours went by. Linda and I had to pee really bad, so we jumped off at one stop and squatted behind a building since a charpi was nowhere to be found. Did anyone look? Who cared. A skirt fanned out easily and nothing was seen.

The bus wound its way through deep canyons with rushing rivers. The driver drove precariously, suddenly braking, lurching back and forth to avoid potholes and the nefarious edge. I clung to the seat in a cold sweat, telling myself to breathe, and in that same breath, loving the madness. The reckless driver took turns too fast, obviously wanting to get the ride over with since the road could give out at any time. Every dip and jolt sent a piercing pain into my stomach. *What the hell! This was crazy! Get me out of here, I'll walk!* Thankfully, we stopped at Lamosangu, where heavy rains had washed the rest of the road out a few days earlier.

An abandoned feeling hung in the air—desolate and sad. The aftermath of destruction would take months to fix. But life carried on—more slowly though, since carrying precious loads had to be done by foot to the villages and homes beyond. The cold, damp air smelled new. A clarity of range struck me as I stepped out of the bus and felt the rubble and grit beneath my feet. The road sat in disarray—ugly debris, ragged edges broken off, unstable, impassable. This was one of the most dangerous roads in Nepal because of the steep slopes. Buses going over in landslides were commonplace.

We continued on foot across a death-defying, swinging footbridge over a heinous river. Since the buses had stopped, the "bridge," at least thirty feet in length and only a few feet above the raging water, had fallen somewhat from the heavy and constant use. A ladder leading up to the damaged bridge hung from one side. The other half of the "non-existent" bridge was limp, knotted together in disappearing strands. We looked nervously at what remained of it, about to fall apart, what might collapse with a light tap. I had heard about bridges like that, but reading or being told about them did not match the fear and courage needed to actually step onto one with a loaded pack. I stared at the Nepalese and Tibetans who laughed, pointed, and clapped at each victory. We clung to pieces of rough rope and splintered wood while torrents of white water churned below like hungry dogs snapping at our ankles. As one of us made it across and awaited the others, time melted into a poem, beautifully tinged with humor and guts. We were proud of ourselves —even more than when we somewhat mastered the language— though I nervously looked back, guessing more boards might be missing on the return trip.

We joined a pack of porters for the two to three hour walk to Barabise. Every once in a while, a glimpse to the other side of the canyon at the washed-out road made my stomach jittery with excitement, the same feeling I got when the power went out. I loved nature taking over—not necessarily in a life-threatening way, but enough to remember who was boss.

We stepped aside as a group of stocky porters, who were carrying teetering loads strapped to their foreheads, approached us on the narrow path. One of them reached out blindly as he kept his head down under the strain of his load. I wasn't sure what to do, but extended my hand and grabbed his like an anchor. He leaned his weight into me, and I pulled him around me with all the strength I had. *Was that appropriate?* I wondered, since men and women were not supposed to touch in public. But he needed help, I couldn't just let him stumble or fall.

He looked up and realized the hand belonged to a white girl! He was old, gnarled, and extremely fatigued. No words were spoken. A nod from him, and he moved on.

Barabise, with its line of inviting tea huts, welcomed weary travelers. Word of a bus leaving for Tatopaani in several hours allowed us time to settle into a corner table and sip tea in a chiyaa pasal (tea hut). Suddenly, the bus pulled up! (Mastering the language? Right!) We grabbed our packs, tossed them onto the outside top rack, hopped on board, and pushed our way inside to standing room only. Everyone looked at each other with agitated glances. The fetid odor of hard-working human bodies surrounded us as we clung to the backs of seats and baggage racks.

Our one-and-a-half-hour ride was a daunting experience, pressed between sweaty bodies, listening to incessant tinny music, fearfully eyeing the harrowing edge of a washed-out road that had many times been put back together with what seemed like glue and rubble. The battered fringe of road was swallowed by the interrupting edge of the windows as I peered over a hundred-foot cliff to the tangled, frigid mountain water below.

"We made it," I said to Carl as we finally pulled into the pleasant town of Tatopaani, its name meaning *hot water.* The place appeared welcoming as we walked up the dusty main road, buildings on either side displaying hanging signs saying "Guesthouse." We checked into a room in the Sherpa's lodge and looked for food in the tiny town of maybe fifty people. Dal bhat satisfied our souls, chiyaa to follow, and candlelight at our table where we stayed up with books and journals. I had read about this area, but didn't know much beyond that. I figured we'd see what we would find and just explore, as we only had a few days.

The night passed fast, black sky and silent as a cave. In the cold morning, mist hung low around the quiet buildings. Hot tea and dal bhat quickly transformed our sleepy mood as we mused on what to do. We headed out across another swinging bridge for a day hike—a little better built than yesterday's—and started up a trail through rice terraces until it ran out. Intuitively picking our way to the top of a steep foothill, a huge valley appeared in gorgeous alpine array. The aspiring view calmed any doubt and frustration I had for anything—and then a voice rang through.

Me walking across a swinging bridge outside of Tatopaani

A spry old man made his way over, greeted us with a handshake, then explained in limited Nepali which mountains were in Tibet and which ones in Nepal. He was a monk who claimed to have been kicked out of Tibet, where he had worked for the Dalai Lama. He now lived in the Dalai Lama's house—a small, sparse hut adorned with pictures of lamas and Buddhists. I sensed beyond his genuine hospitality and childish command of life an extremely disciplined nature. Outside, he showed us around his little plot with a garden and flapping prayer flags. We sipped salty Tibetan tea and spoke in Nepali about the world and what he was doing there.

"How long have you been here?" I asked.

"Dui barsa." ("Two years.") He held up two fingers. We could only catch a few phrases, his accent very thick. "I miss Tibet very much." His eyes turned cloudy, he shifted on his heels. "But I live my life here and carry on the work."

"Have you ever tried to go back?" Carl asked.

"Hajur, tara (Yes, but), it is too difficult. This is my life now, here, on this mountain." He smiled, looking into our eyes. "What do you do?"

"We are students," I answered, "studying Nepali language and culture."

"Why come here?" He patted the ground.

"I wanted to get closer to the mountains, and we have a little time. Soon we go to a village to live with families."

Throughout the conversation Linda sat quietly, then asked about the troubles in his homeland. He answered honestly and candidly. He had tried to go back many times, but was met with great trouble, and anger had filled his body for a long time, but no longer. He began to see his life, and the reasons why his dharma was in Nepal, which he didn't get into.

"How do you keep in touch with it all?" I asked.

He smiled and tapped his forehead, then got up and beckoned us to follow him, showing what he ate and how he existed in that high mountain abode. The long silences between comments were not uncomfortable, but made us wish we could communicate better. How many visitors crossed his path, I wondered, envious of his simple life? He kneeled with such ease on the tip of a narrow rock and gazed at each of us. His eyes sparkled. Adept in the martial arts, he leaped off his perch in a playful kick.

Carl and the old man wrestled in Tai chi-like moves around the circle of rocks at the edge of that great world. The man's infectious smile settled on his wise face as he sat again, in a squat position, back on the pointed rock. We pressed hands together in namaste, and pointed to the setting sun. When the air chilled suddenly, the man grabbed a wrap and followed us a little way down. He pointed to a better route than the one we had taken. We said goodbye, but I lingered for a moment to watch him slowly make his way back. He turned and waved. I held my hand up, our eyes locked for an instant, and I wished to be like him. Maybe I could return and be his student, live up in the mountains, drink butter tea and meditate on world peace—or at least inner peace. I waited until he turned.

Linda and I swam in a waterfall on the way down while Carl went on ahead. A quick dip, the cold ice on our skin squeezing every organ in our bodies, and we laughed with abandon. Back at the lodge, where we stayed a second night, we hungrily devoured dal bhat.

Trekking near the Tibetan border

I wanted to step into Tibet, so the next morning we walked the few kilometers across some of the most beautiful and exhilarating vistas, where magnificent waterfalls crashed to the ground in thunderous rolls and viciously spit cold, blue-grey water. Mountains rose in a surreptitious haze, and I walked, as if in a trance, to the Friendship Bridge that linked the border town of Kodari to Zhangmu in Tibet, and eventually to Lhasa—even the word conjured mysticism and intrigue.

The guards on the bridge stopped us abruptly. They held up white-gloved hands and barked orders we couldn't understand in Tibeto-Chinese.

"Go back," they yelled.

"Can I cross the bridge? I just want to step into Tibet," I pleaded in the politest Nepali I knew.

"No. Go back." He looked at me hard. He thrust a hand, pointing toward where we came from.

"But—"

"Go!" he commanded, eyes lit with fire, gleaming in anger. He moved his body, almost bumping into me. He was the same height, stocky, and severe. We tried again to ask permission, but they were not interested in American students. I just wanted to cross the bridge and come right back. I wasn't a white girl with gold hair defecting. But I didn't push it. I did not want to add to the already delicate matter of international borders, or worse, wind up detained.

We came from the valley of the Sun Kosi River, innocent and trouble-free. White peaked mountains were our expectation, the pilgrimage into my destiny from where I may never have come back was in full throttle, but that border guard had stopped us. I might have bribed him if I had had the privilege of time, or at least the knowledge of my rights, as well as an inkling of his language. We headed back into the deep gorge where the Sun Kosi River cut the earth as it gushed down in tumultuous drum rolls, rhythmic to our own footsteps, walked along the dirt road, and then finally took a night's ride out of there back to Tatopaani.

The bus was packed, so we rode on the outside top rack with the luggage and bundles. The river rumbled alongside the road, accentuating the darkness, thick and mysterious. A strange calm graced my nerves on that broken, treacherous road. I let go completely, leaned back, and felt the bus go buoyant beneath me, as if it floated through the canyon. The indigo sky swallowed punctures of light that sparkled and pulsed and was made even brighter by the fiercely cold air. Blackened hills rose in silhouettes on either side like the massive thighs of an earthy god, speckled with little dots of fire from lighted homes, reluctantly nestled into rugged and ominous heights. It was magical.

Late in the night, we got into Barabise, bought tangerines, and then walked for an hour or so on the trail through rice fields in the dark. Linda was tired and couldn't go on much longer, so we found a secluded spot on a rice paddy, laid out our bags, and fell asleep.

The black night swelled silent with stars, the nearby river gushed and rumbled, rocks hit each other at the bottom in knocks and thwacks. That powerful current churned endlessly, like a stormy ocean. I slept lightly until five a.m. when we all awoke and started out. The moon, still and bright, lit the path of worn rocks smoothed over from hundreds of thousands of feet who walked that ancient, intrepid artery, glistening in obsidian-like hardness, and the river sparkled in a show of frenzied gurgles.

We reached Lamosangu and waited for the bus. Carl had decided to return to Kathmandu, but Linda and I wanted to stay the night at Dhulikhel, where we'd had our mid-term retreat. The over-crowded bus rolled along in a topsy-turvy way, like a jolly, one-man band. One mother held two young children on her lap, and an older child stood next to her. I caught her eye, motioned with my hand toward one of the little ones on her lap, and talked to her in Nepali.

"I could hold one on my lap, if you like?"

She gratefully nodded and said in Nepali, "Go nani, go go go, it's okay," and pushed a little girl about two years old to my outstretched hands. I hoisted her up, smiled shyly at her, and said a few words. She looked at me, wide-eyed, then grasped my finger, held it tightly, and leaned against my chest. Her mother glanced back often. We jostled along for almost an hour; nani (little girl) fell asleep in my arms. As we pulled into a small village, the mother turned to me.

"I get off here. I come back," she said quickly as she carted off her children. I leaned toward the window and saw her call out for her bundles, which were handed down. She came back, bent down, lifted the sleeping child into her arms, squeezed my hand, and said, "Dhanyabad didi." I looked at them outside. We waved to each other, and the bus drove off. I stood up and offered my seat to an old lady while I leaned against Linda's seat. Thirty more minutes to Dhulikhel.

Dhulikhel was the last large village before the Tibetan border, situated less than an hour's drive southeast of Kathmandu. It served as the main destination for food and water along the ancient route between Nepal and Tibet, where people traveled back and forth for trade. It housed mostly Newar, and some Brahmin, Chhetri, and Tamang families scattered amidst narrow streets of buildings with traditional Newari carvings on doors and windows. Its layout was based on ancient Hindu doctrine, in which each structure embodied its own meaning and amity, truly part of their remarkable sense of spiritual order.

We checked into a room, unrolled our bags on the bed to air them out, and headed for the showers. Simple dal bhat for me while Linda ordered a Nepali version of pizza with an egg softly cooked in the middle. The young girl who brought the food remembered us from the retreat and asked what we were doing. We caught a few of her words as she told the cook in Nepali, "Two of the students are back from that school trip. They just came from Tato." The cook graciously came out and offered his famous rice pudding. I nodded excitedly.

After a delicious repast, Linda and I took a sunset jaunt on an easy trail up through shrub oak trees and mountain views that would unwind any discontented soul. We walked in silence until we settled onto some large rocks.

"What a great trek. You just want to do that all the time?" Linda asked.

"I do," I said. "Yes, I do. How lucky to have met that lama up on the mountain."

"Do you think his story was true, about living in the Dalai Lama's house?"

"I don't know. Probably. But even if it wasn't, I want to believe it."

On our way back, the sun set into surreal mauve stripes across the immense sky. We relaxed in warm beds where Linda opened a book to read with her headlamp, and I my journal, accompanied by candlelight. The guy from Café Namaste never came up between us, and I decided not to ask. It didn't matter. I read the pages I had written last night about a concerned dichotomy that existed within my mind—of who I was and what I did.

JOURNAL ENTRY: December 1987, Tatopaani, Nepal.

I am not one to take things lightly and often take the blame for everything. I feel the pain of everybody, and have a hard time separating myself from the anxious energies of the world. I know what moving into a new family entails, and I am trying to mentally prepare for it. But as much as I invite change and want to live in poverty, I'm also scared of it. I can't hide and not deal with the world. I want to be part of it, but am introverted and unaware of the motives that really command my thoughts.

I kept thinking about the lama's disciplined meditation. He doesn't seem to hide from the world even though he lives away from everything. The pain and discord he felt so many years ago while dealing with being kept in a country other than his own was brutal, it seemed. But I could see in him, that it was one of his great teachings.

No MATTER what my thoughts or worries were, I looked forward to the village stay. A shower in the morning and porridge with bananas warmed me and reminded me that I loved Nepal.

We meandered through the quiet streets of Dhulikhel, its old temples and narrow lanes so beautiful and interesting. A little chiyaa pasal (tea hut) tucked outside an ancient temple beckoned us for a cup of sweet tea. The woman working there, excited about conversing in Nepali, waved to her husband and son as they arrived and joined our table. Knowing the language immediately dropped the barrier, especially since the sincere interest we had for their culture was heartfelt. We asked the time, and looked at each other about needing to catch a bus.

"Where you go?" the husband asked in Nepali.

"Kathmandu," I said. "Our school starts again tomorrow."

The husband offered us a ride since they had a load they were about to deliver near there. We paid for the tea, said goodbye to his wife, and followed him down a few streets to a dump truck! The son insisted he ride in the back, but we waved him off and climbed onto the dusty load, settled into a soft pocket near the cab as they handed up our packs, and we nodded at their concerned look through the cracked glass. They dropped us off at a gas station on Ring Road, where we caught a taxi to the base house.

27

EARLY THE NEXT MORNING, VIKRAM, A YOUNG MAN DRESSED IN blue jeans, running shoes, and collared shirt, picked me up from the base house in Kathmandu where we had gathered, awaiting members from our village families. He was a Gorkha soldier, now my older brother (or dai), on leave for a few days, and he spoke English fluently. He would be my escort on the long journey to the remote village of Tangting, a seven-hour hike into the hills outside of Pokhara.

The Prithvi Highway, 174 kilometers long, stretched west from Kathmandu to Pokhara, the second largest city in Nepal. The heavily used road offered access to religious temples, river cross-ings, the Tribhuvan and Mahendra Highways, and towns at important junctions, such as the small, historical town of Gorkha, the origin of the famous soldiers whose motto, "Better to die than be a coward," is as tough as the eighteen inch long kukri knives they still carry. Huge mountains skirted the ride where loose muddy cliffs often fell in tumultuous landslides that washed out the road and bridges. The deeply cut valley of the Madi River offered sights of Machapuchhare and the Annapurna Himals, and plenty of time to daydream on the eight-hour journey to Pokhara. We got in late, checked into a guesthouse, and ate dal bhat in a small café.

"My village is very different than Kathmandu," Vikram, or dai, meaning older brother, as I called him, said, eyeing me carefully. We spoke in English. "There is not much to do there."

"I am happy about that. Shankar said I could help your family with collecting wood and whatever is needed," I said before remarking on how good the dal bhat was.

"You like dal bhat?"

"I love it," I said. "I love all the food here."

"We eat a little differently in the village," he said. "You might like it, too."

"When did you join the army?" I asked.

"When I was eighteen, ten years ago." He wiped his hand and pushed his plate away. "I like to travel. I don't like village life."

He paid. We left and walked back to the guesthouse, a long, lopsided, white brick building, painted heavily in red trim, just off a busy street. The host opened a door to a dorm-like setting where men and women slept in different rooms on small cots. We said goodnight and went to bed.

Pokhara was a beautiful area that boasted some of the highest mountains in the world only thirty miles away: Dhaulagiri, Annapurna, Manaslu (except Machapuchhare, which was only ten miles away). The next day, he showed me around, paraded me off a bit, which embarrassed me, but I played along. He had spent years training in other cities, such as Hong Kong, and unabashedly talked about the women there. We were both nervous, but did he honestly think that impressed me?

He was slick and fast-talking, inflated by his travels and combat experience. I was in a strange position of feeling respect and congeniality for him, apprehension and excitement about the experience ahead, and frustration of knowing more than Vikram on so many levels—or so I thought. He, too, felt strange having a white girl at his side in his hometown, showing her off, and explaining the situation. We acted polite and courteous towards each other. Still, first impressions can be so judgmental.

That night we went to a cultural dance show inside a large tent. We were packed together, kneeling on the dusty ground. My arm accidentally pressed against a young Nepali guy on the other side of me. He shyly pulled away and whispered to his friend. In Nepal, I only clashed on the outside because of my white skin, so people checked me out, looking closely, inquisitively. On the inside, I was a peasant, a villager, a mountain girl. I loved hard work, plain food, and simple living.

Language may have been a barrier in that country, but in that musty-smelling theatrical tent, smiles and hand gestures became the template, friends were born, cultures compared, and countries were borderless. The audience embraced me as one of them. They turned and smiled. Some pushed through and asked my name and what country I came from. It appeared I was the only westerner there, and as much of the show as the dancers on stage.

The colors of the costumes and the music exploded in red, orange, and turquoise against brown skin and make-up. The piercing trill of the bansuri and saarangi flutes, with syncopated beats of the madal drum, mesmerized all of us as the stage transformed into artistic, life-changing energy. When the dance finished, uproarious applause and yelling filled the darkened space.

We got up to go, pushed by the crowd. Vikram looked back to make sure I followed. Hands quickly grasped mine and then let go. Different parts of me were touched, indecently sometimes, and when I looked to see who it might have been, I couldn't tell.

We spilled out through the cloth doors into a cool, dark evening. People Vikram knew came up and asked him about me. I understood a little, and responded when I could. They laughed at my Nepali, with invitations to their houses. Vikram politely thanked them, but declined, as we had to get an early start the next day.

A bus the next morning took us northeast from Pokhara, where we transferred to a jeep that made its way to Jhaundu through an open valley. A few people laden with heavy baskets waved as we passed. A woman sat outside a shack and stared when we stopped as the road turned into a wide footpath. A young man atop the jeep easily recognized my pack amidst the earth-colored bundles, grasped it, but it slipped from his hands and crashed to the ground. A brown liquid trickled from one side of it, like dark blood.

The anti-parasitic and immune-boosting tincture specially concocted for Third World travel had smashed. I bent down to inspect the shattered brown glass inside the pocket. The herbal smell was strong as a large puddle stained the dust. I pulled the broken bottle out; a quarter of the liquid was still there in the bottom. Appalled, Vikram yelled at the incompetence in fast, clipped Nepali. It embarrassed me.

"Shit," he said first in English, then in Nepali, "You imbeciles, what are you doing? What is wrong with you? Get it up, get it up!"

"It's okay," I said calmly in Nepali. I looked up at the poor kid on top of the jeep, and then to Vikram. "It's okay. It's okay, Dai, really, I don't need it."

Suddenly the broken bottle was snatched out of my hand by the old woman who had watched the scene from her porch.

"Didi," I said in Nepali, going after her, "it is broken glass—very sharp, very dangerous."

She cut me off. "Hoina, hoina, dhanyabad." ("No, no, thank you.") Her cracked voice and pitiful face implored release. She patted my hand, gingerly coveted it in the folds of her skirt, and smiled sheepishly, half her teeth missing. "Good, medicine, is good," she croaked in some dialect. One of her eyes was grey, the other deeply pigmented brown and black. Conspiratorially, she blinked at me and hobbled back toward her dilapidated shack. I let it go.

Vikram calmed down after I repeated over and over "not to worry." He hired a porter to carry my backpack. I protested, being a seasoned hiker able to carry my load. He insisted, and the destitute guy who took the job stepped up, agitated and worried. He fumbled with the shoulder straps, carried it a distance with a pained look, then gave up and somehow strapped it the traditional way across his forehead. I felt sorry for him. He looked weary, as if he had just returned from a decade-long pilgrimage. I told Vikram again that I could carry it. His curt refusal silenced me.

"Vikram Dai, I've been hiking since I was very little, carrying my own weight. My mom and I backpack in the mountains in

America all the time. It is something I love to do." I said this in English to make sure I said it clearly and he would understand.

"Ho Bahini," he said, breathing heavy up the steep, rocky steps. "I understand, but now this is a long walk, and we can talk, and you must save breath. It is okay. It is good work for him to carry your pack. He gets paid for this work. Do not worry so much." Vikram carried nothing but a small daypack.

Up flights of rough-cut rocky steps, the narrow dirt trail led around grassy knolls and huts, but the route was remarkably unpopulated. Around a bend, a deep ridge appeared, its opposite face at least three hundred feet away. The steep valley dropped to a rushing river where a swinging bridge with many broken and missing wooden boards, worse than the one at Tatopaani, hung across the raging Madi Khola river hundreds of feet below. The metal cables were the only strength the bridge offered. Vikram looked at me, then stepped onto the rock portal at either side of the cables. He held the rope railings and walked across without stopping or looking back. On the other side, he waved. Glad not to have my pack on my back, I tentatively stepped onto the first panel of wood, looked ahead at Vikram, who smiled and waved me on. I clutched the rope on either side and did what he did—I went forward and did not look back or down, a difficult feat since so many boards were missing over the dizzying, out-of-focus foam far below. Gingerly, I stepped onto the planks as a stab of fear chilled me. But once over the middle part, about thirty feet from the end, I breathed deeply, finally enjoying the thrill. But I did not stop until stepping onto solid ground—safe.

Vikram slapped me on the back. "Ho Bahini, good job! No more of those, just trail now." He could see my relief, smiled genuinely, and stepped onto the trail. We stopped a couple of times to chat with his friends and take short breaks. Late in the day, after hours of hiking, he decided to stop and try to get me to eat a specially prepared meal at one of the houses. I didn't want to be a bother, and figured we'd just get to Tangting, so I declined every time he suggested we stop, but now he called out for food at a lone house near the river, one it seemed he was not familiar with. A

Tibetan woman appeared. Vikram said something in Gurung, very different from Nepali. She looked puzzled for a moment, obviously not accustomed to serving strangers on the path, but waved for us to sit down on a thick wooden bench, and disappeared inside.

After a long wait, she came out with two plates of dal bhat, then retreated quickly into the house. Vikram stood up and called to her.

"Didi, masu (meat), masu, okay?"

"Not for me, Dai, please don't bother."

"Didi," he squinted his eyes and puffed his chest, "masu," he called out to her in a definitive tone and pointed at me, none of which I understood, but I knew what he was doing. Twenty minutes later she brought out a small bowl of sinewy shards of black meat floating in a heavy broth. Vikram smiled, helped himself, and then handed it to me.

"Dhanyabad Dai, tara no khane." ("Thank you, but I do not want to eat it,") I said.

"Sobha," he said with a concerned look, "you need it. We still have a long way to go." I realized he meant well, so I put a few pieces on my plate, tasted one, remarked on how delicious it was, and then finished in silence. I felt awful for that woman, who probably had very little. Meat was scarce, and there we were enjoying all she had. I doubted Vikram tipped her.

We moved on, the porter far ahead, into the atmosphere of Annapurna IV and Lamjung. The path ascended steep hills until, finally, it leveled out, curving round. I spotted a house here and there, and farther on many white houses with authentic shale tile roofing perched on the steep hillside. Children ran toward us, pointing and giggling, as we finally came to Tangting, a terraced village perched at seven thousand feet, which didn't seem high compared to the rest of the Himalayas. I loved the name. It sounded like a song.

Tangting gaun (village) consisted largely of men who served in the Gorkha army, including Vikram, who was gone a few weeks at a time. The women were known for their weaving.

Tangting village seen on right hill in front of the massive Annapurna 2

I followed Vikram on the uneven, rocky pathway down some steps and onto a flat—about twelve by thirty feet long—pounded dirt terrace. It was early evening. The porter had something to eat and drink from Vikram's family, then was sent on his way. Where, I wondered?

I sat on the front steps while a discussion took place inside, all in Gurung, between Vikram and his family. A young girl came out with a bowl of black, hairy-looking root things that looked like taro. I looked up at her questioningly. She said something I couldn't understand, knelt, peeled one, and popped it into her mouth, then ran inside. Quick chatter and giggles fluttered out the open window. I hugged my knees and leaned against the rough wood siding, tired, but so happy to be there, feeling naked again. I tried one; it had a delicious, mild taste, like a starchy mountain potato, but with a better consistency. They called it pidhaalu.

About two hundred and fifty households lived in Tangting, mostly Gurung, derived from the Tibetan word "grong", which meant farmers, one of the indigenous peoples of Nepal's mountainous areas who lived at high altitudes. Upon entering the village, we'd walked through an area where the untouchables lived, Vikram informed me, a caste of people lowest in the Nepali system of identity. Gurung had different meanings; it was not only a language, but also a group in the caste hierarch according to the mulukhi ain, known as alcohol drinkers, or matwali. Tangting had the classic look of a tightly-knit, hard-working, authentic mountain village. I had stepped into a fairytale, nestled on a hillside, surrounded by mountains and thick forest. Annapurna 2 commanded the view. That night it turned pink and blew my mind.

I was grateful to Shankar and Dave (our leader back in Kathmandu). I was where I'd wanted to be all along—as far away as they would let me go. Even though the first week would be strange, harder than my Kathmandu stay because Nepali was not the village language, but Gurung, I was content to be somewhere totally different.

So many giggles and shy looks. Vikram went out of his way to be kind, translated everything, showed me where I would sleep, and explained the bathroom situation (which was outside below the courtyard out in the open, and as you did what you had to do, it tumbled down, seemingly into the paddies below—no charpi, no outhouse, no nothing). Later, I could tell he was remarking to aama how much I enjoyed the food and would be no problem. She smiled widely, delicately looked to me, motioning me to come to her. She inspected my face closely, and then laughed and pointed to my nose ring. She squeezed my shoulders and nodded her head in approval. I was introduced to everyone, and then we sat down to dal bhat.

THE NEXT DAY aama and didi dressed me in "proper" Gurung clothing: cholo, a long-sleeved, fitted top, fastened with ties in front, lungi, a tubular piece of colorful fabric or skirt, no band or elastic at the waist. You stepped into the wide opening, then folded the front to form a pleat, which gave ample room for leg movement, and underneath was worn a similar, yet lighter lungi or cotton slip, similar to a petticoat. The lungi and petticoat were held secure with a wide, vibrant, turquoise-colored belt of sturdy material, or parko, wrapped tightly around the waist several times, the end folded into itself. The outfit was finished with a wrap tied around my head. The morning meal consisted of bhat (rice), saag (cooked greens), and goat meat in my honor (not a daily staple).

Aama and I in Tangting

Vikram rattled off in Gurung to the others while repeating to me in English about showing me around the village. I waved to aama. She waved back. Vikram led me over the cobbled stone pathway that wound through the village. He explained the structure of the houses, their white-washed exterior, dark wooden beams, and heavy shale roofs different from the brown mud, brick, and thatched roof houses I'd seen on the hike up and on my trek before coming to Tangting. We came to an open area and a small stone building. Children rushed to the open windows when they heard our voices.

The head teacher joined us at a table outside the school building. He spoke in Nepali and English, asking me to sing an English song. My mind went blank, but then I sang, "Mary Had a Little Lamb," with gusto. They watched in rapt attention, hanging on every word, then applauded and shrieked. They asked what it meant. I wished I had thought of a more grown-up song. Its meaning stumped me, but I explained it as a children's song. They wanted to learn it with the verses written down, and then they taught it to me in Gurung.

Later that day, I sat on the porch in the sun, watching aama (mother of the family) spin wool in a mesmerizing, steady movement.

"Aama, tapaii nata gota." ("Your family,") I asked her in Nepali, and then recalled, "Baa, angreji (English) father," and then, "Vikram, dai, older brother."

"Ho Sobha," she said, lighting up, and then continued with the rest as I interjected the English word for the one she told me, "Ra (and) bhauju." She laughed.

"Vikram's wife," I said. "Tara (but) bhauju means sister-in-law."

"Ke?" she asked. I repeated it several times as she sounded it out. She waved me off with a smile as if to say, *that is too long and too hard to say*! "Didi, Kamala," she said.

"Ho, older sister," I said, and then, "ra (and) dui bahinis (two younger sisters)."

"Ho Sobha, Jamuna ra Seti, ra angreji?" she asked.

"Younger sisters," I said. Such beautiful names, such a beautiful language.

The next morning after bhat, Kamala heated water and said, "Nu houne?" ("Wash?") I went outside to see what that entailed as aama pointed for me to come. She laughed and pushed my head over, then dumped a pot of water onto it. Kamala handed her a bar of soap, and they both scrubbed, exclaiming about the color and the curl. Strangely, in that village, many women had frizzy hair too.

"But not gold like yours!" I assumed they said in Gurung while pointing to my hair and rubbing it between their fingers. "You take medicine for that?"

"Hoina," I said. Did they think blonde was not natural?

"Her eyes are blue." Kamala gazed into my eyes and told me to blink.

"Didi," I said, "I was born this way. They are naturally like that." I said it in Nepali, as Kamala understood some. I made a mental note to relay this to Vikram next time he was home and explain to them that I did nothing to my hair or eyes. Aama then motioned me to sit in the sun, let it dry, then brushed and braided it.

When she was done, I followed her as she led baisi (water buffalo) down a trail through the lower part of the village to feed on grass. She suddenly squatted and fanned out her skirt, and a trickle flowed into the grass. She looked up at me and snickered. A great way to pee in public—skirts were so versatile!

We left the baisi in a small grassy area and continued on the smooth crafted paths and steps—stone slabs that seemed to connect all the houses in the village—as we followed them to pupu's (aunt) house to join a group of women sitting outside weaving and spinning. I squatted quietly near her, smiling when I heard my name often—I was a hot topic. I'd been told I was the first white person to live in their village. The deeply wise and kind eyes of those women placed me as one of them, a woman on my own path, sizing me up to fit into their world.

On our walk home, aama pointed to a pile of cow dung and said its name in Gurung.

"Yo gobar, Sobha, gobar, angreji maa ke ho?" ("What is it in English?")

"Dung," I said. She nodded.

I sat in our courtyard while her hands pulled apart tufts of coarse wool, copying her motions as she eyed me. When large, shredded piles accumulated in two baskets, she gathered one up, I took the other, and we walked to the village spigot—a busy place. There may have been only one other in the entire village. The water never stopped, but trickled in a steady stream onto a pile of smooth rocks. Submerging the baskets into the flowing, cold water, she stirred and separated the hairy clumps with sticks until the water ran clear. She repeated the word for dung several times in Gurung, but I didn't understand. Looking at me quizzically, she got up, grabbed a piece of stinky cow shit, walked towards me with her wild hair and sparkling eyes, and shook it in my face, laughing hysterically.

"Gobar, gobar, gobar!" she repeated again, "Ke ho, ke ho?" ("Is what, is what?")

I answered, "Dung, oh, dung, dung." We broke into laughter.

The next day, to prepare for bathing my body, I donned the lungi I'd brought for that reason and followed Kamala, my didi (older sister), to the village spigot. As I doused myself in the frigid water, I could hear muted giggles and feel the stares from onlookers in the houses just above the stone wall that backed the washing area. I had become used to the nakedness in Kathmandu in Maya's courtyard since privacy was an unknown concept—especially in Tangting, as the villagers strolled by on the common path that passed right at the edge of the water. Children squealed at my white skin, and the chatter became a buzz. I was not humiliated, just cold and uninterested in getting to the areas that really needed a rinse.

Later, bhauju (sister-in-law/Vikram's wife) and I set off for Siklis village across the valley. From far away, the houses looked flattened. Their roofs glinted like rectangular copper pennies in the intense sunlight. The village sat directly opposite Tangting, and we had to walk several miles down the mountain to the river, then up the facing mountain to reach it. Bamboo grew along the way, its exotic stalks lining the trail. Both communities, located in the rural Kaski district, were beautifully terraced and rich in tradition. Unlike Tangting, Siklis was more accustomed to foreigners, as it is Nepal's largest Gurung village and a destination for trekkers that avoid the bustle of the Annapurna circuit. (Though during my stay in 1987-1988, it seemed quite desolate.)

In that region, they followed shaman and Buddhist customs for marriage, death, and dealing with most aspects of life in general. We stayed with friends or family of bhauju's, and were given tea and sel roti (fried sweet bread) as soon as we stepped inside. The loud chatter of the women buzzed around me as they inspected every fold and wrinkle, each pushing another out of the way, their dark, happy eyes peering closely at my skin, touching my face and clothes. Some held my hand for a moment, squeezed it, and smiled so sincerely that I returned the same. They were not hesitant or nervous, and I felt at ease as they remarked on my nose ring, tugged at my un-pierced ears, and laughed as they looked into my eyes saying, "Nilo, nilo, nilo!" ("Blue, blue, blue!") I lowered my face in amusement and shook my head at the riotous display. They sat me down, brushed my knotted, curly mane, remarked on its color, then their dry, rough, warm hands rubbed ghee into my scalp and braided it tightly with a black hair tassel that extended down my back, making my hair appear much longer than it was.

They were beautiful women, decked out in worn, colorful cholo, lungi, and wraps, numerous rings weighted down floppy ears, and had an unflinching expression: strong, sure, and brave. Several of them stepped back to inspect. I smiled self-consciously. After quick words of approval, they decided I'd been transformed into someone traditional-looking enough to be allowed to follow them up the narrow village paths. Why did we leave the happy kitchen with yummy fried bread? They were on a mission, silent as we walked in single file.

Buildings seemed to grow out of the ground and disappear in an unending perspective only because we turned into a low, black opening of one that had no windows. It took my eyes a moment to adjust as I gasped from the heavy but pleasant smell of incense, so thick my lungs opened inside out and I felt every cell in my body melt. Here, too, I was the only white person. The women pushed me to a wall where I sat away from them, tucked the lungi around my knees, and looked delighted at the people near me. Only breathing could be heard in the still, quiet room. We sat there for a long time.

People squatted side-by-side in a circle with children nestled in their laps. A thin old man resting in the center sat cross-legged with red powder on his forehead. Cones of cooked rice, molded in narrow mounds that looked like household sized funnels, were stuck with flowers, and formed a circle around one larger cone connected by strings from that to the other cones. The configuration formed a shrine poised before the old man—bowls of food, colorful scarves, flowers, and other objects also adorned the area.

As if out of a dream, a woman with short grey hair started to chant and sing in a low, raspy, unearthly voice. Her crooked fingers moved occasionally in front of her somber face. The incantation intensified. The room vibrated. The assembly swayed to the chanting, agreeing in hums and nods. A Jhankri (Lama priest), or shaman, entered, ringing a bell and began to mumble incoherently. The woman with grey hair, possibly a Dhawabong (witch doctor), suddenly got up without breaking her beat, delicately lifted a string from the rice cone, hung it around the old man's neck, and returned to her seat. My eyes followed the strings. When one moved, she repeated her action. As entities, spirits, or guides were called upon to assist the old man into the next world, the strings would move— though not a breath of air stirred in that low-ceilinged room.

The ambience took over like a drug. When the last string had been moved and tied around the man's neck, the chanting intensified. Suddenly, yet with steady movement, the grey haired woman looked directly at me. Her lips stopped moving. Her snake-like eyes glistened as they held onto mine with a magnificent, powerful lock. I wanted to look away, but her piercing diatribe commanded my attention as she wrought dancing devas, shadows, and devils in a powerfully contained, flexuous, yet discreet movement—a single move that connected her hands, eyes, and aura in a concealed, forceful transference. A bewitching presence stirred within me as something shifted.

Suddenly, she smoothly retreated without movement, just a withdrawn expression. She continued her chant. I was released and averted my eyes. Pieces of me, held together by virgin threads from my past, and all that I knew, disintegrated, fell away, dissolving any substance I clung to as her invocation was imprinted. The gaze of that crone, that goddess, that sorceress, stunned and partitioned Sobha/Roanne into shards of spirit, and I floated free. The villager I had now become hummed and swayed, completely aware of my white skin, yet, part of that silent crowd. I merged in that stage of the old man's death.

The Lama priest splashed water on the old man's face and hands, then put his own hands on the man's face and chanted to what sounded like, "*Sha, sha, sha, sha . . .*" repeating it louder and louder as the whole room joined in. "*Sha, sha, sha, SHA, SHA, SHA, SHAAA, SHAAA, SHAAA, SHAAA . . .*"

It went on and on. I was mesmerized. The old man's face

gleamed with heavy droplets of sweat, and the thick heat generated in the room affected us, leaving our faces and bodies wet with perspiration.

The chanting ended. After another long silence, the women gathered around to cut up the food. The old man ate it first, followed by everyone else, slowly getting up to take bites. Between chuckles and hushed voices, they all finally made their way into the bright sunlight. I sat zoned out, still slumped against the wall. The women who had brought me came over to offer pieces of pressed rice cones, and motioned me to follow them back to the house.

We sat around the kitchen eating a fresh batch of sel roti, the fried bread made from a loose batter of ground, soaked rice, milk, and honey or sugar, then skillfully squeezed into a narrow ring directly into boiling ghee. Turned once, a delicious golden brown donut sizzled, hot and fresh, one after the other, fried and stacked in lopsided piles on numerous plates. The honey for the bread was collected by Gurung cliff bee hunters, an incredibly dangerous procedure, a tradition kept alive for thousands of years. With no protective clothing, the hunters climb cliffs on hand-woven rope ladders to sedate the bees with smoke, then catch the combs in baskets. That task was made more difficult by the number of stings endured during it!

Many people gathered around the small kitchen and crowded into the doorway to see the white girl with gold hair. Bhauju, sweet and calm, smiled throughout. She was tall for a village woman, hefty around her middle and her arms—muscular pillars that endured an exhausting life of devotion to her husband, I sensed. Protestation and disapproval were not options for a village wife. I never understood that kind of allegiance. Bhauju had amazing endurance. She wanted children, her own home, and love, I was sure, but culture and tradition bound her heart. When her husband, Vikram, came home, the constant labor ensued, washing his jeans, stiff and new, barefoot, in cold water with a bar of soap. The blind adherence toward the patriarchy was maddening, but that was me. For her, maybe, it was customary.

In the early evening, I went out for some fresh air. Across a small area outside the house where we had first arrived, I walked slowly in my rubber flip-flops, which everybody wore, on rock and mud that dried hard from the sun. I needed to digest my earlier experience of that cold, dark, deathly room. My skin was chilled. An ache fringed secretly at my heart, as if I was holding back a secret no one should know, one I had held onto for so long.

Away from the houses, an old woman sat under a ragged tarp. Curves of loose, wrinkled brown skin in a stained sari hung from her bony frame. She pointed a finger at me and smiled so wide I fell into its wildness. She frowned at a deep cut on her foot, black with infection, then back up to me with yearning, hollow eyes and a slight hint of inhibition. I had pulled out a tube of toothpaste from my parko, ready to brush my teeth. She pointed to it, and then to her foot. In the few Gurung words I had learned, I protested, yet nothing convinced her that my toothpaste didn't heal.

"Is from America. Is good," she said desperately in English.

I hesitated, warned her it was not what she thought, but then relinquished that tact, knowing it could not do much harm, and squeezed a small dollop on her dirty, chewed-up toe. She smeared it deep into the cut, thanked me, and I turned to go, sad my communication wasn't better.

After brushing my teeth, I propelled the foamy paste in a thin, vaporous spray as I had learned from an outdoor school many years ago, seemingly the best way to distribute our chemical waste into nature.

Cumulus clouds billowed in a corner of the darkening sky. I sat there, peering beyond the rippled fields and distant mountains, probing into my own mind, into the intricate tunnels the death ceremony had found, then closed my eyes briefly, stood up, and went back.

I DIDN'T KNOW we would be in Siklis for more than one night, otherwise I'd have brought some other things, especially my journal and pen. The women were kindly, and scrambled to find one small, torn piece of paper while bhauju found a pen.

I watched them grind flour on a jato—one woman stepped on a large lever made of wood with a bulbous hammer end, another woman kneeled and pushed grain into the hole where the head hit. The pumping and pushing work continued until many cups of flour, fine enough for chapati or roti, were produced. The oldest woman motioned to me to give it a try, which I did for a long time, happy to give them a rest from the huge amount of work they did.

The remaining days were spent helping the women cook and pound flour for bread as they kept making piles of the fried rings, distributing them throughout the village for the continuing festivities. It may have been Maghe Sankranti, similar to the winter solstice in the States, which marks the beginning of the harvest season, or it could have been a celebration for the death ceremony.

Bhauju disappeared for hours at a time to do puja or something. I wasn't clear where she went or what she did, but one of the times she took me to wash at the spigot, in the public area, amidst all the eyes of the village, motioning me to splash myself several times with the cold water.

"Again?" I asked in Nepali, hoping I could stop the polar dousing.

"Ho bahini, again," she said, laughing, taking the container and pouring it over my head. Others, also soaking themselves, laughed and pointed and said encouraging words. It seemed a more serious wash, and must have been connected to Maghe Sankranti, since ritual washing was done at that time.

When she was gone, I'd watch and talk with the women, gaze at the mountains, and take notes on the piece of paper they had found for me, filling it with the tiniest of writing.

One of the days, primitive rides and traditional dances took place on one of the cleared terraces. A remarkably crafted, hand-driven Ferris wheel made from wood and rope, about the size of a playground merry-go-round turned on its side, was set up so the children could sit on little ledges of wood while the men turned it. Flowing pieces of white material tied to the rails of the wheel blew in the wind, carrying the joyful giggles of children going up and around. They motioned me to ride it, which I really didn't want to do, but they insisted, so I sat, the only one, for two turns, and then I pleaded to get off.

Music from drums and flutes, puffs of dust rising from dancers, and more stacks of sweet roti filled the festive scene. I walked around the village, exchanging easy phrases in Nepali and a little Gurung with villagers, then found myself several terraces above the festival. Suddenly a sharp sting of a stone hitting my leg made me look up. It came from a group of children sitting on a high wall above me. They continued throwing more small stones, and I wondered if they knew *what* I was? Had they seen many white girls meandering around their village before? I rattled off in Nepali and English and made faces at them, which made them squeal and run away. The stone-throwers didn't follow as I returned back down the stone pathways to the party and evening meal.

Bhauju and I left on the fifth morning, a trail of children— possibly some of the same ones from the day before—following us part way down to the river, before we made the steep climb back up to Tangting.

28

—————

THREE WEEKS INTO THE VILLAGE STAY AND WE WERE comfortable with each other. I knew what to do, where to go, and how to be. Dal bhat, lentil or mung beans and rice, the staple food of Nepal, was a favorite, especially while squatting on the cold mud floor, eating without utensils, right hand only.

Village food was refreshing. Rice was not the main grain in many high mountain villages, but rather black millet. They pounded it into flour and cooked it into a dense, viscous mush called dhindo that stayed in the stomach for hours, truly an endurance food. I loved the salty, spicy cooked saag (greens), sometimes served as gundruk, the leaves of saag half dried and fermented, small handfuls of roughly popped corn, and pindhaalu (boiled taro root). Although the constant frustration of constipation persisted, the food was clean, simple, and my system reacted remarkably well to it.

My Gurung sisters gathered around late at night, after the evening meal, to wash the plates and pots outside with water and ash. Chores were set up around the dying fire. They had no problem giving me work, and included me in all they did. An extra hand meant an easier time for them.

Aama spun wool while we hunched over photos I had brought,

barely discernible in the low, butter-flame light. The villages had no electricity, another aspect I loved, a darkness I often experienced in the mountains when backpacking. In fact, village life was like an extended backpack trip: simple food, lots of exercise, austere sleeping conditions, weathering the elements, and crystal clear beauty. Absorbed in my photos, they came to me with unabashed comments and questions on clothing, food, houses, and landscaping in a mixture of their singsong voices in Nepali and Gurung.

"Everyone has a car at the house? What is that?" Bahini pointed to our greenhouse.

"It is a room where plants are grown during cold days in the winter," I answered.

"It is cold here and we plant," she said. "Do you drive every day?"

"I rode a school bus with many other kids. I lived far away, and the bus ride was more than an hour long."

"You wear pants all the time? Do all girls wear pants?"

"Yes, most of the time."

When I couldn't answer well enough, which was often, they worded it differently or got up and did a charade to get the point across. I'd return the gesture in some form to their shrieks. Aama shook her head at the hilarity. She couldn't help but join in the silliness. They were wonderful, positive, and full of energy. Their bright eyes kindled interest in everything.

The language, such an obstacle, made me crazy. Was that why people across the centuries had gone to war, because of a lack in communication? Had we never learned each other's languages, which led to misunderstandings that grew out of control? I'm sure there was more to it than that—greed for oil, water, land—but communication made life so much easier.

Unfortunately, it wasn't easy to learn Gurung. I looked at those little girls. The youngest one was very open, the other a couple of years older, and the middle child, seemed somewhat troubled and angry. I wondered what their future would be?

Darkness and fatigue took over, and as aama rose, we followed, brushed our teeth outside, and went to our beds. I lit a candle to write in my journal. The two bahinis squeezed together at the edge of my bed and watched me write, no words spoken, until aama called to them. The house was approximately thirty feet by twelve feet, and had two floors connected by a four-foot covered porch. On the base level, the kitchen area was at one end, and sleeping quarters on the other, where I slept. Everyone else slept just beyond my bed, up narrow, wooden stairs. The roughly cut house appeared smoothed over from years of use. Its earthiness held the smells of pioneer living: smoky cooking fire, matted wool, compact mud floors, high mountain breezes, and the human body, always hard at work.

The morning dawned cold and bright and I ran in place to get warm. Kamala laughed while she spread a mixture of cow dung, mud, and water on the porch floor, a common practice for cleanliness and purification in Nepal. The sun took its time rising, and when it did, I stretched and danced. Kamala called to aama to come look at their crazy American daughter.

Tangting perched on the side of a mountain that dropped steeply in rippled terraces. A distant waterfall could be heard amid the chirps and gurgles of chickens scurrying in the courtyard. Since most village houses had low ceilings, I entered the kitchen bending over, then sat opposite the open cooking fire where aama hummed as she stoked the fire and cooked dhindo, the millet mush. With no chimney, the smoke floated and disappeared into the drying racks above, blackening the wood ceiling and upper stone walls. Bhauju came in and took over, rapidly whipping the thick, dark glop. In serious conversation, she and aama discussed the day.

I watched as plates were served, and ate in silence. Outside, we brushed our hair. I braided Seti's, the youngest sister, before doing mine. Her little head was held firmly as I pulled the brush gently through, as I knew it could hurt. But she waved her hand up to me, rattling off in Gurung, "It's okay Sobha, it doesn't hurt me, don't worry."

Aama looked over while pointing to her hair. "Ke baancha?" ("What to say?")

"Brush hair," I said. It continued in a litany of body parts as we exchanged in English, Nepali, and Gurung. Then aama pointed to her eyebrow and laughed mischievously. I pointed to my eye and asked for the Gurung word. She cocked her head, paused, then exploded in laughter. We never got through that one. Maybe I had said something inappropriate?

The giggling died down. She looked at me, two inches from my face, then went on about something. Big wisps of her black puffy hair stuck out at the sides and held me in rapture. A large beaded necklace hung heavy on her breast, and her stained, yellow teeth were wide apart, many missing. "*From eating that popcorn,*" she said. She knew everything simple and real. Her wild look, wrinkled forehead, years of hard work etched in bright brown eyes, unleashed a childish resiliency, beautiful and open. She was a handsome woman, stronger than I'd ever be.

SHANKAR, the Nepali affiliate who worked at the base house, along with our trip leader, Dave, would visit tomorrow or the next day. They had given me an approximate arrival time before I left for the village. My family was giddy with excitement, planning festivities, a lot of work for what I thought was not an important event.

A group of the villagers sacrificed a bhaisi (water buffalo) for Sobha's teachers. The killing occurred right in the yard, leaving long grass mats stained with blood. Large pieces of the dead animal's body were placed neatly in a pile. The spectacle attracted practically the whole village. Men ran about with khukuris (long, curved knives) in their muscular hands. I never got to know my baa (father) very well, as he was usually gone for long periods of time tending their large herd of sheep. But he was an important man, and on that day, he led the kill.

Pieces of raw, reddish-purple jellied blood, jiggling atop mounds of rice, were handed out. I, considered part of their "clan"—and an important one on that day—was given a large portion. Ugh. What to do? I had to eat it. I gulped it in two large bites then scooped up the soupy bloody rice and chased it with rhaaksi. The crowd cheered. Meat was rare, available only once or twice a month. So the feast had been (well, sort of) in my honor, with dances, song, and tika. A young man named Ajay, along with others, urged me to dance. I did my best to follow the moves.

Ajay, a bronzed, extremely fit, twenty-two-year-old man from a nearby Gurung family was one of the best dancers in the village. He wanted to learn English, and I Nepali, which he spoke as well as Gurung, so we met when he could, mostly at night after the last meal. He would kneel at the side of my bed as I sat on it, wrapped in my sleeping bag against the cold, and we conversed, mostly in Nepali. He had a wonderful smile and a relaxed way about him. When the butter lamp died, my flashlight standing on its end took its place. I flirted respectfully, yet still yearned for just one kiss. Still a virgin into my second year of college, I would serve as a perfect Third World bride to that innocent, unsuspecting youth. He worked hard and had the status of being a strapping young man belonging to one of the more affluent families in the village.

Ah, the village, and its intricate codes I'd never know about. Just one kiss. It would be okay for me, just one kiss—but for him? It possibly meant engagement. I knew that. Sort of. I was nineteen. What did I *really* know? In America, one kiss was like shaking hands. It didn't mean courtship, it didn't guarantee love, it didn't do anything but start a long life of yearning, joy, and angst . . . or so I thought.

Villagers teased me about our evenings together and suggested an arranged marriage. My aama brought it up often. Her determined words actually lured me to ponder the possibility—a union that would forever join Tangting's heritage into American destiny. And I, in my naïvety, actually considered it. What if I *did* marry Ajay? What kinds of customs would I have to adhere to? What kind of man was he really? Would I ever know?

I'd be tied down to that village. Crazy. Or, if we lived in the States, the huge change he would have to make would be forever. Divorce or separation was not something taken lightly in Nepali culture. Certain ways were demanded and expected of women there, many of which I would be agreeable to. Of course, I could not commit to something like that.

But Ajay was handsome, with an infectious smile, and deep brown eyes that completely absorbed me. We laughed, conversation was easy, and I loved village life—but no, really Sobha, no, no, no. It was not possible. Ever! Even though, I thought in a remote corner of my mind, Shankar seemed to be pulling it off.

29

SHANKAR ARRIVED IN THE LATE AFTERNOON. A ROMANCE HAD evolved between him and a former student in the program years ago, and they had married. They seemed an odd couple, but then it's hard to judge when customs of love and relationship were different in the States. Displays of affection in public were taboo in Nepal. The restraint required of couples must have been a real struggle and a source of contention throughout their marriage. She came with Shankar to Tangting, quiet and reserved. The hike was obviously difficult, but she replied it was beautiful, and a nice respite from Kathmandu.

The bhaisi, or buffalo, had been divvied up, and a portion cooked for the evening meal. Shankar handed me a pile of letters, a chocolate bar, and Merry Christmas hugs. Had Christmas come and gone already? I hadn't noticed, and never missed it. Ajay came over after the meal to visit. I hadn't spoken so much English in almost four weeks. It was fun to hear stories of the other students and receive news from home in my letters—such a faraway place. I had removed myself emotionally from blacktop America, the white population, quality time, and refined food.

My Gurung family looked at us like the first time I had looked at them when they spoke Gurung so fast. Aama told Shankar I was a daughter of the house who helped out all the time. Bhauju conveyed how impressed she was that I could walk so fast and keep up on the return from Siklis village. I hadn't realized the difference of pace until Shankar came, where I sensed an urgency in his speech, his clipped movements and impatient gestures common in city folk. I felt part of the Gurung people, protective of them and their natural ways.

The next morning, we waited for Shankar and his wife, who had slept in. Shankar eyed my plate of dal bhat, seemed to check the amount in some mental notebook, and remarked on the weather. His expression concerned me. He then took me to meet his family, who lived nearby, as well as other friends, and, lastly, the head Panchayat of the village, similar to the mayor of a town.

"Shankar, you seemed surprised by the amount of dal bhat on my plate," I said as we walked over the rocky trail to another house.

"It's a lot," he said flippantly. "Are you satisfied?"

"Ho," I replied.

He stopped and looked at me. "Is something wrong?"

"No, not at all. I love it here."

Maybe I do eat too much, I thought. Each family member had the same amount. Food wasn't abundant, and actually village fare nourished me well enough, even though I *could* eat more. Eating clean, without access to snacks and sweets, took a period of adjustment. It's good to go with less and use up old reserves, to be empty. Instead of eating when I felt depressed or confused, I had to move through it. I had it easy in the States, where food was available everywhere. It had been my addiction. Tangting village time forced change and turned my energy in other directions.

I shared the chocolate bar with my family that afternoon as we looked at photos Shankar brought, before they packed up to leave. Vikram was leaving with Shankar to go back on duty, but first he proudly showed me photos of himself draped with Japanese women in bars. He had been sure to point out the city lights, and big times. Poor bhauju—his command was her life, a long and lonely one. Her reticent, sweet face and brooding eyes held many unspoken thoughts.

Seti, one of my bahinis, and I waved goodbye at the edge of "Shangri-La" as they left. I felt no pangs of homesickness, nor a need to leave. We skipped back and heard Ajay, sitting on the wall of his courtyard eating an apple, yelling something from above. His joyous smile and handsome face captured my heart. I waved back. Seti said to say, "Waay," so I did. They laughed. She motioned me to say it again, but louder and longer, so I did, encountering more peals of laughter all around. What was so funny? They wanted me to repeat it over and over as we skipped back home, and so I did. I never learned why.

* * *

EARLY THE NEXT MORNING, seated quietly on the floor, aama reluctantly ladled less dal bhat onto my plate. Bhauju ate giant scoops of dhindo, the black millet mud, dunked in watery dal.

"Ke bayo Sobha?" Bhauju said, cocking her head to one side, her muscled body in a tight squat on the cold floor.

"Nothing," I said in Nepali, smiling, shaking my head. She and aama exchanged quick words.

"Hoina," I said loudly, "I don't want more than my share. Everything is okay. I feel good."

Aama stared at me for a moment. "Ho Sobha."

Dhindo was cooked into a thick, viscous paste and eaten to provide bulk in the stomach to stave off hunger, often consumed by the Gurung people. They didn't give it to me, though I asked to try some. Bhauju put a small dollop on my plate. It was considered simple food, not refined enough for a white girl. I tried it and nodded. She laughed. Its heavy, grainy, earthy taste smeared my mouth like mud mixed with grease—tasteless, not chewable, only meant to be swallowed, like an oyster. I kind of liked it.

Bhauju worked all day, long hours of hiking into the mountains, barefoot, searching for leaves to bring back and feed the animals. Hard grunt work, up and down steep, muddy trails. In her sweat and exertion, a freedom must have dominated, for out there she was her own woman carrying her own weight. I accompanied her on many hikes, loading wood and leaves on my back, secured with a strap across the forehead.

That morning, Seti, and a girl from next door, came along. Their chatter sifted into the background. I still did not understand much, so my mind wandered. Occasionally, they would ask me something, often starting with the same question in Gurung and Nepali intermingled. I'd get the idea.

"Are you okay, Sobha?"

"Oh Didi, thakai lagyo tara sanchai cha." ("Yes sister, I am tired, but happy.") They would giggle and mock me in a sisterly way. I didn't want to show or admit that it was hard or that I was tired. I didn't want to receive compliments for fear of appearing conceited, though it must have looked comical at times. But hiking in the mountains, energy and drive were second nature, and I had no problem proving it. Carrying heavy loads since I was a kid—backpacking with my mom in the Green Mountains of Vermont, then in Grand Teton National Park and the Wind Rivers in Wyoming—was great fun and gratifying work. However, during my time in that village, I would learn the mountain people had far greater stamina than I, and that humbled me.

We moved up the increasingly steep hillside in a clipped walk, all of us barefoot, listening to monkeys cackle from trees in secretive little chortles. After an hour, bhauju left with others who had appeared, and I stayed with Seti and the other young girl. For three or four hours, we cut wood and large leaves from trees for the buffalo and sheep back at the village, stacking them into big piles until bhauju returned laden with a huge load of leaves for me to carry. We tied them together, hoisted it onto my forehead, and I followed the footsteps in front of me down the mountain, arriving home by dusk.

The next morning, I went again with bhauju and Seti to the same verdant area, except this time bhauju motioned me to follow her. Like an expert, she quickly cut large leaves from branches, looking like a samurai with the curved knife in one hand, the other grabbing and throwing leaves into piles for me to stuff into large woven baskets, or dokos, carried on our backs secured by a namlo, or strap across the forehead. We worked non-stop until numerous loads were packed tight, and many more awaited further assemblage. She called out a few times until Seti and a few others came through the trees, and we all returned the same way. I was elated to be with them on those important trips, even though it saddened me. The forests were rapidly being depleted because of that technique, making erosion a constant problem. They needed to go farther into the hills to find food for their animals since they could only carry enough for a couple of days. I went on many of those excursions, another pair of legs willing to do anything.

As a kid backpacking with my mom, persistent problems and elusive emotions surfaced in the wilds, and they became a routine place for us to hash things out. We'd laugh, cry, or just relax. I heard it in the sound of the conversation between the girls in the Tangting hills. Hiking up the steep ridges, their chatter private and important, probably about things that bothered or frustrated them. They'd turn back and smile, always repeat the same words in a friendly way throughout my stay in Tangting,

"Thakai lagyo?" ("Tired?") they asked.

"Ho, Didi, tara sanchai bayo," ("Yes sister, but happy,") I replied.

They had a remarkable walk, almost straight down hillsides on steep, rocky, muddy trails, keeping their knees constantly bent and only stepping their feet out. Most of them buzzed down and around in fast-paced, focused, steady movement—a sight to behold! It should have been an Olympic sport. I practiced with Seti in short breaks between gathering leaves. She'd show me, then I'd scramble down, make my way back up, and she'd hit my legs and giggle. Then I'd watch her buzz down with such speed and precision, such stamina and agility!

EVENING ALWAYS DESCENDED SLOWLY as tired muscles, forgotten in the bustle of the day, awakened—a good feeling of hard work accomplished. A full moon shone into every crack with a strange brightness as little forest creatures must have been running around commiserating on Gurung dharma, or whatever aspects of Tibetan Buddhism a full moon brought about. The Gurungs were largely influenced by Buddhism, and followed many of its traditions.

When aama asked me to light the oil lamp, I reached for it, mistakenly bumped and spilled it—precious fuel gone. Oil, expensive and used incredibly sparingly, laboriously carried up from the lowlands. How could I have been so careless? It soaked into the smooth mud floor. I choked up and shook my head. A moment of silence saturated the room. Baa came in, a fluster of how to deal with it. He looked at me, placing his dry, gnarled hands on my shoulders.

"Sobha, it is okay," he said in Gurung, and smiled through troubled eyes. "Do not worry."

I felt his sincere reaction.

"Can I give you rupees to help?" I said in Nepali, and ran to my room, grabbed my wallet, and ran back. He waved them off, as if offended by such an offer from a daughter of his household.

"Hoina, hoina, no, no!" His words were strong. "Sobha," he said again, "it is okay." With a nod and another smile, he walked out of the room. Tears welled in my eyes, aama smiled, the bahinis came in to hear what had happened. I'm sure the whole village knew about it before morning. Kamala came in with a pail and rag and smeared the muddy-dung solution over the stain.

VIKRAM ARRIVED the next day from Pokhara. He and I were invited out for bhat (rice) at a relative's house. A first course of roti, curried potatoes, mula (daikon radish) cut up with red pepper, and chiyaa made me happily satiated. Then a full course of more bhat, saag (cooked greens), chicken, and achaar (chutney) followed for two hours. We ate in animated conversation that largely included me and all the escapades that surrounded the last couple of weeks. Vikram would raise his eyebrows, look over to me, grin and nod, and then more talk, all hand gestures, food, and laughter. I had never experienced a large family with all its dinner table antics, but had always wanted to. Their warmth spilled over in acceptance as our eyes met briefly, either with a smile or inquiry. I felt genuinely part of the tribe.

On the way back to the house, I followed Vikram to a point where I could find my way, then he said he was going to visit another friend. I continued on alone until I heard my name. Kamala and a few others were gathered around her. "Sobha," she said, obviously pained, "what is this?" She showed me a piece of old newspaper with green spit on it.

"Didi, is this from you?" I asked in Nepali.

Another girl who spoke more Nepali than Kamala answered, "Ho Didi, she is sick. She gets this a lot."

Kamala pointed to her head, stomach, and the spit. Her eyes pleaded for some kind of reassurance that I would know what was wrong and could assist with any medicine.

"Didi, I don't know." The spit was bright green. It looked like anti-freeze. I shook my head helplessly. I didn't know what to do.

The other girls spoke quickly in Gurung, then the one asked me in Nepali, "You have medicine to help?"

"No," I said while feeling her hot, dry forehead. "I don't know what it is. Do you feel sick, like throw up?" I motioned my hand coming out of my mouth.

"Ho, ho." Kamala closed her eyes slowly, nodding her head. She was floating in pain, quickly losing the ability to be around such commotion. She leaned back against the rocky wall.

"Chiyaa ra aduwa tara no chinni ra no dudh, ho?" ("Tea with ginger, but no sugar and no milk?") I told the girl who spoke Nepali. She nodded and said they would prepare it.

"Dherai aduwa!" ("Lots of ginger!") I said as she left. After more heartfelt exchanges none of us could really understand, and apologies from me, I left them for my journal, where emotions of inability and frustration poured out.

. . .

JOURNAL ENTRY: Winter 1987, Tangting, Nepal.

There is a part of me that just doesn't understand deeply, and a part that pulls away from being close. I am afraid of being vulnerable, and I hold steadfastly to an imaginary strength that shows as callousness and detachment. I'm sorry for it, but don't know how to cross that bridge. I'm learning how to communicate and be my own self in the world. But youth gets in the way—that tangled web of intellectual know-it-all and intense naïveté.

The women are close in Nepal, physically and emotionally. They trust one another, whole-heartedly, and look into each other's eyes, holding nothing back. I have trouble with that. My sisters left me after the divorce and I grew up alone. I'm an outsider. I became secretive and defensive. My mom and I are close, but that is different. The expectation of Kamala, a sensitive soul whose presence in my life has helped to soften that loss so long ago, pushes that boundary. She is offbeat but unlike Maya (in Kathmandu) who has also been an important influence. Kamala is an earth child, deeply intuitive and serious. Her hand on my shoulder, and her persistent strength is unwavering, until today, when pain and confusion filled her pleading eyes.

"SOBHA," aama called suddenly, "aunos." ("Please come.") I put my things away, she repeated louder, "Sobha! Aunos." Her commands were usually accompanied by her deep, gurgled laugh. I wondered if aama knew what was wrong with Kamala?

"Ho Aama," I said, running to her. I didn't ask about Kamala.

She wanted me to separate wool, which I did, and would have done anything to help out more. She had shown me many times how to hold the bow and flick the clumped, dried wool I had cleaned days before. The wooden part was held with one hand, the string flicked with the other, and the une (wool) on the floor or ground awaited the action of the bow and string that separated it. Throughout the rest of my stay, calluses had formed on my thumb and forefinger from doing it for long periods. Tomorrow I would spin it, and then the grey, brown, and white balls were measured, rolled, and set up to weave. We were alone at the house as I worked at the wool for an hour, then ran in and got my camera.

"Aama, take my picture?" I held up my camera for her to see. She sat in the courtyard, separating corn from husks.

"Eh?"

"Would you take my picture doing the wool?" I said in Nepali, waving the camera. She grunted, got up, came to the porch, and knelt beside me.

"Picture Sobha, you want picture?" she replied apprehensively.

"Ho Aama. Here, like this." I showed her what to do. She held the camera as if it were a live bomb, giggled nervously, and was very cute as she got into it. The first click startled her, but then she was okay and took several good pictures.

"Now me?" she asked, handing the camera back. She took up the bow and started to flick the wool, looked up, smiled, and held her position.

"Okay, perfect." I clicked away as we both laughed.

She hobbled back to her seat near the corn, then yelled, "Makai?" ("Corn?")

"Eh?"

"Corn pop?" she actually said in English.

"Ho, ra tapaii pani?" ("Yes, and you also?")

I followed her into the kitchen. She stoked coals, heated a pot, put in a small handful of over-sized corn kernels, covered it, and waited for them to pop while shaking the pan and smiling at me.

"No eat for me," she said, pointing to missing teeth, followed by a hysterical cackle. She emptied the half-popped corn into a bowl, a small handful, pushed it toward me, and walked back out to her work. I sat on the steps and chewed it as best as I could. The delicious flavor of corn, its chewy kernels, filled me happily.

"Dhanyabad," ("Thank you,") I said while watching her stoic body sit, shucking corn into wide, shallow baskets, picking out damaged ones.

Aama took photo of me 'flicking' wool on front porch, Tangting

Aama spinning cleaned and 'flicked' or separated wool into yarn

Pupu (aunt) beginning weaving process for baakus

30

TANGTING'S WEAVING HERITAGE WAS KNOWN THROUGHOUT THE region, specifically for baakus, a heavy woolen cloak that kept one warm and dry, a staple worn by practically every man in the village. The rest of the day "flicked" by into wool bundles under intermittent cloudy skies. Annapurna Himal (Tent Peak) offered strength and courage to quietly let time pass into the disappearing rhythm of village life—a dying art form in the fast-paced, efficient realm my body belonged to. Unfortunately, I grew up in a society more interested in accumulating junk instead of turning the country solar and ridding the land of fossil fuels. Opposition against the norm had always been my motto, even in high school, where I put my left hand up, instead of my right, during the pledge of allegiance.

So much time in the high mountain Tangting air gave pulse to the break-down process, yet barely enough time to dissolve the conflicting shards of my upbringing—of who I was, who I was evolving into, and how I handled life. Life meant sacrifice, but also beauty in many more ways than being near the Himalayas. I wanted to see life as something beautiful, not just a difficult passage. The Gurung community lived ruggedly and fully. Their lyrical, hard-working nature pierced a keen sense of aliveness in me and awakened a range of flexibility. Even though conflict surfaced often, barriers were broken, and we became cherished friends.

Tangting weavers, from left to right: friend, pupu, aama, me

But my white skin, a constant reminder of America, ceased to fade, no matter how many leaf-collecting trips I participated in, and the certain departure, exciting and comforting, always at the back of my mind, grieved me. The closeness developed through hard-earned work and learned communication would be gone once I left. The reality of leaving, however, also helped me get through the tough times, and appreciate the wonderful times.

I became painfully aware of my impact after getting back from another trip to Siklis village. Kamala, the eldest daughter, in her early twenties, embraced me easily, as did Seti, the youngest sister. But Jamuna, the middle one, did not. She remained angry in a quiet way. The evening meal had started, but I had to use the charpi. Tangting had no squat toilet or outhouse, just a spot in the dirt at the end of the courtyard. On my way back to the kitchen, Jamuna pushed me into the side of the house, seething with angry words about me being privileged, lucky, and rich.

"You, you, I hate you. You have everything, you, you!" She jabbed a pointed finger into my chest.

Devastated and confused, I looked at her, wishing to express how I felt for her and her situation.

"Bahini—" I said, but she cut me off.

"I am not your bahini, you are not a daughter here!" Her tousled brown hair, matted into braids, fell on a faded magenta wrap as she poured out more words I couldn't understand, whispered in hatred, like a snake. "I hate you, I hate who you are." Our exchange was in Nepali.

I choked up, tears welling, but I held back from crying and dried them on my sleeve. I didn't know what to say.

"I am sorry Jamuna. I will be gone soon."

She walked off quickly, disappearing around the corner of the house.

I sat on the steps near the kitchen, hacked mucous that had been gathering internally for months on the clean diet and rigorous exercise, and spit it out. A skinny hen bustled over and ate it. I spit again, and more came over, enjoying the raunchy phlegm. It disgusted me.

Dusk reconciled with day, alpenglow settled on Annapurna, coldness crept in, demanding a wrap. My arms and legs bristled in the chill evening as I was called in to dinner. Settling into a squat, I ate in silence, overwhelmed from my encounter with Jamuna. Where was she? Did anyone care? Why weren't they asking? The affection for each other just minutes earlier bitterly dispersed into taciturnity only I seemed to have. I felt compassion and a new sense of awareness for Jamuna. I had stepped in and taken the small amount of energy and attention from her hard-working parents which should have been given to her.

What did Jamuna have but a long life of duty? She had every right to be angry. I wished I was adept with language to take her aside and help. She was one of millions of young Nepali girls stuck in the rut of servitude and oppression—or so it seemed to me.

Holding bhat together with dal in my right fingers, rolling it into loose balls, and then quickly putting it into my mouth strangely made me think how toilet paper was not a luxury, but everyone had a left hand, and used it for ablutions. That duality simply showed the flexibility of living in Nepal: make do with less.

I finished quickly and excused myself.

In a frigid room, I sat on the edge of my bed and wrote, questioning my place in that house, in Nepal, where I paid to live with families, learn their ways, and they mine. Why hadn't I just gone alone to experience this verdant and rugged country? Then I wouldn't have met these incredible people and experienced this amazing village life.

But, Sobha, if you hadn't come, you might not have been the blame for furthering Jamuna's turmoil . . . But it might have nothing to do with me. What is life about? Sitting in a room and not trying? Exploring? Pushing? Being pushed? We affect each other, an inevitable part of living . . . of traveling . . .

I never told anyone of the encounter with Jamuna because nothing could be done about it. From then on, I tried to keep my distance from her. In hindsight, it was an unavoidable incident, and taught me two important lessons: my impact on others, and empathy. Little did I know how this laid the groundwork to the next rhythm of scenes that would test my desire for selflessness and the unfolding into deep soul work.

THE NEW YEAR always marked a fresh start. I liked the opportunity —new beginnings, a second chance—but this time I missed home. Not being able to talk easily with my Gurung family was hard. In certain situations, just getting a few words out appeared futile. Increasingly, I felt it wasn't worth it, and remained quiet more often. I did what was motioned to me, eating with the family, left hand tucked out of sight, right hand scooping up dal bhat. I tried to abate my growing frustration of not being able to communicate well with the idea that being there was a time to be by myself without the daily grind of going to school. But the rigorous demands of village life, homework, and being part of a foreign community often filled every moment with exhausting monotony.

Kathmandu's fast pace, constant activity, looking over my shoulder at crazy cars and incessant honking, was delightfully far away. The village held more than being surrounded by the Himalayas and living with humble people. I realized I needed to wind down, not just from Kathmandu, but from my revved up Western existence. Nepal's atmosphere of devotion to the soul and a higher awareness filled my impatient, industrious need for movement and busyness. I slapped my bare feet in those reflective puddles following bhauju, listened to aama, and cleaned wool. Days went by like filler in a movie, a medley of growth, beauty, and change.

At times, wonderment and optimism were dampened by being laughed at, chatted about, and stared at. All those eyes peeling me down, leaving me naked while I smiled until they went away. One time Vikram came to see me while I was writing. I had the urge to cry and just talk in English, but I held back. I didn't want to concern him, or suggest anything was wrong, even though he and the others must have felt my withdrawal. The Buddha said that life is suffering caused by craving, which could be overcome. Happiness could be attained through the Eightfold Path—perfect understanding, perfect thought, perfect speech, perfect action, perfect livelihood, perfect effort, perfect mindfulness, and perfect concentration. *Not in my lifetime*, I thought, but how was it measured? If the Gurungs followed the Buddhist path, then what had happened to that dharma to which they were supposed to hold fast?

Ah Sobha, I tried to reason in my head, *we are all human, let it go*. But again and again I had become the center of comic relief, and as time wore on, I wasn't able to make light of it.

I knew things I did were funny, different, and awkward, especially in Tangting, where a day's walk up into the mountains from the big city of Pokhara, across rope bridges, was something the villagers had held together by hope and tradition. Possibly I was one of the first whites some of the villagers had ever seen. Half the time they got me to say things just so they could laugh, their fascination contagious. I didn't think people who lived or stayed in their own country realized how easy it was. No one wanted to have that uncomfortable feeling of insecurity, and if they felt it, they hid the emotion, usually by pretending to be strong—at least that is what I have gathered.

I wish I could have lightened up at this point in the journey. A dream that night helped me see it all a bit clearer, though, unfortunately, my behavior didn't change.

31

I AWOKE AS THE DARKNESS QUICKLY MELTED AND SUNRISE GLAZED Annapurna like a pot in a kiln—radiant! While brushing my teeth, between the edge of the courtyard and the formidable mountain house that I called home in Tangting, a dream filled my senses.

JOURNAL ENTRY: January 1988, Tangting, Nepal.

Dream: I was in a city with a girl in a beat-up station wagon driven by a man. We came to an impassable, narrow bridge, so we got out and walked. A well was beneath this bridge, next to a cliff that had many faces carved into the side of it. A band similar to the Grateful Dead performed on a stage. People swarmed around dancing and selling beads, scarves, food. Babies in small hammocks, seemed abandoned. It made me angry and sad. A man sat on a platform, a kind of guru, and we had to give him money. People believed in him. The man with us gave him seven rupees. I walked away and jumped into a river, fully clothed. The water felt like liquid glass. It was an incredible sensation. In the next scene we were in a plane, flying fast until it seemed we were about to crash, but when we hit the ground the plane turned into a bus on a dirt road.

. . .

THE DREAM CAME into focus as I stared at Tent Peak. I questioned religion and society's rules. The Himalayas were the attraction to that little land-locked country, bordered to the north by China and the south by India.

What colored a country? Why did they tika, or apply heavy black eyeliner to babies' eyes? Why the endless bangles and rings hanging from any piece of available skin? Why the caste system and rigid gender distinctions?

"Sobha, waay! Kasto cha?" ("How are you?") Ajay shouted as he ran by.

"Ajay!" I waved excitedly, and he was gone.

"Sobha!" Aama called from the kitchen. I stayed outside, brushing my teeth and rinsing my face, preoccupied with my thoughts.

I didn't understand. Too much hypocrisy surrounded the church. I grew up in Wyoming, where I experienced the nature-based "religion" of the Native Americans. *That* made sense to me. The dream seemed to illustrate my frustration about how humans distorted spiritualism in the name of religion to fit their ideology. After being in the river of that dream, my own belief system almost crashed (the plane), then carried on as a bus that could have meant I was making a big deal out of nothing. Could I just drop the endless barrage of questioning and brush it off?

By all means, Sobha, laugh with them, don't go against it. Annapurna, universal goddess, give me strength to rise above my problems, give us all strength!

The caste system in Nepal has been an ancient social layering of inequality, in my opinion, which may have been a necessity a long time ago, but it's essentially unequal and limiting. The highest caste in Nepal is Brahmin, then Chhetri, and on down the line to untouchables—a convoluted arrangement where one's identity was predetermined before birth. My village family in Tangting belonged to Pangilama, an offshoot of a supposedly higher caste. The indigenous Gurungs came with their own myth of origin and clan system —clan being different from caste in that some of it spills over into caste concepts, yet clans carry strict notions of bloodlines and endogamy tendencies.

Casts were institutionalized by the Aryan Hindus on the plains of India, and the notions moved into the hills with migrants and refugees that became Paharis (hill Hindus). They gradually entered Nepal and became the Nepalese Tibeto-Mongolian ethnic groups of the Hills. All this was eventually written down in the national law code called Muluku Ain. The old Muluku Ain is still at work in Nepal, despite the notion of caste being officially discarded. In it there is a three-division hierarchy as well as sub-divisions, called jaats, which can be loosely translated as 'people'.

I didn't believe it was fair to be treated unjustly just for being born into a certain household. But fairness was not part of that order. I had no idea of the true implications, but sensed it was a severe and hostile prejudice, silently manifested in complacent acceptance. The archaic classification suppressed the country's growth and development. This beautiful nation was locked into its past—how could any change occur? Did they *want* to change?

Untouchables were hardly seen. They labored twice the hours, in worse conditions, with half the amount of food. The two meals a day in a regular home, consisting of dal bhat and a vegetable side, plus an afternoon snack of a small handful of toasted corn flour or something equivalent, usually fed me well enough.

Although, the other day I was so hungry I snuck into the kitchen and uncovered the rice pot only to be caught red-handed with a chunk of pressed rice. Baa (father) appeared out of nowhere and yelled something. Aama came in and they talked feverishly.

Completely ashamed, I bowed my head and stood silent—a naughty child, as shown by aama's disappointed look. For all I knew, stealing food was considered a horrific fault, or maybe it brought in evil spirits. Baa's quiet words with her got me off somehow. He placed a few twigs on the leftover embers from the morning fire, cut the block of rice into chunks, heated them briefly on the burning wood, and handed them to me. He smiled and walked out. I ate them, completely dejected. They were delicious, with black char speckled from the fire, but I didn't enjoy them. Outside, aama spun wool. I apologized profusely, said I would never do that again, and went to my bed.

. . .

JOURNAL ENTRY: Tangting, Nepal.

If the untouchables have less, how much less? I was so hungry just now, I stole some rice from the kitchen pot. I wished I had asked. Being a woman, a foreigner, the language barrier, the cold—sometimes the food is barely enough and I feel so much for the less fortunate villagers. I am a guest here. I try to respect their rules, their lifestyle, their culture. Oh Sobha, just a little bit longer and you'll be on your own. Beneath the magic and strength of Annapurna—what a name, the giver of food and nourishment, lies such poverty and hunger. I wasn't starving, just hungry—and I like to feel hungry, empty, and then eat dal bhat, wholesome food, easy to digest. But I want something more—hunger for life, for me to know my passions and do them with integrity and strength no matter what anyone says or thinks. Maybe the dream and thoughts of a nation being locked into its past, is a reflection of me, right now. My reaction to the poking fun is merely old emotional debris of being left when I was little. It's my psyche showing me—Look, this is what's going on, see it for what it is, it's not necessarily being done to you, it's just old and in the way and you can change.

I WALKED OUTSIDE. Aama was not there. The quiet courtyard felt expectant. Annapurna caught my wince, as if she had thrown me a blow. *Be courageous,* her presence advised. *Be honest,* the cold wind challenged. *And above all, be present.*

"Sobha, aunos!" ("Come!") Aama called from the kitchen doorway.

"Ho Aama." I went in to her. "Annapurna himal costo ramro!" ("Annapurna, so beautiful!") I pointed at the beauty.

She smiled, shook her head and turned to go back inside. Had she forgotten the rice incident? Surely not. Had she forgiven me, as a mother does?

I followed her to a pile of cleaned wool, needing flicking, or separating.

"La, Sobha." She pointed to the bow and walked away.

My BACK and shoulders ached from collecting and carrying wood and leaves. I wanted to ghumne (wander) with my book and pencils. Every time they pointed at something of mine—clothes, hair, speech —they talked and laughed about it. Communication continued to be quite basic, but the intrigue had worn off. Monotony had set in, as well as the true and often cruel guise of human motives. Like children in a schoolyard, picking on me became frequent—or maybe it was my sensitivity and fatigue. I tried to remember it was no big deal, to let it go.

Later at night, I'd break down in the pages of my journal.

One evening, I watched as the fire swelled and retreated, faded and leaped up again. I sat in the kitchen beside the last embers as words swirled out of the heat, forming a poem. My bahini talked and talked, whether I listened or not, then grasped my chin and pulled it up to her round, jolly, yet concerned face, and said, "Sobha, Sobha." She grinned, then skipped out. Finally, I was alone with my journal, a pen, a light, and my soul.

JOURNAL ENTRY: Tangting, Nepal.

What is behind my thoughts? Where do they come from? It all has to do with me in the world, and how I interact with it. Is what I am thinking just my ego? Am I spoiled? Selfish? Sick? Do I complain too much? Or just nineteen about to turn twenty? This kind of energy swirls around in all individuals thinking their own thoughts, calling out in pain, needing help, wanting justice, ideas, answers. Like the wool spun, thoughts end up, piece by piece, on a spool, a certain color and texture, a purpose totally dependent on the hands that take it up. In the English language "I" and names of people are capitalized, but not in Nepali bhaasa (language). The importance is not on the person, but the collective.

SCUFFLING feet and singsong voices broke into my solitude as aama and Kamala began to prepare the evening meal. They were busier than usual, quickly answering my inquisitive look and broken words —guests were coming, kaka (uncle) and his family. I put my things away and returned to help with the cutting, then settled down to watch, lulled by their voices and the dim light. An hour went by, people arrived, the common stares, points, and questions directed at me flowed, and the meal was overtaken by talk about the white girl with gold hair.

As usual, whenever people were visiting, aama tried to get me to say something. Everyone always laughed, but that time, didi and bhauju joined in. Then aama asked me to get some wood. I went outside, returned with an armful, and they all laughed. Aama had wanted me to hand her the piece next to me, but then she said some things which I repeated, not understanding what the hell she'd said. Everyone howled. I got up, rudely stepped over the meal, and left the room. (The floor is the table, everyone sits squat style, plates on ground, eating with their right hand.)

I walked across the courtyard and down the path. Moments after, footsteps pattered behind me. Bhauju came to tell me bhat was ready.

"Sobha, aunus." ("Come.")

"No khanne Bhauju." ("I don't want to eat.")

She looked at me softly, and said again, "Sobha, aunus." She put her hand out for mine.

No I won't, I thought to myself. "Hoina Bhauju, malai bhoko chaina," ("I'm not hungry,") I said, knowing it wouldn't get me off, but ke garne? (What to do?) I'd probably have everybody in the room asking "Ke bayo?" ("What's wrong?") I was tired of them, frustrated by my isolation, sick of being laughed at, angry at my childishness and inability to get past it, and that night, I didn't want to eat.

She stood there with her hand out. She knew. She knew all about hardships, unfairness, doing things she didn't want to do.

"I don't want to," I repeated in Nepali.

"Ho bahini, I know. Now come," she responded in Nepali. I took her hand. She squeezed it. I followed her back. There was no way out. I swallowed my pride and let it go.

I ate the damn rice. I was a good daughter of that Gurung household, under a dark shale roof, in the midst of the Himalayas, and really, only friends surrounded me. I told them in the best way I could how difficult the language was. They nodded and agreed. Cold eyes melted into interest, and I felt an acceptance, a step onto a different reality. In that moment, I shed a piece of self-centeredness. The conversation moved off me and onto the weather, Nepali politics, and family. When the bahinis said goodnight, per aama's prompting, I took the cue as well and tailed behind after a gracious, heartfelt good night to all attending. The three of us brushed our teeth outside, peed, and whispered subha ratri (good night).

I was in bed, clock ticking on the shelf, shadows cast by the candle dancing on my covers. I anticipated writing in my journal and then sleep, the luxury of comfort from my warm breath on my writing hand. My clothes and braids always carried a slight smokiness from the fire that mingled with the day's turmoil.

I closed my eyes; blackness cloaked my soul. Tomorrow I decided to take off by myself, to do my own thing. I needed to get away.

32

THE NEXT MORNING, I DRESSED QUICKLY, BRUSHED AND BRAIDED my hair, and went into the kitchen. I briefly mentioned a few words to them before leaving, saying that I wouldn't be back until late. Aama looked at me, confused, nodded, and said, "La." She did not seem to understand, and I was afraid if I tried to explain too much more that they would stop me. It was chilly and damp, so I grabbed another wrap on the way out.

The wind gusted as I hastily made my way beyond the buildings of the village and into the trees, following the well-worn path I knew from collecting wood. After cresting the ridge, a faint trail followed along the forested spine for about half an hour until I came to a small, rocky outcropping. Perfect. Tangting huddled far below in objective distillation, one of many smoky, but vibrant villages tucked into the foothills of the vast Himalayas.

I hunched down onto a smooth boulder, wrapped a wooly shawl around my waist, and waited for Annapurna to wake up. She looked sleepy, slowly removing a thick blanket of clouds, and stretched in the early dawn. George Winston played in my head as the moving melody invaded my body, filling the gaps, pushing out old feelings. The grass moved freely as did my hair that I had released from its braids, and my choked-up thoughts merged together in a phantasm of flowing words.

I gazed at the mountains, budding like lazy giant limbs from mottled green valleys, soft in their perspective, as gentle streams sprang from secluded leafy niches. Trees towered in cliques, undulating in a persistent breeze that ebbed behind and below me, and I felt a lightness of being. My hand wrote, free of will, like a river rolling down a canyon. My mind howled at the world among many thousands of others, crying out in the same way.

JOURNAL ENTRY: Tangting, Nepal.

Why does everything affect me? Why do I let people walk all over me and not say or do a thing? Have I walked over others, unaware of that trespass? Why am I scared? Is that why I am here, to learn how to be strong? In a way, village people are lucky. They are not exposed to the craziness of western culture, and I know the younger ones fight it. At least they are daily exposed to the rigorous demands of physical labor. I love to work, but I fight it, even though I feel better when I eat less and work hard. It burns up some of the emotional turmoil, and uses up some of that energy.

I RAMBLED on page after page, shaking my hand when it got tired. Annapurna finally stepped out of the fog and appeared boldly before me. Hima meant snow, and alaya, dwelling, and in Sanskrit, Himalaya meant "abode of the snow." More than one hundred mountains above 23,600 feet nestled in the foothills, bordered on the north by the Tibetan Plateau and the northwest by the Karakoram Range. What a dazzling sight. Those magnificent mountains made my heart gasp every time they stole my eyes.

I leaned back against a rock, looked over the land, and drifted into the folds and creases of the paddies below. Such an enormous expanse between where I sat and Siklis village across the valley. Small binoculars helped me pick out the trail where a few people, as tiny as ants, walked by the river. I shut my eyes and remembered the other night in Tangting, when I sneaked out for a moonlit walk. I leafed through pages in my journal and found that entry.

JOURNAL ENTRY: January 1988, Tangting, Nepal.

It's the full moon and bright outside. Outside is a funny word—perhaps there is an inside and outside to the outside. As I walked along the stony path, I stopped for a moment and looked at the moon, followed its aura where it fell upon a tree with no leaves, just twisted branches telling a story of a village long ago, of children's faces and dirty hands. Cows and dogs walked by and people rested at the base of its trunk. It emanated calmness. This tree, that never moved, held magic; the knowing stance of a person who had been through many years and looked at a child with compassion because of the trying times the child must go through, of being young in such a big world, of looking for something, whether it be the kite in a tree or the quest of 'who am I.' The tree looked alive, black and tall, with a deep hissing wind through the holes in its rough skin, and the moon showered its light in droplets. All questions are the same, they just happen in different stages of life. And sometimes one question takes several years to answer, or is never resolved . . .

I am grateful for my family here. It is hard for them, too. They have opened their life, let me in, shared their house and friends. Such a short time to accomplish what I long to do in this country.

A BREEZE softly caressed my arms and back. Annapurna poised in warm and discerning support of this past and present outpouring. The rocky ground numbed my bony bottom and forced me to get up and move around. I did a few yoga sun salutations, then tinkered around on the penny whistle, but its high, melodic, tinny sound didn't give the comfort of a guitar or piano. In this great and distant tundra, its sound echoed in the huge expanse, quickly losing itself in breathy recesses. I sat down in my secluded spot and quickly plunged back into my thoughts.

I came to Nepal to be in the mountains. A visit to the Himalayas breathed in every pore of my body, and I had to see them in person. I also wanted to live in poverty, be forced to have less, but actually doing that was much different than talking about it. This experience was whittling my human condition down to a basic, neural edge.

I'd always wanted to experience something big. Nepal delivered that—especially the village—since it was my request that I be placed as far "out" as possible. I really wanted to be turned inside out. *But could I handle it?*

I escaped to get away from the catalyst of being exposed, poked, and questioned, to revive my objectivity, to see a wider view. Did it deliver brevity and bequeath a sense of nourishment? Yes, I just had to get away from them and regain my footing.

From eight a.m. to just before dinner, I'd been alone, on a rock, high up on a hill, with my flute, journal, sketchbook, schoolwork, and music—alone for one whole glorious day. I hadn't experienced that since before I'd come to Nepal. It was cold and almost dark when I returned. My family had been worried about me. Inside, sitting beside the fire, I debated whether or not to tell my reasons for going. When it was just aama, I told her in as much Nepali as I could speak, knowing she wouldn't understand much of it.

"Aama, I had to leave today to be alone and think about things. I get laughed at so much for everything I do. I get frustrated and cannot talk about it. It makes me not want to be here. I know you barely understand what I am saying now. I'm sorry I don't know your language better to explain this, but I had to go."

"Nanu," (term of endearment) she said softly. Didi, bhauju, and bahini came in. I smiled at them while wiping tears quickly away.

"I will not do that again. I am sorry," I continued. "I know you all are trying hard, too, and I thank you so much for it." I touched my heart and smiled.

Aama reached for my hand, held it, then let it go. "Sobha," she began, "when Shankar was here, you spoke English and we didn't understand. You laughed and looked at us. I worried you didn't like something."

I remembered that time with my teachers, but it wasn't about them. I had looked at my family then with a mixture of emotion, sorry they couldn't understand, and at the same time reluctantly happy, as if to say, '*See, this is how I feel all the time.*'

Aama nodded. I was moved by her depth of communication. We figured it out, I got it off my chest, and the next days were better.

That night, I had a different kind of dream: I was swimming, big black doors opened onto black water, a dark forest, and a dark sky with stars. Even though everything was so dark, I felt brightness, a lightness, and freedom. Then an image of me falling down stairs that circled around and around and being scared, but I put my arms out to fly and felt okay. Again, everything was dark.

The first image was reassuring, the second, not so. Had I just overcome one obstacle to face yet another?

33

THE DAYS WENT BY MORE QUICKLY AS WE CLEANED, SEPARATED, and spun wool. I sat in the courtyard, near the ledge, where the next ledge and hundreds after rippled in rice and millet paddies. Aama and her women friends worked wool with their proficient, bony fingers and babbled in Gurung, so most of it sounded like chattering birds. However, listening to them relaxed me. I liked those times when nothing was expected of me. My thoughts could drift, and sometimes I understood a word or a phrase and tossed in a small comment. The ladies would nod and smile, remark to aama, then ask me something in Gurung and fragmented Nepali.

"Sobha," one would say, "are you married?"

"Hoina," ("No,") I said, which they knew, but they loved to ask again and again. "Tara," ("But,") I continued, "maybe a nice Gurung man for me?" They loved that and cackled, slapping each other on the arm.

"Ajay, ho bahini, Ajay, ho bahini, ho!" Aama nodded toward me.

"Ho Sobha, and you stay and live in Tangting!" another woman said.

"Ho Didi," I replied, "and walk the mountains like you do, eat dhindo, and dance!"

"Sobha loves the mountain," aama would say, and wave her hand toward Tent Peak. She didn't roll her eyes, but there was a saucy hint of impertinence to her usually sweet demeanor.

"Ah." The women would turn to look. "Sobha, you teach our children and stay."

COUNTLESS MORNINGS AFTER BHAT, I spent three or four hours washing wool at the spigot. I squatted on the edge of the rocky, hand-built basin, about five feet square, submerging the bamboo basket that held clumps of wool while water filtered through. I'd swish with my hands or thin bamboo sticks to separate and agitate the clumps of wool. Losing myself in the water, watching it move, thinking, letting time evaporate until the ache in my knees and shoulders brought me back. The intense, numbing cold pained my already freezing hands, forcing me to stand and jump up and down. After some feeling returned, I blew on them, squeezing them between the backs of my knees and calves before continuing again. Old women watched from their ledge that overlooked the watering hole, pointing and smiling, occasionally laughing or mumbling to each other.

Since the day I had taken off alone, something clicked. We fell into a familiarity that was beyond anything that could have been planned. The foreignness had dropped. I accepted their ways and released the petty derisions and hang-ups I'd had.

Aama looked at me one evening, her eyes illustrious and serious, and said, "Sobha Lama Gurung," giving me their last name in nodded approval.

One evening soon after that, aama, bhauju, Kamala, the bahi-nis, and I stayed up late in the kitchen, stitching wool baakus while the young girls did their schoolwork in the dim light of butter lamps and dwindling fire. Even though Jamuna (the middle sister) was not in school anymore, she still did schoolwork when time permitted. With my help in taking up the slack, she could spend time on letters and numbers. Lately she had seemed more tolerant of me.

Precious wood used only for cooking, not for warmth, had been generously used that cold night as an exception, and we were having such fun together, none of us wanted to go to bed. Kamala asked about me leaving. The village stay was nearing its middle mark. I would be gone ten days for the mid-term retreat. Our conversations were always in Gurung and Nepali.

"Sobha, what will you do?" Kamala asked.

"We meet in Kathmandu, then go on a river trip, and then to the Terai. Have you been?" I asked in Nepali.

"Hoina, only Pokhara," she said. "But aama has, when she was young."

"Sobha," aama asked, "you ride elephant?"

"Ho Aama, I think so. Did you?"

"Ay, Sobha," she said. "You come back?"

"Ho Aama." I smiled coquettishly. "Unless you don't want me."

"Ah Sobha," she said, putting her baaku down. "You come back and stay."

The fire died out. Bhauju covered it in a thick layer of ash, we put our things away, and said goodnight. They all passed the place where I slept, except the bahinis stopped and knelt by my bed, pointing to my journal. They loved to watch me write lines in English, then in Sanskrit. I tore the page out and handed it to them. Aama called for them to come to bed. They grabbed the paper and ran upstairs. I put on every piece of clothing I had, including a wool hat, pulled my bag around me, and blew out the candle.

34

At dawn, two days later, I left Tangting under a grey sky. I wished for a simple Gurung-type school bag with its long strap secured to my forehead, much more comfortable than a bulky back-pack. Since I only needed a few things, I decided to leave my pack behind and took a small bag I had purchased at a market in Kath-mandu. After waving goodbye to my family, Seti led the way as far as she was allowed. A woman looked up as we passed by, an untouchable. Her modest and unbiased eyes convinced me yet again of the nonsensical (or so I thought) caste system. Seti turned to leave after a hug, her wave an inwardly turned hand with fingers wiggling as if motioning me to come. That wave implied courtesy and respect as opposed to the palm facing outward, which was consid-ered rude.

No vehicles or roads led to any of the villages surrounding Tangting, only footpaths. I hummed and sang, loving the freedom. Better than that, I had somewhere to go, and looked forward to it as well as leaving behind, only briefly, a place and a family I had grown fond of.

Ripples of hills descended in unison from the high elevation where I stopped to look around, the still, quiet setting appearing distinct and unveiled. I looked around, turning my head to listen. The air had a vacuous silence. The slight breeze felt light, as if my skin was being picked apart by tiny air particles. Before I fell into total blissful mountain oblivion, a bell from a bhaisi (buffalo) clinked, then again more loudly. A lighter clink followed. I shivered and smiled. It was the only sound that broke the silence, and at that moment I stood alone in that vast land. Energy of the earth swirled invisibly, and the atmosphere tantalized, real and visceral.

I was there to experience life, every grain of it. Nepal's sanguine interior and opulent receptiveness embraced me. It simply became another episode of life among people who spoke a different tongue —disclosing its ephemeral, tumultuous, bizarre, and gruesome anatomy. Was it a difficult passage of age and integrity? Yes, as well as the simple question, *what are you doing,* in that clipped, singsong cadence the Nepali people expressed—the same inquiry I challenged myself.

A fork in the path veered off. I wasn't sure I was taking the right way. I followed it until a hut appeared behind a small grassy hill. An old man sat outside on a bench, pouring milky liquid from a large rustic container into small, glass bottles. He saw me wave, then motioned for me to come down, where we chatted in Nepali.

"Namaste Dai. I'm on my way to Pokhara, and wasn't sure which path to take, but I think it's there." I pointed back to the way I came.

"Ho." His smile encompassed the world, and he patted the seat next to him.

"What are you doing?" I asked, pointing to the apparatus in front of him.

"Amilo dahi." (Sour yogurt.) He filled a cup with the clumpy, white liquid and handed it to me.

I looked at the dirty glass, curd sliding down the outside. It smelled rank. I graciously accepted it, and sipped the concoction modestly as he explained the trail system. I asked if he lived in that house.

"No, no, no. I live in—" He waved up into the hills. I didn't catch the name, but smiled and thanked him for the drink, which was not bad. I finished it.

"I have to go. Pokhara is far, still. I meet my school in Kathmandu."

"Where from?" he asked.

"Tangting."

"Ah, Tangting." He chuckled. "Far. You walk alone?"

"Ho Dai, alone." I pressed my hands together in namaste, and continued on my way.

"You come back?" he called after twisting his body to look at me.

"Ho, in ten days. I come back and live again in Tangting."

"Ho bahini ho!" He gave me a quick nod and a chiseled smile.

THE SWINGING BRIDGE I had crossed so long ago with Vikram swayed before me. Distant river thunder rumbled ominously hundreds of feet below, beckoning through the wide cracks in the precarious slotted boards. I looked across—saw no one. The cables on either side vibrated in anticipation as I stepped out boldly and commenced the dare. Without looking back, I breathed deep, stepping quickly as the end got closer. Once my feet stepped onto the smooth, chunky rocks on the other side, I turned and yipped, throwing my hands up in the air, and laughed rakishly into the enormous chasm.

The well-worn path lazily wound past infrequent houses and pastures. My feet skirted large rocks in the trail, easily tripping on a few as the vistas and incredibly rich air swept me lucid. Throughout that delicious passage of time, I realized I was so fixated on being free that the thought of it had stopped me from attaining it. I went to Nepal to live in poverty and see the Himalayas, but that was only partly true. I had also gone to experience freedom in a safe setting and to connect with the people—*the people*!

Existing in a place so opposed to what I knew made me see, firsthand, life outside of *me*. Nepal's exotic canvas made it easy to examine the anomalies, but once the freshness wore off, the daily grind remained, and being the same person was strangely mundane. Then frustration had crept in and I'd lost sight of the simple plea-sure of being here. I'd held onto the goal so tightly, put up such resistance that it prevented me from seeing ahead—until it didn't. My mind needed enough time to find solace in the uncompromising tenacity of the village, and that solace was found as the barrier of language halted ego and intellect. Communication had been at a bare minimum, and we'd learned to get through to each other. The level of living became quieter. I was forced to stop, observe, and absorb.

The path began to widen into a rough road. People appeared more frequently. Small buses came and went a few times a day, and I waited a short time for the next one. I reached Pokhara around two in the afternoon and wandered through the streets of the bohemian city. Its stunning panorama of Annapurna and Macha-puchre presented an unbelievable backdrop to the bustling center of peddlers, artisans, and expats—locals who pushed hashish, purses, money-changing, tickets—everything that could be bought or sold. I listened to them, then shot back in Nepali a flood of incredible conjugations and syntax, and smiled at their amazed faces. Some-times we'd converse like old friends, and some glared at me with a stony face.

The bus station was my first stop. I bought a ticket for the next day, then looked for the guesthouse where Vikram had taken me on our way to the village. Her door was locked. I found another one nearby that had beds for fifteen rupees (less than a dollar, what a deal!), and a few more included a plate of dal bhat. The rotund, gregarious didi who ran the place was a true mistress of ceremonies as she decisively directed traffic in her establishment. She looked me up and down doubtfully, wrinkled her nose, and was shocked I could speak her language so well.

"Didi," I said, "I need a bed for the night."

"Listen to you!" she remarked. "You sleep in the same room as everyone."

"Okay, no problem. And dal bhat?"

"You want bhat?" Her lips curled into a smile. She wiped her hands on a towel and set them on her hips.

"Ho Didi. I love dal bhat."

She shook her head and beckoned me to follow. Her murmured words trailed down the short hallway, pungent from incense. I was sure she wondered why a single white girl wanted to stay at her place. The co-ed sleeping room contained about thirty cots, had a high ceiling, and was decorated with pictures of gods and goddesses.

"Pick one. Bhat at six. You want me to wake you up?"

"Ho Didi, at five. Is that okay?"

She nodded.

"Dhanyabad." ("Thank you.") I pressed my palms together and bowed slightly.

As the evening wore on, her place filled. The bright lights and loud conversation were a shock from the village. I had been away from "civilization" long enough that the harshness flustered me. I was the only white person, but felt like one of the bunch since no one stared or pointed. Pokhara was a well-known destination, a gateway to the Annapurna circuit and other outrageous, famous treks. In that cheap little guesthouse, eating with my right hand at a long table with other locals, and looking like one of them—aside from my white skin and gold hair—I felt confident, knowing what I was doing, being able to do it, and having a blast.

Later, a sleepless fatigue crowded the clamor, and I slumped on a bunk in a far corner. The thin futon and bulky sleeping roll wrapped me in warmth against the chill. Half the beds were occupied, each of us sequestered upon those small islands, travelers and workers of certain fates and destinies, moving at different times through the motions of getting ready for bed.

Suddenly, I felt alone. I missed the quiet, dark, seclusion of the village. I grabbed my journal.

JOURNAL ENTRY: January 1988. Pokhara, Nepal.

Perhaps I don't feel free inside and that is what I constantly push against. Perhaps the opportunity and security of living with families in this ritualistic society actually gives me full rein to explore the wilds and desires of my mind in the raging beauty and truth of Nepal.

THOSE FAMILIAL BOUNDARIES, rules, and monotony provided grounding, firm and absolute—even though in that same breath I fought against those institutional pillars. In looking so hard for my path, my own resistance accumulated. Being in Pokhara, getting around on my own, speaking the language, knowing the ways and quirks of those people, I realized an unrestrained and complete immersion had taken place.

Why can't I just accept things the way they are and get out of my own way? Aren't those the stories I had always heard about—people meeting their dream partner or job only when they had forgotten about it and involved themselves in something else?

I brushed my teeth, organized myself to leave soundlessly early in the morning, and curled back into the comforter with my journal. Lights were out at ten p.m. More people came in that night, slowly filling the room. I woke several times in the dark to sounds of shuffled steps, muted rifling, and heavy breathing. Eventually, sleep permeated every unanswered question in my body, and I dropped into a deep, dreamless stupor.

35

A ROUGH SHAKE ON MY SHOULDER AND A SMILING FACE AT FIVE a.m. woke me. Tea and a chapati on a little corner table in the kitchen was accompanied by the didi's warm conversation in Nepali, which went on too long since buses don't wait, lengthening the already late start I would get.

"You live in Tangting?" she asked, rolling a chapati.

"Ho Didi. This is delicious, thank you."

"Why Tangting? It is far and cold, ho?"

"Ho Didi, far and cold. I like far and cold."

"You from America. Why Nepal?"

"I love the mountains, and your culture. I came to see your way of life and learn from you."

"We are good?" She looked up for a moment while still expertly rolling and cooking on the open fire. I told her a few highlights of why Nepal was so wonderful. She handed me another warm chapati as I got up to leave in the early light of a brisk morning.

The short walk to the bus station in a slight drizzle matched my mood. The buzz of bicycles and scooters kept me jumpy and cautious. The bus arrived on time. I settled into a window seat and relaxed for the eight-hour ride. I'd be in Kathmandu by late afternoon, time enough to visit Maya in Chabahil, and catch up on my journal at Pumperknickles.

The commute in those over-crowded, battered buses was long and noisy, and it stopped often along the road to let passengers on and off. Sometimes the driver would pull over, open the door as someone would step up half-way to talk rapidly in friendly banter, oblivious to the schedule, then, after a few minutes, we'd move on without them. The ride was dangerous since the brakes on those Third World clunkers were dicey. In fact, some part of the engine broke down a few times on several trips that I'd endured before. There was an underlying recklessness that triggered a latent survival mechanism in me, and I was ever alert on those journeys.

The bus pulled up to a busy area. Sun shone warm on the dusty curb, where women sat eating raw mula (white daikon radish). A few seats in front of me a woman leaned out the window and joyfully chatted with friends. One held a short knife and cut a huge slab of mula, then nudged a little girl standing next to her, who walked over and handed it up to the woman. She thanked her while absently peeling off the thick skin, then flung the skin, hitting the little girl on her back in a playful game. The little girl picked it up and threw it back. They chuckled. The woman with the radish asked her age, and remarked with wide eyes how big and pretty she had grown. The girl blushed and hid behind her mother. The woman on the bus crunched into the mula. It sounded refreshing. Her white teeth chewed the juicy, pungent vegetable. She nodded to the girl to get her another piece. It made me salivate for such a simple treat. I looked back and forth as the women conversed, lively and loudly, dressed in worn, beautiful saris.

That brief engagement carved a memorable image in my mind about Nepal—its lightness of being, even under brutal working conditions, rigorous adherence to primitive mechanisms, hunger, disease, unchecked industrial growth, faces lined with mirth and hardship, and the beauty of the rugged Himalayas. The unique Nepali culture had woven together all that it is, since before the religions began, as a sacred, natural identity. Nepal is the birthplace of the Buddha. Even in the wake of inevitable atrocities, the people are the gems that shine through. Century after century their legacy holds true to namaste: *nama* meaning bow, *as* meaning I, and *te* meaning you—literally to say, "bow me you," or "I bow to you." It can also be interpreted in part as "na ma" (not mine), an interesting twist or modesty in the desire to reduce one's ego in the presence of another. The hands are pressed together at the heart, and the gesture affirms a soulful exchange. Self-sacrifice, compassion, modesty, and kindness are only a few words that express their incredible, open hearts. Those women eating mula shared lineage into humanity's most desirable element: healthiness. Their culture still demanded physical labor in all aspects of living, and consumed primarily whole grains and vegetables. One part of the country's magic surely came from their traditional diet.

Nepal's absence of refined and/or stimulant snacks made me seek out mula, and I formed a love affair with it. The larger roots were almost sweet and juicy, whereas the smaller, or more narrow ones, were spicy. They were the best antidote to over-eating or consuming too many oily or heavy foods. They joined my daily staple that could be peeled, deeming them safe to eat raw, along with the apple-tasting bananas and tiny tangerines.

36

I ARRIVED IN KATHMANDU SPACEY AND TIRED, BUT SOON FOUND my friends and became invigorated by all the talk in English. Our shared experiences had a touch of bragging excitement, but overall, a newly found confidence and maturity could be felt from all of us. To learn, to absorb, to change—the village had become a panacea for catharsis.

The retreat schedule included a three-day rafting trip down the Trisuli River, and then a couple of nights at Chitwan Lodge in the Terai jungle. After the quiet solitude of the village, standing around bright orange rafts at the edge of a cold and boisterous river in the middle of Asia seemed odd. After an hour and a half drive out of Kathmandu, down river from Naubise, we reached one of several launching points. A few Nepali men and older boys helped with life jackets and rafts, and off we went.

It was an exhilarating ride. Along the way, we took a quick dip in the cool water. The rapids were exciting, but nothing like the "Lunch Counter" on the Snake River in Jackson Hole, Wyoming. When I was a kid, my parents owned a gallery in Crabtree Corner next to the Lewis & Clark Expeditions. In the summers when they had an extra seat, I would sometimes fill it. Rafting was familiar, but the unpredictable nature of white water scared me. When younger, the adventure was thrilling, and I loved getting wet. After so many of those trips, I'd had enough. But, of course, riding a river in Nepal held a different wildness that exposed the land in contrasting angles and revealed a different kind of professional Nepalese.

The first night we pulled out just north of Mugling, a crossroad junction of the Trisuli and Marsyangdi rivers. The crew anchored the rafts on the beach. Tents were set up and a large fire burned warm and bright on the sandy bank. A disappointing American meal of spaghetti with tomato sauce was spread out for the white kuires, a derogatory term for foreigners, instead of the rustic, outdoor Nepali camping food I had hoped for, whatever it might have been. A few of us chatted with the river guides, a lively and fun-loving bunch, English-speaking and savvy to Westerners. After dinner and clean up, they gathered down the beach around their own fire and made dal bhat, but welcomed us for conversation.

One of our students, Carl, asked if he could share their dinner, which they cheerfully doled out. I found myself talking to one of the guides about America, our lives and our dreams. He hoped to study abroad after a few more years of rafting and saving his money. We stayed up late, and as I walked back to my tent, I looked over my shoulder at him, silver-gilded in the moonlight. He waved. I returned it, even though the darkness stole any definition, then slipped into the tent, changed, and wriggled into a bag. Juni mumbled something, probably sarcastic about hoping I'd had fun, then wrapped the bag tighter around her and floated back to sleep.

I lay awake, soothed by the gurgling water, its rolls and swirls glissaded in murky dialogue. That guy was nice, and it was fun to speak English to someone from Nepal who had his own ideas and seemed free to do what he wanted.

I awoke early, before most of the others, and emerged into a chilly, clear morning. The crew had a fire going where I warmed my hands after taking care of toiletries in the area they'd cordoned off. Two of our students were sick with giardia (an awful parasite found in contaminated water, food, and on some surfaces, that infected humans and animals), and a taxi took them to Chitwan, where we would meet the next day. The young man I'd talked with last night came up to me as I stood near the fire, still sleepy and almost hypnotized by the rushing river.

"Did you sleep well, Sobha?" he asked quietly. His eyes beckoned me but only for a second, then he looked away.

"Yes, I did. And you?"

"Ho, it was a good night." He smiled again, nodded, and left.

The canyon's steep rocky faces moved slowly by. My fingers made lacy lines in the river, and conversation in each raft was subdued until a water fight broke out. It was warm enough to enjoy tuna salad and peanut butter and jelly sandwiches while banked on the side, only to push out again into more water fights. Our gregarious energy instantly stopped after the warning to "hold on" shot out from one of the guides. A succession of rapids, a gushing torrent; the rafts jumped and swerved through them. Another beach-night spot, and I turned down the fried chicken for dinner for bhat, tarkari, and chapati with Carl and the crew, which, again, they welcomed.

I found myself alone a second time with the enchanting young Nepali man. We sat under a woolly blanket off to the side of the rest, who were drinking something other than tea. Our conversing trailed off. His hand moved toward mine and my stomach jumped. He moved in fast. We kissed passionately, but I pulled away abruptly. His spirited and ready eyes didn't seem to care who was around or what they thought. Did they see us? Hear us? He leaned in for another kiss, warm, soft, sensual. His arms lingered around me. Again, I pushed away.

"No, I cannot do this," I said in Nepali.

"Why not?" he asked, pulling me in again.

Because, I thought to myself, *I do not want to appear as a loose woman from America, where sex is easy, and—no Sobha! No, no, no!!* But I answered differently in Nepali.

"I don't want to do this. It's not right. I'm sorry."

I ran toward the raging fire where my friends were drinking tea, sharing stories in inebriated companionship. I stared into the fire, its furnace of jagged black wood licking and spitting like a dragon. I closed my eyes, took a deep breath, and another one. *What am I doing?*

Carl looked over in a knowing way, his eyes questioning. I gave him a bug-eyed look, then sat down and leaned against another friend. She was eating something while pontificating on how much she missed bacon wrapped anything and chocolate brownies.

Why did I do that? I thought. It happened fast, was probably harmless, but still, I was sorry. The noise coming from our quiet, respective village selves shifted quickly into a lusty and rowdy bunch in that camp, echoing off the narrow canyon walls and energized by the babbling, mysterious river.

The next morning during tea, scrambled eggs, and toast, while the crew dismantled camp, our teachers briefed us on the day. After a few hours on the river, the trip would end in Gai Ghat, followed by an hour and a half bus ride to Chitwan Lodge in the Terai, where we would spend two nights. My eyes met with the young man from last night, his downcast and distant. I got into his boat and rode with friends. After I handed him my life jacket, we said good-bye. He studied my face with stony depth that unlocked me. I felt a plunge into my chest, soft and stabbing. Maybe he doesn't tryst like that often? Maybe what we had was something. Maybe he is as innocent as I, and maybe he was merely swept towards me as I was to him?

We loaded into the waiting bus, I at a window seat, following his moves in and around the rafts, packing things up. The bus pulled away. He looked after it. I couldn't wave, cautious against being seen and questioned—or teased. Then we were gone. I never saw him again.

37

THE PLAINS OF THE TERAI, AT OVER THREE HUNDRED FEET IN elevation, stretched across the southern part of Nepal, a totally different place compared to the popular Himalayas. Those Gangetic flat lands were diverse and distinct—sub-tropical weather, ethnic groups, and agricultural fields where most of the food for the country was cultivated. The dress, language, and social traditions differed from their rugged neighbors located only a few hours away. We bumbled along in the noisy bus, mostly in silence, as travel often made most of us retreat and reflect within the jangle of displacement, passage, and change.

The Chitwan Lodge, or "Heart of the Jungle," nestled in the Dun Valley at the convergence of the Kali Gandaki and Trisuli Rivers. It was believed a third and spiritual river joined them, and all formed a major tributary of the Ganges. Nearby, Devghat was considered by the Hindus as a holy place to die, and served as a hermitage of meditation.

In the same partnership as our last retreat at Dhulikhel, we settled into our shared rooms before gathering outside in a court-yard tangled with large leafy plants where tea awaited. As we talked about the river adventure and what was going to happen in the next two days, the two students who were sick, and had arrived the day before, joined us. They seemed somewhat better, or at least rested. A German couple sipped their tea, and a small Australian trekking group talked quietly at their table.

The unfamiliar humidity settled into my bones in a restless way. Something was different in this section of Nepal, and it made me uncomfortable. Maybe it was the presence of large mammals only a few feet away in the jungle, or the locals who were naturally taller, darker-skinned, and mysterious. A tension of superiority reigned. Who was in control? Definitely not the elephants, who were beaten and tamed into submission to serve large numbers of visitors wanting a lope while spotting other unique and more elusive animals. Chitwan, Nepal's first national park, had been established in 1973, which covered three hundred and sixty square miles. In a lush monsoon climate, the park was biologically diverse. Its flora and fauna included the deciduous Sai trees, acacia, and sisam trees, as well as an abundance of deer, sloth bear, monkeys, wild boar, jackals, cats, snakes, crocodiles, even freshwater dolphins, and a slew of other creatures.

I had never been a safari enthusiast—quite the opposite, in fact. I felt more comfortable and intrigued by high, craggy mountains. But as I tromped through the enormous height of elephant grass to spot an Asian one-horned Rhino or a royal Bengal tiger—my only knowledge of that majestic cat had come from the side of a Celestial Seasonings tea box—my curiosity was piqued.

I felt small, but in a different way than in the shadow of my beloved Himalayas—possibly because being on the back of an elephant was daunting. We gathered around the tour guide instructing us on how to mount these gentle creatures, which he said were easy to ride. His assistant led one of the huge animals over to our small circle. Its ragged skin and sad eyes made me want to cry. It fell to its knees, bowed its head, and the assistant easily perched his body upon the curved trunk. The elephant hauled him up swiftly, where he grabbed hold of the back of its ears and landed in a straddle behind the gentle forehead of the gigantic beast.

Elephants were the largest herbivorous animals on the planet, and its only predator? Humans. How sad and depressing was that!? Elephants were capable of complex emotions and had amazing memories. Imagine that massive personality, her expression of the struggles she experienced, the entrapment, the daily dust and exhaust. It broke my heart. I could see the detachment and pent up emotion in her tired eyes, covered in the life she had unluckily fallen into, truly a beast of burden. It was why I couldn't go to zoos. The look in the animals' eyes made me crazy. I knew what I saw—the clench of manpower on their delicate and fragile souls.

We took turns getting up on the trunk, or had the option of a ladder. I chose the trunk, but seeing another student expertly maneuver it inhibited me. Everyone had a knack for something that you just didn't know about until you did it. One of hers was obviously that, and I was impressed.

I sheepishly walked up to that massive, grey, wrinkled being, put my hand on her shoulder, whispered, "I know how you feel, and I am sorry," then put my hand on her trunk and did it, but not quite as nobly as the student before. For some reason my middle sank and bent over as the elephant lifted, and I grabbed for something, but nothing was there. The guide yelled, pointing frantically. I didn't understand, but miraculously recovered as I somehow sprang up on top. Three more students followed, as well as our guide. Our group mounted and rode four elephants, spaced evenly apart in a row, looking like a movie scene. Settled into the bamboo baskets atop the elephants' backs, we trundled through thick jungle and pungent grasslands, plunged through deep, muddy waters, and traipsed into the nether lands of the Terai.

THE RIDE WAS a discombobulated display of four huge feet in a slow, syncopated gait. It wasn't my thing, but at least I could say I'd ridden an elephant, seen a few rhinos, a tiger, and a handful of beautiful birds. Still, I had a hard time enjoying something that pained another species. My mind wandered to the rafting guide's sensual eyes and soft kiss, his conciliatory rumination on what he wanted to do, and the fleeting excitement of feeling friendship on another level. Lulled by the elephant's movement, swaggering back and forth, forward and around, until each lope shook me back to reality.

The elephant ride on our retreat in the Terai

The guides were alert to follow any movement in the tall elephant grass, exhaustingly wanting to fulfill photo wishes of the rich white people. We were a different group, though. We spoke their language, didn't take many pictures, and asked if we could help brush the elephants down and see how they were fed. But still, it was a pastime of the wealthy—wasn't it?

The rest of the retreat was mellow, not much planned except evening gatherings around dinner talking about how the village experience had deepened our awareness of our place in the world. Shankar spoke sensitively about his visits to each of the villages, what he had seen, and how differently we reacted to our families. I thought of mine: Kamala's health and mysteriousness; Jamuna's hostility and sad situation; my hike into the hills with weight balanced from my forehead; Ajay's dancing and nightly conversations; aama's patient, wise eyes; writing practice with Seti; cold, dark nights, intensely quiet; the death ceremony, difficult and arduous conditions; Tangting, its beauty and intimacy—ah! What life renders in the wake of mortality, in the presence of exposure, in the excitement of change.

In one more month, the program would be over, and though a wrap-up at the base house would end the program, officially the Chitwan retreat brought it to a close in an informal manner.

Latent fears unleashed a deeper set of questions. What next? For many it was clear, but for me? Nepal had substantiated a distrust and dislike of the normal education system. If not college, what would fulfill my need to do something worthwhile? Could I find something I loved to do, and would I achieve growth and insight?

Nepal had cracked me open, the bright light piercing through old debris and reflecting on elements I didn't quite yet grasp. How could I harness that newfound knowledge and funnel it into something worthwhile and fun? A career? A path? A job?

Being away from the village with its life of duty and my wish to fit in brought an understanding of how I interacted with people, a little stronger, more conscious of my surroundings and the people around me. I missed home, thought about it at times, and felt it in my heart rather than seeing it in my mind.

Shankar talked of visiting one of the students in her village and how she had it so together, gathering things to help with dinner, assisting with the cooking. I had never even thought of helping with the actual cooking. I didn't think to ask. It felt off limits. I could barely hold myself together. Embarrassed at my behavior, I fell into destructive thoughts, but then an inner voice said, *But you climb their mountains and help carry their weight, and you keep up with them and wash their wool . . .* We all had strengths, but it was always easier to see my shortcomings.

On the trip back to Kathmandu, wrapped up in our own thoughts, the bumps and jolts of the bus loosened us up as we each thought about the return to our villages after the freedom of the retreat. Our teachers had brought suntalas and keras (tangerines and bananas) along. The pungent smell of the peel made me breathe deeply with pleasure. They pointed out vistas along the way, and I relaxed into the dry, flat scenery.

We would have two free nights in Kathmandu before heading

back to our primitive lives. Most of us looked forward to the austerity of village life, even though feelings of apprehension and congeniality vied for attention. I felt resistance about going back into the cold, tedious infrastructure of the village with its established routines. I had learned and gathered and exchanged enough, and was ready to fly in my own direction. With that admittance, I gazed more peacefully out the dusty window, observed workers bent over in fields, lifting long handled tools, digging into the earth. Sowing seeds took persistence. Skill happened in its own time. I smiled at my own clichéd analogy, but felt its truth. There was no rush. The village experience would never happen again, so the little time I had left would probably be the most important, and possibly the best.

When we arrived in Kathmandu, Langtang and Jugal Himals magnificently stole the scene, and I resolved to let the ripening of that whole Nepal experience reveal more and more . . . and more.

It was my birthday the last evening before returning to Tangting, a celebration I always enjoyed, although I was shy and didn't care for being the center of attention. A traditional Nepali restaurant fed us a sumptuous dinner, then my teachers and fellow students surprised me with a chocolate cake from a favorite Thamel café. My sweet tooth didn't go by undetected, as it was a definite weakness. I cut the cake into small wedges, only sharing three quarters of the dense indulgence, knowing I'd devour more of it on my own later! One last toast to the whole crazy and wonderful experience of Nepal, then we dispersed into the Kathmandu ethers. Moving into my twenties marked a turning point into a new decade of growth. I felt special. I had made the right decision to be in Nepal at that time in my life.

A few of us stayed in a guesthouse to have absolute freedom, staying up late at the Namaste Café where Linda and the owner were definitely having an affair. Another student too had hooked up with one of the rafting guides, and they had a room somewhere. That's what adults did. I was not naïve to it, just surprised. Why didn't I have a room with *my* rafting guide, or at least a date for tea? Was I upholding some kind of good-girls-don't-do-that kind-of-thing without some form of courtship ideal? Was I a prude? Why not explore? What held me back?

I am a virgin Sobha, I haven't done it yet.

Yes, I know, but it doesn't mean you have to get married!

I knew that. I was just scared. Was it safe to fool around in a Third World country? Could I handle that kind of intimacy?

What I couldn't handle was my incessant questioning, checking, measuring, judging. I judged myself to the point of frenzied craziness of not knowing what to do, who to talk to, or where to turn. And the amount of time and work to pull me out of that kind of introspection isolated me and tore into any shred of self-esteem.

The rest of us played in that ancient, holy city. The choked streets crawled with people and curios, fascinating and simple, hanging from tiny, closet-like storefronts. The aromatic scents of curry and urine, diesel and incense, forever imprinted Nepal into my memory. The next morning, I enjoyed the rest of that dense, sweet, chocolate birthday torte for breakfast while packing up.

I had a decision to make about school in the spring. Did I want to go or not? It sounded good not to go back and instead work in Jackson Hole to see where that might take me. Maybe in the summer I'd do a course with the outdoor leadership school, Outward Bound, or spend the money for college on a course or a job I really wanted to do. My heart was not into the small campus schoolroom in Petaluma, California.

What did I want to do?

On the way to Pokhara, while traveling with Carl and a few other students in a night bus, the clunky old thing pulled over for dal bhat at two in the morning. Two of us shared a plate—yikes, how jutho (dirty)! Eating from the same plate was considered polluted for others. In the middle of that little café, my friends sang happy birthday to me and revealed yet another cake. I blushed and tried to stop them, but they made me endure it. The place hushed, then everyone clapped. The cake was awful, waxy and gummy, made to look like a western masterpiece, but concocted with horrifying ingredients. We shared it with everyone on the bus, much to their delight.

232

Later that day we rented bicycles as we explored Pokhara, bought fruit at the side of Phewa Tal (lake), the second largest in Nepal, with Machapuchhare reflected on its surface. A tiny island sat off center, with Taal Barahi, a Hindu temple, hidden below green, bushy trees. Carl walked out to a dead tree that rose at least twenty feet above the lake's surface, climbed it, and perched like a hawk surveying the area while we sat near the water's edge. The gentle lap of water, the glowing setting sun, gave way to silent reflection until a swift, brisk chill had us walking quickly back to our guesthouse, the same place where I had stayed before the retreat.

The didi remembered my face as we entered the narrow, wooden doorway, pointing a distrusting shake of her finger at Carl for some reason, but invited us in, and we paid for cots. Dal bhat with a bunch of other Nepalese was fun and boisterous, then we were off to bed early. My big toe throbbed from a minor accident earlier that day when Juni stopped her bike abruptly to point at something. I'd rammed into her back wheel, fell down, and scraped my leg and toe on the rough asphalt. A large chunk of skin had torn off and it was infected. I didn't have anything with me, so I cleaned it off with cold water and wrapped it in toilet paper for the night.

The next morning, I cleaned it again and the didi gave me a bandage. A stroll down a street, suggested by her, displayed quaint cafés: tea and toast, round tables, comfortable chairs, and an eclectic ménage of foreigners lounged over books, newspapers, or engaged in impassioned discussion. We joined the scene for a couple of hours, catching up in journals, reading, and talking about what we were going to do when the program was over. They planned to return to school and attend the last quarter. Mine was to squeeze in as many country stopovers as the flight would allow, and maybe defect! Juni and Linda were interested, and said they might tag along.

At eleven o'clock we said goodbye and went our separate ways to the high hamlets of order, beauty, and work. I caught a van to the trailhead, waved to the decrepit lady who snatched up the broken tincture from last time, and started off at a quick pace. About an hour later, the ominous swinging bridge came into view, beautiful to look at, but realistically dangerous. My stomach tightened, hands squeezing around the strap on my forehead (I had purchased a traditional woven bag, similar to my bahini's in the village). I breathed deeply. I had to cross it. It hadn't been repaired in my absence—surely it hadn't been in a long, long time. It moved in its own rhythm, slightly enough to disengage my hips from my legs in a puppet-like way.

An old woman arched over a cane, carrying a large load, sat chewing on a piece of something near the bridge. I looked at her, put down my bag, sat down after asking if that was all right, pulled out a package of biscuits, and offered her some.

"Bujae, (respectful term for older woman) are you crossing the bridge, or have you already come across?" I asked in Nepali.

"Nanu, I cross, but rest first." She chuckled and pointed to the biscuits.

"For you." I handed the package to her. "I too cross to Tangting."

"Tangting? You?" She laughed, then fell silent, gathered her things, stood up slowly—I leaped to offer a hand—she nodded, and turned toward the bridge. She became an agile, miniature creature, gracefully connected with the world around, and expertly, without hesitation, made her way across without stopping. Once on the other side, she turned, waved with her free hand, then hobbled along. I followed, and once on the other side, I did not jump in triumph, but moved steadily on, as if it were no big deal, merely part of the moveable feast before me.

I caught up with her, pressing my hands together. "Namaste Bujae, ramro sanga." ("In good step.) She smiled so big, her face looked like an old dried apple.

Many of the hills on the way to Tangting were transformed into steep and lengthy stairs built from hand chiseled, heavy, square slabs of rock, secure in their placement. Ascending those flights made carrying heavy loads easier, stepping was more secure, and mud ceased to be a problem, especially during monsoon season, where rains relentlessly flooded the area. I enjoyed the conditioning as it slowed me down, strengthened my legs, and increased my endurance. Hiking was the best exercise. I liked its simplicity, a peaceful, meditative rhythm.

My mom instilled a love of the mountains and the importance of exercise—but not in a gym. Rather in the high elevations where trees grew gnarled and leaned to one side to compensate from extreme winds and weather, where assonance of the tundra to the dissonance of the mind could find equilibrium, one that would disengage the mundane and interfering nature of civilization and shoal the profound breath instinctive in each one of us. I was completely in sync when above tree level, and was too often muddled when below. But, strangely, I became inert when in the throes of either one to remember to be real to who I was and how I felt. I guessed age would bring that wise old self to fruition.

I breathed deep and stopped to look around. I was high enough to see the Himalayas pressed into the sky, unreal and fantastic. Their breathless beauty gave energy to life. I was getting close, and it was a good thing, since my legs were tired from the walk. A distinct chill arose quite suddenly as the sun dropped behind the rugged mountain skyline, and I knew the day was folding in. Finally, the last rocky platform above a long flight of stairs marked the entrance to Tangting—that place of breathless intuition where time seemed eternal. Cold, expectant air filled my quickened steps. I made my way through the familiar walkway to *my house.*

38

"SOBHA, SOBHAAAA!" MY NAME RANG OUT FROM A FEW HOUSES as little children ran on terraced courtyards, singing that familiar name louder and louder. I waved to them before disappearing onto the neat and familiar patio. The white girl with gold hair had returned.

"Aama, Kamala? I am back. Are you here?" I dropped the bag onto my bed, then met them at the opening to the kitchen.

"Ho bahini, Sobha is here."

Everyone but baa came out and hugged me. I followed them into the kitchen, where steamy dal bhat sat like a pile of gems on their plates. Aama hastened to fill another one.

"How did you know to make enough?" I asked, pointing to the bhat.

"Sapaana (dream) Sobha. You came to me in my sapaana," she said, putting down the metal spoon and patting her head to stress the emphasis of her dream.

I had gifts for everyone, but waited until after the meal. Ajay bounded into the room, smiled full and bright, with his soft voice and beautiful way. He said in Nepali, "Sobha, Sobha, Sobha, how was the big city?" He sat down next to Seti and poked her. She giggled and poked him back.

"Dai, it was good, but I missed this village and all of you. The food here is so much better, and the night is darker. How are you? What is new?"

Someone got married after I had left. They were sorry I had missed the festivities, and especially the dancing. Ajay got up and did a little jig, then he said goodnight. We cleaned up, I told them to wait. I followed Seti, where we squatted next to each other, fanned out our skirts, and giggled. She was cute. I knew I'd miss her. Then I returned from my sleeping area with a bundle in my arms.

For aama, a large beautiful cauliflower, and a piece of her favorite sweet. It tasted like sour, watery goat cheese, sweetened with too much sugar, on a crumbly base—not too bad, but definitely an acquired taste. A small sack for each of the bahinis was filled with pencils, an eraser, a coin purse, a few candies, and that dried fruit thing I'd learned about during the urban stay. Churas (glass bracelets) and pretty scarves for Kamala, aama, and bhauju, and a new hat for baa. I had thought about bringing kerosene, but decided against it.

Early the next morning I felt sick—all that cake and rich food in Kathmandu had finally caught up to me—but I dressed hastily and got moving outside in the cold, doing my morning chores. Once inside, waiting for a plate of dal bhat, dark shadows disappeared into the cold vespers. Bhauju shoveled giant scoops of dhindo into her mouth, the muddy black millet stuff dunked in watery dal. I passed on it. The sick feeling went away after I started hiking at a quick pace to keep up with bhauju and Kamala.

"Are you okay?" they asked in Gurung.

"Ho Didi. Thakai lagyo, tara—" ("Yes, Didi. Tired, but—") I said.

"Tara sanchai cha." ("But happy.") They laughed, cutting me off, knowing what I would say. That was the funniest thing to them.

For about an hour and a half we climbed high enough to see Machapuchhare. I told them to stop and look at that amazing mountain. They obliged, but were more amused by my enthusiasm.

It felt as if two to three thousand feet of elevation had passed beneath our callused feet. Their pace was faster than usual, and we got up into new territory, higher than the usual forests, and onto the arid plateaus of the Himalayas.

We collected wood all day, retrieved long branches that Kamala cut and piled into neat bundles. I never understood the method of the carefully crafted bundles, but there certainly was one. After stuffing our dokos and starting back down, my head hurt, and the descent became difficult. The namlo across my forehead cut into my sweaty skin. As I had done many times before, I wondered, *Why am I doing this?* Because it built character and stamina. I wanted to crack that "nut" I had been carrying for years, the one that inhibited me from coming out of myself. *That's why Sobha.*

Mom taught me that when you are tired and the backpack on your back is heavy, but you have miles to go, follow the person's feet in front with your eyes, and your steps will ease into the rhythm and ground will be covered. That is what I did, following behind bhauju and Kamala in a steady march, slightly hypnotized by their sure step, and Tangting finally appeared.

THE AMBIANCE of the evening peeled away another layer of my turmoil. Aama touched her forehead and pointed to mine, where a deep red mark grooved my white skin from carrying the day's load.

"Bahini ho!" she said, her aged body nimbly squatting-walking at the same time around the low-ceilinged room, the few kitchen utensils placed neatly behind her, shiny kasouri (metal cooking pot), and in her hand a dhawo (long, ladle-like metal spoon) filled with spicy lentils.

The wind blew through cracks in the walls. Thunder from distant hills boomed like a child hitting a hollow drum. Voluminous clouds crawled over each other—the wrath of heavenly power swirled and billowed. A storm moved in. I looked at my two young sisters and pointed to the sky. They echoed its force in a rattle of continuous oh-oh-ohs and then giggled.

238

"Why the oh-oh-ohhhs?" I asked in Gurung.

"It answers the thunder," they said seriously.

I put my book down and chatted with them about weather, animals, and repeated colors to each other in a little game we made up to memorize them. A shadow passed the doorway—was it a large bird? I hadn't seen many. Perhaps a lone Griffon, Egyptian Vulture, or Golden Eagle had spread its wings against the slate grey sky, yearning for its home in the rocky temples. It circled in large, lazy, determined rings.

Me on the ledge in front of our house in Tangting

The girls left at aama's call. I went outside to sit on the steps that led up to the kitchen and watched the change under the surging storm. The bird vanished into the hilly, tree-filled expanse. An almost full moon hung in desolate charm, like a kerosene lamp in a dark house. The damp air from imminent drops of lonely mountain tears was alive with the music of pensile memories—*my* memories. I could see the breadth of precipitation move in quickly, washing the land in its powerful exhale, then disappearing slowly into the valley.

39

My days at Tangting were numbered. Instead of counting them, I concentrated on my schoolwork. Aside from language studies, we had to write a profile of the village we lived in, including the population, industry, environment, ethnic groups, and more. Each of us had a project of our own choice. Mine was learning the process of wool gathering, washing, spinning, and weaving.

Another day collecting wood with Kamala brought a different experience. We left immediately after eating bhat—the pressure to get into the hills and work, work, work clearly felt urgent! I wondered why? Maybe a storm boiled. Aama knew I was curious, and tried to explain, but for some reason she became agitated, so I stopped her in Nepali.

"It's okay Aama, no need. I just follow."

"Ho Sobha, tara no," she said. "Much work, other people wait."

After walking for an hour, we rested with five other Nepali men who were working for our family, chopping and carrying wood—that was the reason to rush. We all moved on to a spot where we'd previously been. There were piles of thick branches Kamala had done, but more leaves, chips, and bark were strewn about. Paths had been cut through jungle debris.

The men chopped while Kamala and I filled dokos with cut wood and carried it a little way to a cleared area, where we dumped it into new neat piles. Back and forth, hours of bending and lifting, under a bleak sky and chilly wind.

"Sobha," Kamala asked in Nepali, "what do you eat in America at work?"

"Different things. I was a baker, and ate a lot of bread and sweet things—too many."

"You eat a lot of sweet things?"

"Ho Didi, at work I did. But at home we eat mostly rice and beans and vegetables."

"I would like to eat a lot of sweets." She chuckled. "What kind of vegetables?"

"Greens, cabbage—banda gobhi, carrots—gajara I think? Lots of tarkari."

"Masu? Hoina?" ("Meat? No?")

"Very little, Didi, like here."

After a few minutes, she asked, "Sobha, what is school like there?"

"I live with other students in large buildings without our parents. We study all day, and do work for the school to help pay for it. We study all kinds of things, depending on what we want to do."

"What do you want to do?" she asked as we stopped for a rest on a fallen log.

"Oh Didi, many things. I want to be a teacher. I don't know. One of them is being with you. This is how I like to learn."

"Ho Didi," she said with a smile. Even though she was my didi (older sister) because of age, it was respectful or endearing to call me that.

"What do *you* want to do, Kamala?"

She looked at the mountain for a long moment, and then said, "What can I do Sobha? I am a woman of the village." She patted my hand.

"Will you marry?" I asked.

She nodded. "Ho Sobha, perhaps."

"When? And to who? Do you know?" I pressed.

She looked back, smiled, and waved me off.

"Didi," I urged, "kahile?" ("When?")

"I don't know." She was serious. I knew her health was not good, but something else seemed to linger. I didn't know, and did not ask again.

We walked in silence. My relationship with Kamala transcended borders of nations and cultures. The trust and unspoken communication defied all our differences. Our bond was a reckoning of my past, as I had lost touch with my two older sisters since the divorce. Kamala was unique. Her kaleidoscope brown eyes encompassed time like it was a dial, turned by a keen sense of awareness. Was it the mysterious disease she endured? An intuitive psychic ability? Or a humble, dire, ethos ordained in some far reach of her enigmatic mind, and in fuzzy detail, she seemed to know the order of things. She saw something deeply moving, as if life had to be lived exactly as it was. Only pain, intense and panoptic, took that freedom and grace from her being; infrequently, yet completely.

"I am sorry, Didi," I said. Perhaps I'd gone too far.

"Sobha, it is okay. Do not worry about me." After another long pause, she said nervously, "What do you do at moon time?"

She was referring to menstruation. I'd wondered if that subject would come up. I told her how I dealt with it, yet while in Nepal, I had not menstruated for months.

"Why Sobha? Are you okay?"

"Ho Didi, it is just from so much exercise and different food, I think. I am okay."

We spoke a lot more, and much was lost in that conversation, but we got through to each other, as we often did. We had grown close, and I was going to miss her.

At a break we prepared khaja (a snack) of chiyaa and dhindo (tea and black millet mush) with a type of hot dipping sauce. The men met up with us for the food. After we cleaned up, Kamala and I hiked to another spot where the men had been and gathered a few more loads. For the last one, they joined us, and we all started down, reaching our houses after dark.

I felt good as we ate rice. My youngest bahini begged me to

teach her more writing in English. With a tired smile, I said, "Ke garne?" ("What to do?") and pulled out paper. We exchanged pens. Her little round face blurted out words while I changed them from Sanskrit to English. Kamala looked over our shoulders while pounding buffalo cream into butter, and aama nodded off. When she jerked awake, we'd all giggle.

40

I WAS NOT AN ALTRUISTIC PERSON. I DID NOT WANT TO COME back to Tangting and bring in pipes to help build a better water drainage system, or deal with the sewer, or build a school. I'd heard of other people wanting to help, grateful for the stay with families—as I was. A bond had been formed that would live with me forever. Their lives deeply moved and matured me. I wished someone would help them, but I knew it wasn't going to be me.

I considered marrying into their village under the guise of dreaming the impossible, but nipped that in the bud. At twenty, anything was possible, right? Little did I understand how karma and the natural order of things really worked. Experiencing the intense friendship with my family hastened my thirst for more travel and discovery—though not necessarily in another living situation. I wasn't good at relinquishing privacy; I was not patient to mandates that didn't make sense to me.

I felt bad about lying to Kamala that day about not getting my period. Menstruation had never bothered me—always on time, no cramps, and of short duration. It was true that in Nepal I didn't have a regular cycle every month, and believed it was brought on by the extreme circumstances. However, I was born in Montreal,

Canada, I moved to Stowe, Vermont, for seven years, and then spent ten years in Jackson, Wyoming. I thrived in snow and freezing temperatures. Heat, most often from a wood stove, warmed our house, so winter was always comfortable and hot showers and baths soothed any discomforts.

Wood and water in Nepal were highly coveted, laboriously gathered, and dwindled quickly. Wood, used only for cooking, did not heat their homes. The austere, harsh cold bit into me in a pervasive tension. After hours of grunt work in the hills, sweaty from the effort, long evenings were spent sewing and studying in cold rooms. Since clothes were rarely washed, they became dry with sticky sweat. The movement to stay warm was my only ally.

The villagers seemed unaffected by the colder months. They took their climate conditions for granted, a fabrication of their hardiness, stamina, and incredible immunity. I, too, was used to uncomfortable temperatures, but my body reacted by holding onto reserves and shutting down—thus the lack of menstruation, which I knew would only be temporary, so I didn't worry about it.

Nepal had strict conditions around menses, referred to as chhaupadi, a tradition that dictated how a woman was supposed to behave during their cycle. Women were to stay away from their families, as they were thought to be unclean or impure. Girls often missed school and were in isolation for days each month. There were horror stories of deaths, rapes, animal attacks, and infection brought on by the subjugation of women in dangerous, often confined places —another atrocity practiced in many areas in the world, not just Nepal, that enslaved women. I lied about having my period the one time I got it while in the village. I did not mention it or make excuses. To go through yet another set of rules, to be ostracized further, seemed pointless, even though I was actively disobeying hardcore traditions as well as breaching my family's trust. Our teachers had explained that during menses, we were considered jutho, or polluted, and we were to eat outside or in another room— depending on the family's preference. Unfortunately, I felt inhibited and reserved, but wished I had honored their ways and abided by their rules.

This custom showed the dichotomy of living abroad. I only went so far to immerse myself in a foreign culture as inequality, servitude, victimization, and a superiority caste system reigned over a servile, antediluvian population. I knew I couldn't change their "system," but I wasn't going to pretend it was okay. I could have argued the point, and in the secluded hills above Tangting, I might have made progress with Kamala, but the language got in the way.

41

MOST OF THE TIME MY HANDS WERE DRY AND PRICKLY FROM THE lack of fat in my diet and the continuous work of washing the rough wool in cold water. A small vial of cream was a last thought when packing for the village, but had become prized property, and now, sadly, I was down to the final drops. Such a small thing gave such great pleasure as I wrapped my thirsty hands around the soothing paste. The smell of the cream brought on a déjà vu of Mendocino, California, where I ran barefoot on the sand and the smell of the salty ocean misted the air while biking in the early morning fog. A burst of memories came back to me—the health food store, "*Corners of the Mouth*," eating steamy brown rice, apples, vitamin C chewables, the bakery, good friends, picking mussels, sitting on the bench above Portuguese beach—Wow!

Annapurna waited patiently as the visions subsided into a soft, sensitive longing. I'd been in Nepal a long time. I wondered if my recollection of this country would be as bright in the years ahead.

"Sobha!" aama called loudly.

"Waay," I said back in the same tone, which made her laugh easily.

"Aunos."

She wanted me to clean two large pieces of heavy material that seemed to be mattress covers. I carried them to the spigot and began the arduous kneading with my feet in the cold water. Over and over, I folded the material with my feet, putting all my weight into it to squeeze out the dirt and soapy water. After a while I thought they looked fairly good, so I gathered them up and went to get her approval. Aama uncoiled the material to inspect my hard work. She took a few brief looks and handed them back.

"Again, again, Sobha. Get it white!"

She understood my shyness and hesitancy, my beginners mind. She was a hard teacher. I trudged back to the cold, rocky spigot to wash the dirty grey cloth that had only been white years earlier. I amused myself that she may have kept it for me to learn the intricacy of stepping on cold, wet cloth to press it clean, or to give me something to keep me busy. Anyway, with limited language ability and needing to be told how to best help them, and then shown how to do it, it must have been tiring for her.

Old women laughed as they perched above the spigot, squawking in their ancient tongue about the white girl with gold hair and how she washed! I threw my head back, smiled widely, and walked over the cobblestones back to aama for another inspection.

"Ho Aama!?"

"Again!"

Unbelievable, she told me to go back again. At the spigot, different women were scrubbing the same type of material, laughing as they twisted their hard-working bodies, telling me how to do it. The old women sitting above cackled, "Back again, Sobha!" and "Oh poor, Sobha." They laughed and laughed.

It was not humiliating, it was basic. I enjoyed being told what to do and learning how to wash in cold water with my hands and feet. Sure, I'd done it a thousand times, but mostly I used washable menstrual pads, hand-scrubbed wool sweaters, and, growing up, we had a small washing machine with a roller to wring water out of clothes by hand, then we hung the laundry up on a line to dry.

I was getting college credit to learn how to wash with my hands and feet! I was being exposed to the judgments of the village folk while conversing in a completely foreign language, one I didn't even learn, and melding proximity of color and race, letting go of inhibitions, feeling at one with a completely opposite culture, and loving it. I put every ounce of sweat into washing that cloth, wringing it out tight, kneading its thick folds, scrubbing like an Olympian—and to my surprise, I got it clean. Women doing the same thing smiled at me. They understood. What a workout!

I was proud as aama nodded her head in absolute approval. It was like being a kid again in an adult body. I had relaxed into the simple, thrilling pleasure of talking about a sapaana (dream) or eating a cold chunk of rice. I didn't have to answer to anyone necessarily, until my Gurung brother, Vikram, was home for a short time and asked me to get him a glass of paani (water). Nicely, but in a matter-of-fact way, I said in Nepali, "You get it."

You'd think I had committed adultery or killed someone in cold blood. Aama raised her finger, a shining fury in her eyes. "Sobha!" She thrust out my name in a force that elevated my sorry ass off the smooth, muddy surface.

I got him a glass of water.

42

MY FREQUENT TRIPS TO THE COLD-WATER SPIGOT TO CLEAN WOOL granted long periods of reflection. I thought humans had common sense, but what good was that unless coupled with intuition? We squelch our inner voice before we even hear it. I thought about all the abuse, poverty, and racism rampant in the world. I knew about it, but living so close to such axioms, where the color of skin or caste of birth made such a difference, broke my deeply poetic view of Nepal. My thoughts became lost and tangled.

I sat up and stretched my aching back, released a loud sigh, and looked at Annapurna. I was part of it, as much as I fought it. How could I not be? My aim was to find my path, my bliss, do good, make a change, even if that change was only in myself. Along the way I wanted to clarify my convoluted past and foster healthy relationships, preserve the earth's resources, and enjoy life.

Why did some people strive for power? Why did others accept the simple things? I did not know. Maybe that went back generations, passed down from parent to child. How can we break old patterns, outdated, primitive ways, or reverse destructive behavior?

The cold water swished into the rough wool and softened it, making it cloudy. The word *Remember*, painted on a plaque above the door at my high school in Mendocino, would float into my mind again, reminding me—

Remember, take a breath . . .

Remember, you have as much to do with everything as anyone else . . .

Remember, look at yourself and why you do things, what are the consequences of your thoughts, your actions . . .

Remember, it takes work . . .

Remember, listen . . .

Remember, listen, *remember*, listen . . .

Tangting gang: bottom row left to right: me, unknown, Kamala, unknown, Seti, behind Seti is aama and to her right is pupu. I have forgotten the names of the others

One evening, the villagers gathered under a large, wooden lean-to where the youth would meet and have fun. Instead of going to a club in the city, rural villages had their own social commons place. The socializing was known as Rodhi. Traditional folk music blared loud from a cheap speaker as a few men and several young boys sat on the side with five interesting percussion instruments called Panche Baja. The instruments included: a tyamko, small kettle drum, played with two pieces of sticks; a damaha or nagara, a larger drum made of leather stretched over an end of a hollow copper bowl, played with hands; a sanai, a short pipe instrument; a jhurma or jhyali, cymbals; and dholaki, a two-sided drum similar to a madal, which are drums made from hollow wood or metal covered with animal skin and played with fingers. Ajay and a few others, dressed in flashy colors and scarves, ran up to the small stage and bowed. He led dance after dance in an exhausting litany of finesse and endurance that must have told a story—though about what, I didn't know. The audience cheered and drank late into the night. I was pulled on stage and made to accompany a few of the easier dances to the amused applause of the crowd.

I tried my best to copy the intricate eye and hand movements and the timed steps, always followed by raucous hoots. Aama shook with joy, but she went home early. It was fun, especially since there was no pressure. They loved my participation, patting me on the back with stern nods of approval. Ajay, bhauju, Kamala, the bahi-nis, and I gaily skipped through the village after the festivities. What a delightful scene. Gurungs loved the merriment of dancing, and they celebrated many times throughout the year, especially around harvest, the changing of the seasons, marriages, and holidays. They believed that life revealed itself in rhythm—the heartbeat, breath-ing, walking, laughter, the way they talked . . . They honored that original impulse, which gave them a sense of immortality. Music dwelt in the heart of Gurung cultural identity.

Ajay explained their unique intricacies on many of our evenings together, adding that the untouchables and all levels of ethnic cultures were allowed into the festivities. I was relieved to hear that the stigma of lineage could be dropped so that everyone had a good time together. Women seemed to be treated more equally in the village than in Kathmandu. They were open, cheerful, resilient, and confident—all Gurung attributes. I thought it was merely hard village life where the men were often gone and women did more of the immediate work, but women were allowed to own property and run businesses.

Tangting's musical performances helped deal with the monotony and laborious rough living, as well as mesh the advent of modern music and technology that inevitably leached into even the remotest regions. It kept the generations on equal ground when the old taught the young, and the young introduced new, outlandish sounds and moves on the stage for all to see and judge—and they judged harshly! Small arguments burst out that would teach and tame the youth. Some broke away from servility and primitiveness, as our teacher Shankar had done by marrying a white girl from America. I wondered if my rafting guide on the retreat had left to pursue his own interests. Or maybe it was to help his family? I would never know.

Beautiful Kamala combing her hair at a break up in the mountains above Tangting on one of our many leaf-collecting trips

The next day I went to collect wood with Kamala. We sat down to eat khaja (snack), both tired from getting to bed late the previous night. She hugged me, and then she stretched to ease her sore back. I suggested a method that could help her and she agreed to try it. I had her cross her arms over her chest and take a deep breath as I wrapped my arms around her from behind. When she released her breath totally, I lifted her up quickly. A deep *crack* from her upper back was the result. She thanked me, looking into my eyes as if she saw the ocean, something she had never seen.

Instantly, I understood how these people and their life affected me. I looked at her, and she at me. In my heart, I felt a wistful sadness. I realized through silent surrender that I would never see her again, nor Tangting. We were two people with lives on different sides of the world. For the short time we were together, I helped, which they respected, and I was grateful.

We hoisted our baskets, and headed up into the verdant jungle.

I WENT for wood again the next day, Saturday (or Holy day), and both bahinis came too. We worked until about one in the afternoon, when looming grey clouds moved in fast, carrying deep thunder and lightning. In minutes, hard, vicious hail bombarded the hillside with lighted, shattered icicles, bouncing off our heads and feet. Baa was working there too, and led us to a small cave.

Khaja (snack) was handed out by Kamala, a small handful of roasted corn flour—strange, but delicious! Unfortunately, I mistakenly inhaled a small amount and coughed violently, much to their concern, but quickly recovered. I remarked on how tasty it was. A bit of flour had dusted my lips and nose, which made them laugh.

The storm built and turned into a dynamic downpour, loud and chilling. After each rumble, the bahinis chortled, "Oh, ohhh, ooohh-hhh." I joined. Baa smiled while he leaned against the opening, peering thoughtfully toward the sky.

Kamala looked at me earnestly and said in Nepali, "If thunder is not answered, it gets angry, and hits harder."

We stayed in that cave for an hour while the storm pounded the muddy area and thunder ripped through the charcoal sky with envy, showing its rollick determination of what was to come. While waiting for the storm to clear, Seti taught me a song, and Kamala joined in. Once I learned it, we sang it individually in rounds. Our voices blended beautifully. Even baa nodded.

The thick, black, soupy sky moved quickly into the hungry

mouths of wind and billowy cumulus clouds. A steady, light rain followed, finally ending in heavy drops—*thunk, thunk, thunk*—from the rocky opening. Baa stepped out and looked up.

"Okay, aunos, aunos (come, come)." He waved to us. His agile, athletic body sprinted like a deer. About in his fifties, he was all muscle, and was imbued with a constant, mild energy. He lived in the hills with many of the other men, a nomadic rhythm of following the sheep from pasture to pasture.

We picked up where we had left off, but I didn't do as well because it was excessively muddy. I slipped so many times they decided I needed to go home early, and I would follow Seti. On my way down, carrying a load of leaves and branches, I lost my footing constantly, and had to take my boots off so my toes could grab the mud to keep me from falling. I usually went barefoot, but my feet were cut and bruised from walking in the hills for many days. The muddy trail was relentless and steep, with no switchbacks (a switch-back is a trail that zig-zags up a steep mountain instead of a straight trail). I couldn't control the weight of the doko against my forehead as it tipped me from side to side. Tears came to my eyes. It was an awful feeling not to be in control, yet I had no choice but to move slowly, steadily, painfully on.

My bahini was amazingly patient and sweet. She felt bad, seeing how hard I tried. Every once in a while she looked back and said, "Ramro sanga aunos (come in good step)." Not once did she lose her step, but rather bounced like a bunny. Were her feet structurally different from mine? Generations of daily physical labor, a lean diet, a lack of machinery, and most of all, a heightened sense of the earth—that was the magic formula.

I was silent for the rest of the trip as I concentrated on every step, holding my breath until I felt stable enough to move forward. I fell down in the slippery, muddy terrain numerous times. My lungi (skirt) was coated in wet muck, calves and arms splattered, and even my face was splotched with gooey mud. Each time, Seti helped me get back on my feet.

After hours of grueling exertion, we reached flat ground. My tense muscles could finally stretch into a relaxed gait as we

approached Tangting, its lilting architecture familiar and comforting. Seti ran ahead, telling aama about our plight. She stood in the
courtyard, a beacon, sensible and concerned, and she smiled as I
walked up to her.

"Oh Sobha, Sobha, Sobha," she said, then yelled after Seti to
help with my load. She looked at me again and said in Gurung, "Go
take off wet things and wash, then come inside."

"Aama, I am okay, I just don't have Gurung blood, but," and I
pointed to the hills, "it is in my heart." I thumped my chest.

I changed into a washing lungi. Resolutely, I trudged down the
path to the spigot and stepped into the flat, rocky basin. Awful,
frigid water ran down my legs, arms, over my face, and down my
chest and stomach. (Oh! What misery!) Once dried and in soft
clothes, I relaxed, though I couldn't control my chattering teeth,
which continued even after sitting down near the minuscule fire in
the kitchen. Chewing on hot food calmed me. My stainless-steel
plate held the usual rice, sautéed greens and lentils, but also two
chicken feet! I picked one up, the size of a large walnut, and chewed
out of pure politeness. It wasn't something I *wanted* to eat, and what
was on it anyway—grizzle, claw, skin? I watched Seti suck, chew, spit
out, and copied her.

During that evening meal, the family was sincerely impressed. I
wanted to be treated like one of them, and the arduous day had
humbled me. In that village, we broke barriers and became intimate
friends, but I was white, from America, of which I would return to.
That difference would always segregate me.

I looked at them, seated in a tight circle around dying embers,
laughing and commiserating. What wonderful, soulful people! Such
wise, hardworking lives spent in austere conditions.

They genuinely said, "Sobha, you are Gurung mountain girl.
Sobha the mountain girl!" giggling and nodding their heads. Barely
a fire, the cold room grew colder, but their warmth and compassion
touched my heart.

THE NEXT MORNING my whole body ached. I scrambled out of my bag into my freezing clothes. Then euphoria gripped my weary heart when I looked outside and saw the courtyard laden with four inches of heavy snow. No one else liked it, so I tried to bring on smiles by stomping around, flopping down into a snow angel, and singing Simon and Garfunkel's song, *A Hazy Shade of Winter*—I didn't know most of the words, so I interjected Nepali ones.

They were not amused. In fact, a strange, impatient, stay-out-of-the-way feeling permeated the house. Maybe it was the cold. My stomach was sore from eating too late last night. I asked for a small amount that morning, and happily ate slowly. Maybe everyone was cranky because of the added work the cold brought on. I decided to ghumne (wander), but told aama where I was going, and strolled over to my pupu's (aunt) house, where I often went in late afternoons. She patted the floor beside her and put up tea. I didn't stay long, but it was a nice stop.

Later, everyone's mood changed. I worked on finishing a few school projects, which included taking pictures of aama weaving and spinning. She cited names of the equipment she used, and I made sketches in my notebook. Later, while separating wool on the porch, I got up every ten minutes and jogged around to get warm. Aama looked at me with a gracious expression that secured the moment like a photo in candid testimony of our mutual appreciation. The few months in Tangting had changed all of us, which her look reflected. I came into their lives, and I would depart. I wondered if she would miss me, and hoped they would think kindly of me.

"Aama," I called from the porch, "aunos." ("Please come.")

"Ke bayo Sobha?" ("What's wrong?")

"Aunos."

"Ho Sobha, ke garne?!" ("Yes, Sobha, what to do?!")

"Here is a map of the world," I said in Nepali as I opened it onto the floor. "Vikram is here." I pointed to Hong Kong. "America is across the ocean. I go to school here." I pointed to Northern California. "And here is Nepal."

She loved to see where her son was posted and its proximity to Nepal. Her eyes deepened.

"Dhanyabad Sobha."

"Aama, this map is for you." I don't think she ever saw where her son worked, how far away he was, or what the world looked like. I explained about planes, how I flew from California to Nepal, and Vikram's route.

She shook her head in wonderment. "So far, Sobha, so far."

"Ho Aama, the world is very big."

She got up, but motioned me to stay. A moment later she came back, handing me a chewed up pencil, and simply said, "Vikram?"

I marked all the spots.

43

A JAY WAS GONE FOR THE LAST WEEK OF MY VILLAGE STAY, AND NO one would tell me why. I asked Kamala and bhauju, but they said they didn't know.

Did it have something to do with me? He had not mentioned anything, and we hadn't said goodbye. Our friendship was only that, but had he anticipated our farewell evening talk? It all seemed mysterious, but I didn't feel I had the right to push for an answer. When a decision of life significance is taken in a Gurung village, it is not discussed much, nor are farewells. It was said that a Gurung should never look back when he has decided to leave.

The absence of Ajay at the end of my stay broadened my understanding of the village and my place in it. Only so much could be communicated on both sides, which unfortunately prevented understanding sometimes. Maybe it went deeper. I had touched the surface of Gurung life, which rippled out and affected each one involved. I had fallen in love with Ajay, and aama, Kamala, and Tangting! But not in a committed way. I wanted to exchange addresses, stay in touch, look into Ajay's eyes one last time and say dhanyabad. However, the ancient code of a spiritually-minded, traditional folk was at the helm, and I respected that.

*My Gurung family in Tangting taken on my last day, bottom row left to right: aama, baa,
Seti; top row left to right: I forget her name, she came with us on leaf-collecting trips, then a
friend of the family, then me, Kamala, friend, and Jamuna*

Communities were built, layer upon layer, and handed down
from generation to generation—beliefs set, customs created. Each
ethnic group had their own set of values and etiquette. In Nepal,
they were part of the oxygen the people breathed in that country.

As much as I wanted to fit in and be treated like one of them, I
would have to *become* one of them. Not necessarily through
marriage, but time, desire, and effort. Even then, would I be allowed
in? Could I accept this rich relationship my family and I had shared
as enough? What more did I need? What more did I want?

In the final days before leaving Tangting, I worked with aama,
finishing a piece of woven material for me to take home. Kamala
sat close, even though she suffered from a headache, or whatever
caused her pained expression behind the piercing smile. On my last
day, even baa showed up, dressed in his best bhoto (vest) and dhoti
(loin cloth), for a farewell photo. The rest of the family dressed in
their finest too, western pink dresses on the young girls (although I
wished they had stayed in traditional attire), and magnificent

cholos and lungis on the women. I took pictures of it all, and the schoolmaster came by to snap a few of us together in front of the house.

I never said goodbye to Ajay. We had spoken of marriage in one of our late-night talks—not between he and I, but of the differences between our countries. I was honest with him about not wanting to marry anyone, and even though our eyes had lingered for a moment, we knew it was not possible.

Bhauju was gone with Vikram, but we had said our farewells before they left. Colorful malas (flower garlands) were placed around my neck. Kamala hugged me tightly several times.

Kamala giving me mala, flower garland, on my last day in Tangting

"Write," she whispered in English.

"Ho Didi, ho." I pressed my penny whistle into her hand and asked her to pass it on to Ajay.

I hugged aama. At the exact moment our energies coincided and then yielded, the hug was complete, and we released. She put her hands on my shoulders and shook them, looked around my face, tugged at my still un-pierced ears, and with tears in her eyes said in Gurung, "Sobha, you will not forget us?"

"Hoina Aama, never."

"You will think of us and say dhanyabad." Her pain, fatigue, and love crinkled her face. She repeated firmly, "You will think of us here, in your life way out there, and you will write to us, and say dhanyabad."

"Ho Aama, more than you could ever know, even in your dreams. You have changed my life."

"Ho Sobha, ho. Now go. It is late, and rain comes."

I walked over to Seti and hugged her. We sang quickly, in rounds, the song she had taught me up in the cave, then I hugged Jamuna. Tears came to my eyes. She squinted and tilted her head. We embraced again.

Baa came over and hugged me briefly. "Go bahinis, take Sobha, go, go," he said in Gurung to the two young girls, who ran into the house to change, then walked with me to the edge of the village. My name rang out from houses where people had known me, my bahinis yelling back to them that I was leaving, then we passed the untouchables to where the path dropped down the steep, rocky stairs. They shouted after me for ten minutes until I disappeared into the verdant land.

"Sobha, Sobha, waaay." I heard their high-pitched voices echoing down the rugged countryside.

"Waaay," I yelled back, cupping my hands around my mouth and shouting into the billowing grey clouds.

"Sobha, waaay," they repeated until rain descended, lightly at first, and then steadily, drowning out all sound. I looked up every so often. The sky had woven with the land in a grey/green watercolor wash, and, alone, I made my way further down the valley.

After hours of quiet, purposeful walking, the swinging bridge appeared, even more treacherous in the rain. I didn't pause. The storm and thunderous river below cushioned my emotions, making the intimidating height magically peaceful. I made good time to the road where I saw a small van moving slowly in the distance. I yelled and waved. It stopped. The driver got out and motioned for me to hurry. Thankfully, they were heading to Pokhara. I arrived just after sunset, soaking wet.

The didi at the guesthouse welcomed me, took my soggy things and hung them in her kitchen. Darkness slithered down the walls and mixed with the spicy smell of dinner. The warmth of the woman's place relaxed my tired body. I sat at the corner table and enjoyed her sweet tea and lively conversation. After dal bhat, I went to sleep.

The next morning one of my eyes had swollen shut, most likely from a bug bite. The didi looked at me, horrified, and chuckled. She pressed a wet cloth onto it and told me to hold it there. It's nothing to worry about, I told her, after keeping the compress on for ten minutes, adding that friends were waiting for me.

Linda waved as I walked into the café, her thick, black eyebrows raised and pale face smiling, and Juni, who I had gone on the first trek with into the Helambu valley, sat in a cozy corner with tea and books, chatting with other travelers across the table. Their eyes widened when they saw my face, looking like I had been beaten up.

"What happened to you?"

"A bug bit me in the night."

"Does it hurt?"

"No, it doesn't even itch. So, what's the plan?"

Before saying goodbye after the river retreat, Juni had mentioned bringing friends to her village because her Newar family had encouraged it. I thought it would be fun, and so we had planned a two-night excursion.

"It takes about an hour and a half to walk to my village. We're going to have crawfish. My family is so excited."

"Crawfish?"

"Yeah, they're so good. We'll help catch them when we get there."

The walk turned out to be pleasant and easy, flat and dry. No hills, no rain, no bridge, and it went by fast. The dusty, wide trail splayed out in ragged veins as we neared her village, the main route continuing gently on around buildings. An older woman rocked under a small overhang. Juni pointed to her house just as the woman recognized her. With great excitement, members of her family came out of different entrances, introductions were made, gifts given, and we settled inside for tea.

In the small, quiet, laid-back village, the narrow and rectangular hobbit-like houses were made of mud and exposed brick. Some were enhanced with hand-cut, latticed windows, making them almost quaint—unlike Tangting whose homes, emulating extreme heights and weather, were constructed of large limbs, white-washed walls, and heavy shale roofs.

Juni's family seemed like islanders compared to the rugged mountain people of Tangting. They were Newars, meaning "inhabitants of Nepal," who originated from Indo-Aryan and Tibeto-Burman ethnicities, and are divided into castes/jaat. Some are Hindu, some Buddhist, and are for the most part syncretic practitioners of religion. All the castes resembled each other, though differences were easily recognized, especially when ancestry was known. The Newar people were considered indigenous, mostly Mongolian origin, the only uniquely urban group in Nepal. They held the kingdoms of the Kathmandu Valley.

Her family spoke Nepali, which made our conversations lively and full. The three brothers were in their teens, and waited anxiously to show us around as well as start the crawfish catch for dinner, since it was late in the afternoon. Small, hand-dug tributaries served as channels to water the crops, which contained the little grey-colored crustaceans. With rolled up lungis and bare feet, we followed along, clutching small buckets and catching dozens of the weird-looking creatures. It was sunny and warm, the mud felt good, and a gentle abandonment found its way into my concerned, lingering thoughts of Jamuna's resolute face, her strong hug, Kamala's pain, aama's kindness . . .

After much preparation and excitement, we finally sat down to eat. With the first bite, I knew I was in trouble. The crawfish tasted like awful swamp meat. Juni chided and jabbed at her family members like long time relatives, all the while feasting on those disgusting things. I tried hard not to show my distaste, but she could tell, and told me not to worry. Linda was indifferent, and finished her plate. I remarked on how delicious the bhat and achaar were. The aama pointed to the fish and then crossed her fingers in front of her nose. I agreed with her gesture, and they all burst out laughing. We helped clean up, scraping leftovers into a pile outside where dogs lapped them up, then sat out under the stars and visited. I was amazed at the ease in which Juni conversed and laughed, so comfortable with those amenable, shy people.

WE SLEPT side-by-side on floor mats with piles of woolly blankets. I was restless, but intrigued to experience another village. The next day we lounged with most of her family under the overhang of their porch. They made a bowl of kani (popcorn), and covered it in melted ghee and salt, which we gobbled up in minutes. Juni had taught them how we ate it in the States, whereas in Nepal it was served plain, so that counted as an extravagant and rare treat. The three of us walked around the village, meeting others she knew, then ventured out of its boundaries and up a hill to a nice view.

"Your family is sweet, and you converse in Nepali!" I said. "That must have been great—mine didn't."

"Mine is similar," Linda said. "Nepali-speaking, also Newar, but my village is a bit farther of a walk."

"I am able to talk to my hajur aama the most, and the youngest boy, Arjun, too. He wants to study abroad like us," Juni added.

"Do you think he'll make it?" Linda asked.

"I don't know," Juni answered. "What was your village like?"

"Tangting?" I said. "It's way up in the mountains. They speak mainly Gurung."

"Oh, that must have been hard," Linda replied. "Juni, what's for dinner tonight, roasted beetles?"

Dinner was a delicious traditional meal heaped onto shiny metal plates and bowls. Their bright faces and endless questions reflected a hardworking, humble, and joyous people, like most Nepalese I met, but this family—and possibly the whole village—seemed more relaxed. I assumed that came from the lower altitude, easier weather, and the less stringent working conditions compared to the higher mountain villages.

"Didi," I could barely get the words out from the spicy sauce I'd just tasted, "yo ke ho (what is it)?"

They all laughed and pushed the bowl towards me.

"Hoina, dherai piro!" ("No, really spicy!") I over exaggerated, fanning my mouth, which made them laugh more. Juni said it was hotter than usual. One of the greatest compliments one can give is to ask for more, remarking on how delicious the hosts' food is.

"Yo tarkari mitho chha, ra saag, ra achaar." ("This vegetable curry is very tasty, and the greens, and the chutney.") I smiled and nodded my head in thanks.

We stayed up late talking to her brothers and a few villagers. They liked hearing about Wyoming's extreme snowfalls and cold weather, and about how we loved Nepal.

The next morning I awoke early and went outside. Juni joined me just after the sun barely crested the hill that we'd climbed the day before. She offered me a glass of warm water with lime. She was amazed that Linda was still asleep. We had to wake her up or we'd miss the midday bus to Kathmandu.

After some kind of deep fried dough and tender hugs, hajur aama took Juni aside and whispered something to her that brought her to tears. This is what I found with most Nepali people when my eyes had greeted her family's two days ago—a warm and humble acceptance. I had met that gaze, that namaste, that gracious and positive encounter, with the same respect.

We departed down the path, wrapped in shawls, our small daypacks secured snugly over the diagonal wrap. We reached Pokhara in an hour.

44

THE COOL KATHMANDU EVENING GREETED US LIKE AN OLD friend. Calling home for the last time, I told my parents good things about my village stay and of my plans to start my long-awaited Annapurna trek. I had been planning it since the retreat, and now it would begin in a couple of days. Finishing my call, I relayed my itinerary for the rest of the trip—returning via Malaysia, Singapore, Hawaii, and finally back at school in northern California. Mom's soft, loving voice sounded worried. I tried to ease her concern, from seven thousand miles away, with an assured tone and definite plans to see her in only a few weeks. They seemed excited, and said they would drive to California to meet me while I was flying home.

I headed to Maya's, my original Kathmandu family, for the night. Nima saw me pull into the courtyard on my red bike and jumped up and down, squealing and clapping. "Sobha, Sobha, Sobha!" she shouted, sitting me down on the steps outside the kitchen, stroking my hair. Maya, Muni, even Tara came down, and we became a bunch of chattering girls. Tara did not say a word, but she smiled.

We moved into the kitchen, where hajur aama stirred a pot. She looked up at me and broke into the dearest, crinkled giggle. I handed her pakka chori (a bundle of vegetables) I'd brought, and she waved to me, patting her side to sit down beside her. One of my brothers was at a friend's house. The other showed up briefly and shyly waved a hello before escaping.

Dinner had always been prepared late, and Maya lit a few extra butter lamps while posing a barrage of questions about the village. They wanted to know everything. I explained and described as best I could, happy to be talking Nepali. The dal bhat tasted refined and salty compared to the village, where it was starkly different— earthier and wholesome. Or maybe in Tangting I was always raven- ously hungry compared to the overindulgent palate I experienced from too much snacking and going out in Kathmandu.

I had brought my sleeping bag so they wouldn't have to prepare bedding. Maya disapproved. I convinced her to let me have my way. She and I stayed up late, talking about experiences in the village that I had not disclosed over dinner. I mentioned Ajay, which she liked hearing about, and the death ceremony. She gently inhaled a cigarette. The smoke dangled like a ghost between us. She provided an objective sounding-board to the impasses I struggled with. Her highly valued and unbiased perspective made me see things differently.

"Did you come here to marry, Sobha?" Maya asked in English. Without waiting for an answer, she replied, "Of course not." She put out her cigarette. "The most important thing is to learn." She emphasized her words, then said in Nepali, "And to learn, you must let go." Her serene character had an uninhibited docility that convinced me of Nepal's power, one that is greater than any classroom.

"Let go of what Didi? I have a lot to hold on to."

"We all do," in Nepali, then in English she said, "When my husband died, my world stopped. But I had to work, and now my work is my life. I help my people. I *love* my people." She finished in Nepali, "Now come, it is late."

The next morning Maya left for work after a long hug and my promise to be careful on the trek. I assured her of one last visit before leaving Nepal. The streets were busy, full of exhaust, steamy smells of curry and urine. Cows leisurely took up road space. Smiles and waves as I shouted back, "Namaste didi! Dai, kasto cha? Sanchai, sanchai cha, ho!" I was free.

The base house smelled of popcorn. One of the students happily popped a second bowl, shaking her booty and the kettle to music. The place buzzed as we all finished papers for school. No computers or typewriters existed—everything had to be hand-written, images drawn and labeled. I did first drafts in pencil, final ones in pen.

Our program director needed details on when we wanted to leave so he could schedule return flights. A few of us planned to spend a long stopover in Malaysia, then in Singapore for me and a few days in Hawaii since I had to change planes there.

45

I HAD PLANNED A FIVE-DAY TREK INTO THE ANNAPURNA Sanctuary, a sacred area to the Gurung people, and a popular destination since its glacial basin was the starting point to major routes to the Annapurna peaks. Juni and Linda decided to join me, even after I questioned them about their experience in the high mountains and ability to hike strenuously for days. I had my doubts, but welcomed the company.

We dosed ourselves with Valium for the night bus to Pokhara and slipped easily into a drowsy trance over the thousands of potholes and numerous stops. We awoke just as the creaky old bus pulled into that eclectic mecca of Nepal, stunningly poignant, with Machapuchhare looking crisp and foreboding in the morning light.

I bargained with a taxi to take us to a point where we transferred to a jeep. The jeep driver probably knew the road with his eyes closed, but for about an hour and a half on a rugged road along a flat valley, he took unnecessary risks, going way too fast. He swerved to avoid people walking with heavy loads, tail-gated slower cars to the point of braking slightly then careening around them with barely enough time to get back on the proper side again. His blaring music added to the stressful ride. The small village of Phedi finally appeared. The driver jumped out and yelled commands as he helped get our packs out, smirked, and casually thanked us in English.

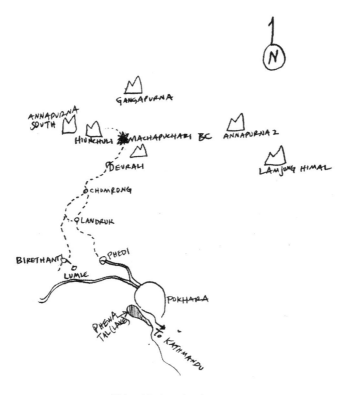

Trek to Machapuchare base camp

The wide stone steps began steeply, very hilly, terraced with rice and millet fields. Rustic hotels dotted the trail along the way, yet it didn't feel touristy. The first part of the day was beautiful. We made good time, but around noon it started to rain and continued for hours, which discouraged us, but we kept on walking to the village of Landrung, a good spot to stop and discuss what to do.

Within twenty minutes, half our tahini and a full loaf of pumpernickel bread had vanished. Linda wasn't feeling well, and wanted to return to Pokhara the next day. Her allergies to everything in the States had made me wary of Third World living for her, but she seemed to have overcome that. Juni was listless, but still interested, and I, of course, was wildly energetic and determined. I looked at my friends. We had all been through a lot, and they didn't need my impatient, over-zealous prompting.

"I want to do this," I began, "but there's not a lot of time, and I don't think it's going to get any easier."

"We know," Linda said, matter-of-factly, folding her thick arms on the table. She was full of Wyoming hardiness.

"I want to," Juni said. "Maybe not as fast as you, but I'm in."

"Does it have to be a marathon?" Linda joked.

It's funny, I thought. I never could jog for as long as I had seen Linda do many times, but I could hike forever. "Let's just keep going and see what the day brings," I said.

It was still pouring late in the afternoon. Our spirits were low, yet we pushed on another hour until a small hotel appeared on the trail in the oncoming darkness. A change of clothes, bags rolled out onto bamboo mats, and tea and rice porridge around a tiny fire warmed us. The didi pointed to a string across the porch to hang wet clothes, and she allowed our completely soggy boots near the fire. Mine got too close and one of them sizzled and burned on one side, the synthetic material curling up and exposing the padding.

We slept well and woke to a marbled blue and white sky. Annapurna One calmly demanded attention, sitting at 26,545 feet, the tenth highest mountain in the world (all the Annapurna peaks reached over seven thousand meters). An exciting spurt of energy infused my achy limbs, and after a few stretches, I was ready to go.

"My god Ro, do you ever stop?" Linda asked, getting out of her bag.

"Something smells good," Juni said sleepily, and turned over.

"Let's get up. It's gorgeous out," I sang out softly. We ate warm porridge in earthen bowls while staring at the outrageous view. A porter jogged up the pathway for Linda, who had asked the didi last night if she knew of anyone. A small, jubilant Nepali man sat outside, shook our hands, and was thrilled we spoke his language. He had been on his way back from carrying loads up to the higher lodges. He picked up Linda's pack like it was a bag of feathers, threw us a huge smile, asked where we would be stopping, and jogged off.

That day was difficult—up and down ridges, gaining elevation, losing a little, climbing again—eight hours through extraordinary diverse terrain, ending in a cold and frosty place called TipTop. Along the way, we met two guys who were trekking. They were amazed at what we had covered in two days, which had taken them four. We all shared raaksi (rice liquor) warmed by the fire and planned the next day. There had been talk of too much snow, blocking the base camps.

I didn't sleep well that night, but felt rested enough in the morning as I stretched before anyone was up. We discussed the day over tea and chapatis. I never considered acclimatizing to the higher elevations, which didn't bother me, but my friends could have used more time. I also hadn't looked into permits. Thankfully, we were never questioned, though I later learned they were needed in some areas.

Machapuchhare base camp was reachable, but an avalanche had buried it under thirty feet of snow. Hiking became easier every day. The higher elevations were exciting, eliciting a buoyancy and incredible energy in me. I felt freest up in the alpine, invincible and subservient, small and infused with joy and insight. My elation from the hiking experience pushed my body forward while the others dragged behind, perhaps from the altitude or the cold. It made me sad that we couldn't go farther and higher because I loved being there. But my friends didn't feel as I did about this extraordinary trip. It wasn't as important to them. Trekking in Nepal had been a lifelong dream of mine. Anything falling short of my plans irritated me. I knew they enjoyed it—anyone experiencing the Himalayas gained vitality and a cherished awe—but for me it was a *mission*. Getting into the heart of those heights unleashed a desire so strong I could barely contain myself.

The trail cut through rich, green stalks that rose from tangled depths. Bizarre and Zen-like, they portrayed incredibly diverse vegetation throughout the area. The Himalayas were at such great heights that the lows were graced in dense rhododendron and bamboo jungles. Patches of snow sent tingles up my spine as we crested ridge after ridge, getting closer to their majesty. A string of old, discolored prayer flags flapped intensely in a bitter breeze. Though ragged and alone, they marked a threshold, a portal, a sacred invitation to a mystical place.

Unfortunately, too many "peak baggers," insensitive, arrogant climbers, and foreigners frequented the area. Their complaints about trail conditions, lodging, and food choices unnerved me—as if they were there to be catered to. Their boasting of how many mountains they had climbed and countries they had traversed was truly embarrassing, and described quite clearly the phrase "The Ugly American," although they were from other countries as well. The locals had no choice but to gratify these westerners in their shiny new Northface and Patagonia clad bodies.

I tried not to let the belligerent strangers interfere with the magnificence of that rugged and bewitching place. The prayer flags symbolized to even the humblest visitor, and should admonish all others, that these mountains were one of the ultimate seductions and masters of destiny, and if one was of the few lucky enough to have the time and opportunity to visit them, then be grateful. The power was there, even more in those tattered flags with barely discernible printed Buddhist mantras, letting the wind and rain carry their message into the world. They added to my already complete mental and emotional free fall into the Himalayas.

The canyon narrowed, rocky cliffs and mountains towered on each side. At the base of those cliffs the Modi Khola (river) roared over smooth, glaciated rock. The water was green, ice cold, hollering and crashing like a rock band. I climbed up on wet snowy ground in steady, even steps. I stopped to look up, and at that moment, from one of the cascading waterfalls, a large chunk of ice exploded on the rocks below, shattering in white shards of glitter, like mirrors. I gasped, took a deep breath, felt the edges of my body interlock into my surroundings like an Escher design, and I became part of the landscape. I then continued onward, my steps floating up through the heavy snow and thin air.

Soon after, a house came into view. It was built out of an overhanging rock, only to serve trekkers since the chiseled platform it was anchored to was no larger than the size of a small car. I arrived alone, my friends far behind. A small Gurung family lived there and sold provisions, warm meals, and offered a few bunks. I bought a package of biscuits and sat down to wait. They were the same coconut-flavored ones I had often bought in Kathmandu—sweet and crumbly, like short bread. The family was friendly and we conversed in the meager Gurung I knew. A few trekkers from Australia hunched over tea and fried bread on the ledge that over-looked the winding, steep trail, doing the same as I, keeping warm and feeling high from hiking in the mountains. They smiled infec-tiously, nodded their heads in greeting.

My friends arrived, a healthy round of tea and more biscuits were bought, and then we set off for Deurali, the last village (or rather hut) before the Machapuchhare base camp. It was cold, and heavy, wet snow clutched the mucky trail. Bright fragments of golden sun peeked in and out of fast moving, dark grey storm clouds. We crossed a glacier, following the deep grooves of earlier hikers, and gained more elevation before reaching a dinky, dark hut that fatefully stood at the top of a long incline. A couple of porters talked outside, acknowledged us with wide smiles as we asked them a few questions, in fluent Nepali, about a helicopter we had heard earlier. Suddenly, thunderous chops broke the ominous sky, and it came into view. They spoke of two people being lost the day before.

The icy wind penetrated the thin layers of my sweat-soaked shirt. I donned my last piece of dry clothing and wrapped a scarf tightly around my head and neck. Juni and I left our packs with Linda, who had paid for a bunk there, and we took off to find a place to sleep. We hiked for about twenty minutes only to find another, very small, closed up hut. A bit further on, a neat little cave appeared, protected in the rocks. We returned for our stuff. Linda could not believe what we were doing and tried to convince us otherwise, but it was too warm and claustrophobic inside the hut. I preferred the wild sparseness of finding my own way. I bought corn flour to make chapatis. Juni and I left, bewildered Nepali faces staring at us.

After closely inspecting the cave, we decided it wouldn't work. We went back to the abandoned hut and forced our way in through a loose window. Our mats were rolled out and I began a fire, as we had found a few sticks of wood in the cabin.

Suddenly, we heard footsteps. Gloved hands wiped the foggy window and a shrouded face peered in. Concerned Nepali voices exchanged quick words. Two guys unlocked the door and came in (the ones we recognized sitting outside the hut below) and asked, in Nepali, what we were doing. I immediately felt ashamed. I spoke to them in their language.

"Come in," I said, as if it were my place to invite. The thoughts I had, just hours ago, about arrogant foreigners taking advantage of these humble people, and now there I was, thinking I could get away with a free night in a place that I did not know.

They were amazingly cool, as if they were disturbing us. We all knew we were wrong, but they accepted the situation, as they could tell we were not out to do damage. The conversation took place in Nepali.

"How did you get in?" one of the men asked in a stern, displeased tone.

I walked over to the window and showed him.

"I am very sorry," I said, lowering my eyes.

"You can stay here," he said, after squatting by the now smoky fire that the other man had put out, "but you cannot have fire. Firewood is very hard to get. It has to be carried from far away."

"Dai, we are very sorry. Thank you for letting us stay. It will only be one night. We will be gone early in the morning." Of course I understood about the wood and what it entailed. I was the only one who spoke. Juni sat silent.

"Okay." He and the other man, who did not say a word, sat for a few minutes asking questions about our school stay, field projects, my family in Tangting, with whom they were familiar, and then they left.

There we were, in that secluded hut. It was cold and snowing, but warm enough in our sleeping bags. We ate raw corn flour, washed it down with ice water, stripped down to long underwear, shirt, sweater, hat, and mittens. Exhausted, Juni fell asleep quickly while I balanced my flashlight, opened my journal, and tracked the day. A human could go for quite a while on little food—in fact, less was better. We had only consumed a few cups of tea, some chapatis, and biscuits that day, and my stomach felt hollow as it sank into the caverns of my hip bones. Thunder, or perhaps an avalanche, rumbled in the stillness. I wondered if those lost mountaineers had been found.

I slept fitfully to the sound of cracking icicles echoing in ripples until the last tinkles disappeared into the hollows of my ears. My body waited as thick wisps of misty breath released from between my lips. Was I asleep, or just deeply tranquil? At eleven thousand feet, the air was clear and easy to breathe as it crossed through membranes deep within my organs, tissues, and blood. The hard, cold, uneven, broken boards beneath me conformed to the rocky, frozen earth they lay on. My body fit agreeably, like melted wax, its torpid muscles disconnected, as if in space.

I floated in timeless awareness until the early morning lifted and a grey light imbued the simple dwelling. Juni asked if I was awake. We packed up, checked the place over to make sure nothing was out of order, and went down to get Linda. She was dressed lightly in the warmth of the hut. We started out around nine a.m., late for the pending avalanche conditions.

Even with long moments of sun and our fast pace, the cold cut through our clothing, and Linda couldn't take it. Her boots were not good (the tread wouldn't hold), and eventually her frustration and fatigue won out. She turned back. Juni and I trudged on and up.

High cliffs rose on either side, rocky buttresses that stretched our necks to look at the towering panorama. All of them were covered with snow and accordion walls of ice, humming an ancient tune that whistled in my ears, making me stop frequently to cock my head and listen. I walked ahead in a feverish pace, passing all the people that were in front, until I was the only one in that vast, white, glacial amphitheater and stopped, thirty feet above the avalanched Machapuchhare base camp in the middle of Nepal—nothing around me, the snow outrageously deep and still, the sun warming my bones. I stared for a long moment. Silence. Absolute hush in that mountain-protected sound room: Hiunchuli, Annapurna South, Fang, Annapurna, Gangapurna, Annapurna 3, and Machapuchhare in a circle ten miles in diameter. The crunch of my own footsteps startled me. My breath deepened, grounding my yearning desire to keep going and renounce everything.

The Himalayas were grand, grander than I could have imagined, so grand they went out of focus, spilling over the ends of my peripheral vision. I called out. The airy depth swallowed my voice. Many others, unknown to me, slogged behind in the knee-deep snowy path, but in that moment, I had some of the highest mountains in the world to myself.

The Himalayas nourished a yearning that would take a lifetime to ripen; one that kept me searching for a purpose, a direction. In the mountains, I felt complete, totally at ease and focused, but amidst people and the responsibilities of life, I was overwhelmed and scattered.

My mind wandered in every direction, the sight so bright from pure, crystallized white. The quiescent space was awe-inspiring. One rock, cold and icy, offered a perch. My camera (a Nikon FM10 35 mm) froze up the day before, so I took pictures in my mind. The mountains were defined. Their shadows moved quickly as the passing sun surveyed its environs, throwing veils of wispy cirrus clouds like wedding rice. I was high—on altitude, on mountains, on snow measured in tens of feet—mountains surrounding me in crisp, white edges, ultra-clear and overwhelming. My throat ached to hold back the impulse to cry out and run into the white, the austere, the unattainable. In the company of those divine, masterful entities whose rugged beauty, awesome heights, and crystalline structures, dangerously intense and unreachable, left me ragged and whole. I turned slowly, taking in the scene over and over again, my boots soaked through, sun so hot and bright, snow and ice melted as if in time lapse.

I pushed cold hands into warm pockets. I was the trekker I longed to be, the mountaineer I fantasized about. I was finally one step more of the woman I hoped to be. I was merely insignificant in the midst of those magnificent moguls.

I was silent, and the silence penetrated my heart like a first kiss.

I sank my heels into that rock until Juni and others plodded up the wet, snowy trail, bringing too many voices, plastic wrapping, and movement to that serene and edgy wilderness.

Soon word came of severe avalanche danger—the warmth was melting the snow fast. We reluctantly headed back. I wondered if those lost hikers had been found yet. Were they stuck somewhere in a crevasse, dangling from a cliff? This was not a place to try to outwit.

We reached Deurali, where Linda had remained and had some soup while the sun left its sticky fingers on the last peak. Just after noon, when snow descended heavily, we packed up and silently started down, each in our own thoughts, each wanting to get down and get warm. TipTop stood forlorn and welcome, wet from rain, not snow. The depressing lower elevation diminished my energy. The muddy trail and intense hiking tugged at our tired legs, and we needed to stop; it was almost five and getting dark.

We were lucky to get as far as we did—besides, it was part of my plan to do with less, experience something bigger, be turned inside out. The glacier crossing was the trickiest, requiring knowledge and skill, of which I had very little. I had experienced traversing a glacier with my mom in Wyoming's Wind River Range, and it had been scary.

My friends went inside the hut. I stood out in the rain, thinking. I'd wanted so badly to do this Annapurna trek, the leader who forever coaxed us on, driving us harder to cover more ground, hike faster, get higher. Why did my friends come along? They don't know what they got themselves into . . . but did I? Yet they followed, with no former experience of backpacking or surviving in the mountains, a place I was brought up in, always more comfortable in the arms of a high-altitude ridge. But I'm happy they came.

The snowy mountains—massive rocky castles—and high elevations were hypnotic. I longed for this isolated life away from society and all it entailed. I struggled with people who were too slow or not really interested, but I continually chose to surround myself with those less passionate about what I was passionate about because of my fear of embarking on my own, to follow impulses so sacred and strong within me. I looked back into the twilight where dark slabs, clean-cut and massive, were outlined in a thousand rain-dropped sky, punctured holes into the heavens, as if a sieve in a misty layer, cleansed my euphoric self, left upon that rock up on the high mountain cirque. And the part of me that stood and looked back, wet through to the bone, submitted to cold sleet that trickled down following strands of wet hair clinging to the sides of my face. Tears joined the descent into a dripping stream. My fingers wiped the salty warmth away before they trickled down my neck.

My trek through the Modi Khola gorge to Machapuchare base camp.
Photo credit Olav Myrholt

"Sobha?" Juni called out softly. "It's wet and cold. Come inside."

I walked up the stairs into the dimly lit lodge that exuded dense warmth, its muted walls and austere structure easing my sense of longing. Boots and socks were already by the fire. The didi heated leftover Tibetan bread while we sat and talked. We devoured the hot, greasy rounds, dividing them in pieces where she had scored them twice before frying. She was familiar with foreigners, their barrage of wet clothes and tired bodies. Her quiet enthusiasm and gracious hosting was even more genuine when we conversed in Nepali. I relaxed enough to let go of that burning urge to drop everything and run back into the white mirage, hoping to find my destiny.

———

THE NEXT MORNING WAS BEAUTIFUL, frosty, and clear. I sipped tea while describing the previous day in my journal. The others had a full breakfast and chatted happily with the didi. Their leisurely pace made me anxious, and we got started late on the trail. Walking back through the thick, bamboo jungle and green bushy trees left us peeling off layers of sweaters and jackets and tying them to our bulky packs. Monkeys swung from branches and the river roared below.

We came across those ragged prayer flags again, snapping in the Himalayan wind. They reminded us once more of the culture and tradition Nepal commanded us to remember. The many feet that had trod that trail deserved appreciation and preservation of this stunning and dangerous area, reminders to heed the advice of seasoned alpinists, many of whom did the work of cleaning up the catastrophic amounts of debris too many others left behind, reminders to show deference to the indigenous people—it's their home.

We moved on, individually calculating our own imperfections, climbing up mountainsides out of the jungle into arid, higher elevations, stopping at lodges for tea or popcorn. At one point when we studied a map to find where we were, we decided to take a new way back, a route up to Birethanti to meet the Annapurna circuit trail as opposed to the Annapurna Sanctuary trail we were on.

From Chomrong, where we had bought potatoes and porridge to make hot cereal, we walked along a ridge in a warm, late afternoon haze. After deciding to camp by a river, I finally got to use the pot I had brought and cooked the potatoes.

"This is delicious," Linda said. A full moon added to the charisma of nearing the end of that unbelievable journey as we all ate out of the one pot with our hands.

"I could eat two more pots of this," Juni remarked. "What else did you put in here?"

"Garlic and some spice, an onion, and whatever that woman gave me at the last village."

"Smells like cumin, or something close to it," Linda added.

We scraped every last remaining morsel, and then I cleaned the pot with dirt and rinsed it out. While we set up camp, young Nepali women and men ran by, chasing after each other, smearing red powder on their faces.

"Where did they come from?" Juni asked.

"It's Holi," Linda said. "My family warned me about it. They like westerners especially, so watch out."

Holi, of Hindu origin, but celebrated by all, is also known as the festival of color, or festival of love. It announced the arrival of spring, illustrating good over evil, even the mending of friendships. Everyone was free game to be pelted and smeared in paint, colorful powder, balloons filled with color, even squirt guns. We were cornered, given tika and smudges of red and blue, then waved at by laughing, sometimes inebriated, dressed up, energetic rioters, running rampant, spreading joy. What a fun culture; beautiful and peaceful, too. It gaily consummated our quick and challenging passage into the high mountains.

The last day walking out, tea huts were strewn along the trail, with outside tables and chairs like a European resort area. Different dialects—French, German, Swiss—filled the space. Pretty people in clean clothing smoked cigarettes, sipped tea, and, in sophisticated airs, talked about the treks they'd done or were about to undertake.

It was all too much for me. I had experienced the guts and glory of true Nepali culture and just finished a treacherous, under-equipped expedition. They seemed to have no idea of the great land they were visiting, and yet I was envious of their ease, their beautiful faces and obvious affluence. Their confidence shattered my hyper-sensitive ego, and so, in determination, I turned my head and walked down the trail.

Nothing happened. No one said anything, or even noticed me. In that instant, the reality of society hit me. How little I had learned or had matured. How easy my bubble could burst. The clink of glasses, romantic excess, deformed the fairytale picture I'd held, unconsciously, until that moment. I quickly pulled myself together as I caught up with my friends.

I found them resting on a rock off the trail, talking to locals. Linda especially had an impressive handle on the language and blew their minds with her conjugations. We all joined in, and had them laughing and inviting us to stay with them. Our limited time didn't allow that opportunity, though. The first batch of our students were soon heading back to the States, and we had to check in at the base house.

46

THE BUS-RIDE FROM POKHARA BACK TO KATHMANDU JUMBLED along those foreboding roads, but I was not concerned with them anymore. Instead, the woman in front distracted me. She threw up every hour out the window; her husband didn't even seem to care as she suffered. Her tired face and sad eyes hid nothing, but with a protruding belly and a child at her breast, energy to protest was not available. When the bus finally stopped to pick someone up, she pushed through the crowd and got off. Her husband argued with the driver long enough to wait for her return. That didn't help her, and she continued vomiting after the bus moved on. I tuned out as much as possible, even though her entrails whisked onto my window, leaving yellowish bits of food and saliva. My thoughts took me away into the insatiable quest to get further into the wild, more remote mountains.

HOLI STILL RAGED as we stepped off the bus into the streets of a frenzied Kathmandu. People looked like they'd walked out of a Jackson Pollack painting, splattered with paint, hair dusted in red and blue, and faces grinning mischievously, ready to pelt and spray. Foreigners were opportune targets, as many walked by completely disfigured by the chaotic color scheme with drunken smiles, unsure if the strikes were in jest or not. I wasn't sure. The hits were hard, frequent, and potent. They were the first blatantly aggressive attacks on our fair-skinned group, showering our clothes as we fled the threatening scene. The ritual of throwing paint-filled balloons and sticky, powdery colors grew feverishly as the day jangled on. I wanted to blend in somehow, convince them I was one of them, that I came from a relatively poor family and America wasn't everything it was cracked up to be. Another hit! Warm liquid trickled down the back of my neck. Another aimed at Linda's back exploded in red dust. The pursuers were different than the ones from the other day in the mountains, and though young, their vicious revenge, probably from their lack of freedom or besieged life, deepened any deference I had. The influence of easy sex, affluent upbringing, and free will dripped from our tailored Nepali rags into their line of sight. I couldn't quite decipher—were they playful, wicked, or envious? I'd had the same feeling when I saw those well-to-do foreigners at the end of my trek. I didn't want to be like them, but I didn't like the privileges they took for granted.

Those Kathmandu "gangs" continued to carry on. Festivals where towns and cities brought their religion alive, in unrestrained pageants of beauty or force, carried the good and the bad of a people deeply rooted in sacrificial mores and ritualistic history. I was jostled; everything I had discovered and cultivated seemed to blow away in that tremulous frontispiece. Smudged in blue and red, humbled into servitude, happy at the assault, I became a billboard. Immodestly, my body displayed the duality of white skin and chromaticism—ahh, mesmerizing for the beholder and the martyr. My eyes absorbed pints of color, awash in emotion, intensity, and devotion.

Nepal blatantly, yet subtly, offered risk, and I took it on, but the end of my journey brought a new perspective. Climbing Swayambhunath's three hundred and sixty-five steps for the last time measured and cut the poignant, personal, and even abstract reminiscence. Memories replayed like the chorus of a song. Over and over, faces, smells, and exquisite imagery came to me as Holi exploded in declaration—love! I had fallen in love with Nepal.

Monkeys screamed in unison from nearby trees, their surges heightening that moment into fervor as I jogged up the remaining steps. Every moment burst with aliveness, the snap of prayer flags, the scurrying crimson robes, the undulating rhythm of prayer-wheels spinning on their axes, the awe . . . the beauty . . . the magic of Nepal.

JOURNAL ENTRY: Spring 1988, Swayambhu, Nepal.

This is far beyond an acid trip I recalled of that image of the children behind that ornate gate before coming to Nepal, and I am still dazed . . . but now, determined. It has dawned on me; I don't want to sit in a classroom. I don't want to write term papers. I don't want to separate into groups and talk about my experience, I don't want to listen to old, wise, curmudgeon faculty members who never really acted on their impulses or intransigent whims. I just flew across the ocean, smelled the burning flesh of a dying man, co-mingled with poverty, ate warm, sacrificial blood, shared heartfelt questions and insecurities with the Nepali people, sweated beneath the largest, most awesome mountains in the world—sit in a classroom and talk about what I had experienced? I don't think so.

I've tasted independence. I've seen much more than a textbook or teacher can teach me. I have to find something that will compel me forward, something that captures my heart; fuels this insatiable quest to go higher and farther to pierce into the boundaries of my flesh in unspoken, magnetic fury.

NEPAL FREED ME. It tore me out of everything I knew. Maybe I didn't fit the newness yet, maybe I fought the cracking of my shell, maybe I wasn't ready for the growth—but I *had* changed. And the rippling effect would continue until the flower bloomed or the ripe fruit fell. I felt the energy. Nepal's powerful beauty and hardworking people accepted me. I burst with emotion. Yes, I had fallen in love with Nepal. I spun prayer wheels, repeating my own mantra of thanks and of hope to Kamala, Jamuna, bhauju, aama, Ajay, Maya, Nima, Tara, and all the patient and beautiful people I had met. Thanks to the Himalayas for their dreamy magnificence and silent companionship—they would forever be a presence in my life. Nepal released a great latent energy, one that was not totally clear, and maybe still tinged with fear. With all that experience and awareness, I sat on the ledge overlooking Kathmandu, not really sure what I felt beyond that powerful love, and hoped I would find my way in the world . . . one day.

EPILOGUE

AFTER NEPAL, I TRAVELED TO MALAYSIA FOR SEVERAL WEEKS, then had brief layovers in Singapore, Hawaii, and finally home. On the airplane leaving Hawaii, I sat between a teenage boy, defunct to anything but his headphones, and an Asian woman in her late eighties who was visiting her daughter in Los Angeles. She offered me a chocolate-covered macadamia nut. Delicious!

"Were you here for long?" she asked me.

"Less than a week. I just came from studying in Nepal."

"You did? Oh my. Nepal. That is far away." Her fragile, aged eyes seemed to regret not doing what she burned to do.

"Yes, it is," I said.

The engine started, lights flashed to buckle seat belts, flight attendants displayed oxygen masks, the pilot's Hollywood voice stated the "ready for take-off" spiel, and off we went into the windy blue ethers. The moment we left the ground, a succession of all I had been through, vacuous and prolific, charged my mind. I had arrived in Nepal naked and exposed, but now naked was my strength. Stripped of the burden to do what society creeded, I felt unattached, powerfully light and excited to take on my life. I was strong, confident, mature. How could I be anything but unconventional when my mind always went deep into trails that disappeared or slid off into a blackness of ideas, forever plunging into rhetoric, creativity, and stress to produce something? I was impatient to become someone, yet reticent to decide.

Easy does it, Sobha.

If I didn't go back to school, what would I do?

Follow my dreams . . .

Paris. I spoke enough French to get by, and could handle foreign travel now. The experience of poverty and spiritualism would be juxtaposed by sophisticated chic and modernity—yet filtered through my eager mind and desire to experience another impoverished population: the impressionistic artist.

I finished that Asian journey as the plane descended into the glitz of California, air-conditioned and gluttonous. The forgotten garish opulence jolted me back from Nepal, where every single person was skinny and brown, and here it was just the opposite.

What did I look like? Sun bleached, brown, wild, and fit.

The white girl with gold hair quickly found a bus to Petaluma and waited outside on the edge of a greasy sidewalk, hinting of cigarette smoke and exhaust.

It was good to be home!

AUTHOR'S NOTE

I hope you enjoyed experiencing this journey with me. I'd love it if you could take a minute and post a review wherever you purchased this book (even a few words). It helps other readers find my story.

If you'd like to learn more about my work since Nepal, please visit my website: RoanneLegg.com. In the years since Naked in Nepal, I've had lots of adventures that will be the subject of forthcoming books.

For the singer/songwriter side of my life, drop by youtube.
I'd love to hear what you think about my books or music! Please feel free to write me at, naked@RoanneLegg.com. I promise I'll answer (eventually, it might just take me a bit of time).

ABOUT THE AUTHOR

 Roanne Legg, professional whole food chef, author, musician, and poet, has had her writing published in literary magazines, anthologies, and books. Her original music has been used in compilations and films (one produced by the Discovery Channel). She has acted, performed live music, dance, and poetry throughout the US and Canada. Trained in the Meisner technique of acting, she also has experience as a film actress and voice-over artist. Please visit her website, RoanneLegg.com, and youtube. She lives in the Pacific Northwest with her husband and son.

Books by Roanne Legg

Naked in Nepal — A young woman's journey in Nepal.
For the Love of Eating — Plant-based, macrobiotic cookbook.
Beautifully Torn — Collection of poems.

Send Me a Kiss in a Storm — Music CD

ACKNOWLEDGMENTS

My aama in Tangting looked me in the eye before I left, on the ledge in front of our house, high up in the Himalayas. She held my face and said in Gurung, "Do not forget us, do not forget to say Dhanyabad." I looked at Annapurna, framed by an azure sky in depths unimaginable, and then headed down the rocky path. I will never forget.

Little did I know over thirty years later I would record that life-changing experience. Little did I know when, after years of trying to locate my Nepali families, especially after the horrendous 2015 earthquake—though I found some, repeated attempts of lost mail left me futile. Little did I know how Nepal was to be the second greatest milestone of my life. Each step from when I left Tangting village to this day, I have thought of Nepal, and cannot express the amount of Dhanyabad I feel.

But mostly to my husband, Brandt, who supports me in all that I do. It is largely because of his reminders to keep at it, his positive attitude, his belief in me and my experiences, and his piercing editorial questions, that this book has come to fruit.

And then my son, Teakki, who makes me want to record my life for him to read one day. His inquiries on how I am doing helped grind out the words.

For Mom and Marty, who have always believed in my talents, and are a constant inspiration.

Even though my sisters were rarely part of my life at this age, they have always been in my heart, albeit buried under layers of emotional debris, never forgotten or without hope of reconnection. I thank you, Karen and Maxine, for the love that has never left our tattered lives.

For Mollie Gregory, a prolific and skilled author and dear friend whose correspondence always started with, "How's the book coming?" Her edit and honest, straight critique was vital.

For Olav Myrholt, his knowledge and experience of Nepal and expert photography helped detail certain places and situations, as well as provide clarifications of the Nepalese people and their culture.

Deanne Martin helped with this book's first edit. She tackled a world of grammatical errors, navigating the story with detail and interest. Thanks to my early readers, Brandt Legg, Harriet Greene, Marty Goldman, Barbara Blair, Germaine Ploos, and Ben Piper, who took the rough versions and offered helpful suggestions. And then Jack Llartin capped the final proofing.

For Heather Feng, Pilar West, and Suzi Adams, college friends whose independent vitality still fuels me. And to all the students who went with me to Nepal, your faces are seared into my memory. Thanks to David Kleiman for initial inquiries about Nepal.

Dherai dhanyabad to my patient, thoughtful, and knowledge-able Nepali teachers, and the leader of our World College West Nepal group, John.

Dhanyabad to Prakash Gurung, for helping me contact family members from Tangting, and is still a connection to that wonderful village. To Ashok Gurung, Dikendra Raj Kandel, and Shanti Bajracharya, who tried to help find family members after the earthquake, as well as answering numerous questions of Nepali words for things I had forgotten. And for your continued friendship.

Immense gratitude to my Nepal families in Kathmandu and Tangting, as well as for Nepal and the Nepalese. Thank you for your beautiful country, open hearts, authentic spiritualism, intensely hard-working life, and opportunity to experience a window into your lives. I am forever grateful.

GLOSSARY

NEPALI - ENGLISH

achaar – relish or pickle made from tomato, radish, or whatever is in season

aama – mother

alu-roti – hand rolled flour tortilla with potatoes (alu) and other herbs and/or vegetables

aunos – please come

baa – father

baaku – hand-woven poncho-like cloak, made in Tangting

bahini – younger sister

bhaasa – language

bhat – rice

bhai – younger brother

bhai tika – during Tihar, an event where the younger brother is honored with gifts

bhauju – sister-in-law

bujae – grandmother, or respectful term for older woman

carpi – primitive toilet

chapatti – hand rolled tortilla (see alu-roti)

Chitwan – the national park in the Terai

cholo – short, cropped, wrap-around shirt worn by women

chura – glass bracelet

churi – dried, pounded rice

dai - older brother, or any older male

dal – lentils

dhanyabad – thank you

dhawabong – witch doctor

dhawo – a metal spoon with a long handle, resembling a ladle

dhindo or **dhedo** – porridge made from millet flour

didi – older sister

doko – conical basket woven of bamboo strips, used for carrying loads on the back with a strap (namlo) round the head

ghee – clarified butter, handmade in most homes

ghumne – wander

grong – farmers

hajur aama – grandmother

jutho – dirty, polluted

jato – circular milling stone on a pivot

jutho – something polluted or dirty

kaja – snack

kani also **makai** – popcorn, or it just means snack

kasto cha – how are you

ke garne – what to do

khal batta – treated stones used like a pestle and mortar for pounding herbs/spices

khiki – foot-operated pestle for milling grain

khir – rice pudding

kasouri – metal cooking pot

kukur – dog

khukuri – traditional knife of Nepal. Also the weapon and all-purpose utility tool of the Gorkha soldiers. Twelve to thirty inches long, the unique inward curve serves as a combination of an axe and a machete.

lassi – sour milk/yogurt type drink, often flavored with banana or spices

lohoro – smooth, rectangular stone used with a silauto to crush spices, ginger, garlic, and/or seeds for making chutney

lungi – wrap worn while washing body, also a wrap, cinched at the waist like a tubular skirt, worn by women

makai also **kani** – popcorn or snack of some kind

mala – flower garland placed around the neck during festivities

maasu/masu – meat

mandala – a term for any geometric symbol that represents the cosmic energy in a metaphysical or symbolic matter. In reference to the Buddhist path, the purpose of the mandala is to put an end to human suffering, to attain enlightenment and a correct view of reality. It is a mean to discover divinity by the realization that it resides within our own self.

momos – dumplings

mula – daikon, white radish

namlo – see Doko

nanu – term of endearment for young girl

paani – water (as opposed to *pani,* which means "also")

Panchayat – the previous non-party political regime

pashminas – Nepali shawls, most often made of wool, used to wrap around the body for warmth

pidaalu – taro root, or mountain potato

piro – spicy or hot

puja – worship, act of prayer, ritual may include making offerings

pugyo – full, enough to eat

Punjabi – narrow pants and long tunic, traditional clothing

pupu – aunt

rhaaksi – local liquor

rickshaws – bicycle taxi

roti – unleavened bread

rupees – unit of currency in Nepal (also India, Pakistan, and Sri Lanka)

saag – cooked greens

samosas – fried dough filled with vegetables, curry, or potatoes

sanchai cha – "Good, I am good" (in answer to *kasto cha*, "How are you?")

sapaana – dream

saris – traditional women's dress

silauto – flat tray-like rock, to hold ingredients that are being crushed by a lohoro

stupas – religious temples all over Nepal

subha ratri – good night

sari – women's clothing, a length of cloth worn draped around the body

sel roti – fried sweet bread

Tamang – Ethnic group believed to be of Mongolian, Tibetan ancestry. They are Lama Buddhists, with their own language and culture; some celebrate Hindu festivals as well

tarkari – medley of vegetables, often cooked with spices

Terai – lower, sub-tropical plains area of Nepal

Tihar – Hindu festival of lights. Laxmi, the goddess of wealth, is worshipped. Celebrated in late September and into October.

tika – decorative mark made on forehead as a blessing

tingshas – small cymbals used in ritual and prayer

Kathmandu (Chabahil) family members:

- Nima and Muni – bahinis/younger sisters
- Maya – aama/mother, but liked to be referred to as didi/older sister
- Tara – possibly Maya's sister
- hajur aama – grandmother

Base house members:

- Shankar – Nepali affiliate who found families for students
- Gopal – caretaker
- Padmini and Shanti – female teachers
- Birendra and Dhikendra – male teachers

The other students:

- Carl
- Juni
- Linda
- Sobha (me)

Tangting family members:

- Kamala – didi/older sister
- Seti and Jamuna – bahinis/younger sisters
- Vikram – dai/older brother
- bhauju – sister-in-law (Vikram, my dai/older brother's, wife)
- Ajay – young man who I talked to often in Tangting
- aama – mother
- baa – father

Made in the USA
Coppell, TX
17 January 2020